Those of us who grew _ our Young Women's experience will recognize the injunctions to ponder, reflect and journal. The Beehive Girl is not nearly so passive! Thatcher's delightful account of time traveling into forgotten skills reveals how active, challenged and ambitious our foremothers were in their vision. At once amusing and reflective, *Beehive Girl* prompts deep admiration for the practices and people that shaped generations of Saints

—Neylan McBaine
author of *Women at Church* and *Pioneering the Vote*

Mikayla Thatcher's *Beehive Girl* is an exceptionally smart, funny, and full-hearted peek into a forgotten Young Women's program in use from 1915 to 1970. Part memoir, part project book (think Rachel Held Evans' *A Year of Biblical Womanhood*, Jana Riess' *Flunking Sainthood*, and Gretchen Rubin's *The Happiness Project*), we follow along with Thatcher as she documents her personal journey fulfilling the original Beehive Girls' requirements as a modern adult. She works on skills like making a piece of furniture; caring for a hive of actual bees (which enthralled me and had me scrambling to learn more); milking a goat, 'doing at least one good turn daily,' and writing essays about Latter-day Saint women. As part of the program she wrote her own hymn! (Bonus: she includes an additional hymn she co-wrote with her husband that is in all sincerity my favorite hymn of all time.)

Because Thatcher didn't automatically know how to *do* these skills, we also get to meet the mentors and friends who helped her, and those relationships were so tender to witness. Through the lens of the project we watch as she finishes her science PhD, moves away from her homeland, and cares for her young daughter in a new place.

Thatcher's writing is so warm and poignant. I often found myself laughing at an aside before tearing up at the beautiful language, experiences, and memories in the next lines that pulled out memories of my own. Beehive Girl is so, so special. I want everyone with any relationship to Mormonism to read it. And the backmatter! It deserves ALL of the heart eyes and more.

—Rachel Hunt Steenblik
author of *Mother's Milk* and *I Gave Her a Name*

BEEHIVE GIRL

BCC
PRESS

BY COMMON CONSENT PRESS is a non-profit publisher dedicated to producing affordable, high-quality books that help define and shape the Latter-day Saint experience. BCC Press publishes books that address all aspects of Mormon life. Our mission includes finding manuscripts that will contribute to the lives of thoughtful Latter-day Saints, mentoring authors and nurturing projects to completion, and distributing important books to the Mormon audience at the lowest possible cost.

BEEHIVE GIRL

Mikayla
Orton
Thatcher

For information contact
By Common Consent Press
4900 Penrose Dr.
Newburgh, IN 47630

Textile art: Brenna Adams
Cover design: Mark Orton
Art direction: D Christian Harrison
Book design: Andrew Heiss

www.bccpress.org

ISBN-13: 978-1-948218-82-5

10 9 8 7 6 5 4 3 2 1

For Jane,
so she will understand where she comes from

CONTENTS

ACKNOWLEDGMENTS

Many of the people who helped me create this book are mentioned in the book itself—another round of applause for all of you. I couldn't have learned to sew or milk a goat or change a tire (etc.) without you.

Then there are the behind the scenes people. Rachel Hunt Steenblik vouched for my book all over the Internet before it even existed. Mette Ivie Harrison encouraged me to do a re-write I did not want to do. My book club and my brother Kyle read the book years before its release and told me it was worth their time. My friend Brenna volunteered a bazillion hours of creative genius to embroider personalized Beehive Girl badges for my book cover. My dad designed the patches. My colleagues, my students, and the good people of Twitter kept asking about my project over the years, reminding me that it was wanted. The folks at BCC Press—especially Cece!—helped me pull everything together for an actual book and an actual launch. I appreciate all of your help so very much.

And finally, there's Nate. My constant sounding board, my first editor, my Manager of Interactions with Strangers, and the person who cared for our Jane while I wrote this book. Thank you, dearest friend, for helping me make *Beehive Girl* a real thing.

MIRACLES FOR
THE LORD

MOST LATTER-DAY SAINT GIRLS are excited to turn twelve, but I was desperate. My friends at school had graduated from Primary long ago: by the summer after seventh grade, they'd already been to girls' camp without me. Twice. I knew every song in the children's songbook and felt way too grown-up to appear in one more Primary Program with the Sunbeams. I wanted to go to fabulous Wednesday-night activities that occasionally included *boys*.

First, though, I wanted to go to the temple. My dad took me to do baptisms early the morning of my birthday— at the Mount Timpanogos Temple, a mile away from our house. I didn't love walking around in nothing but a large towel, going without the makeup I usually used to hide my intense acne, or having a nosebleed in the font. Still, it was special to be twelve, in the temple, and alone with my dad. Special dad time can feel rare when you're the oldest of six kids.

My ward's Young Women President came to visit me and my parents the very same week. "Congratulations! You're a Beehive now!" She taught me about the many elements of my new life as a "youth." I thought I was already an expert, but my peers had never mentioned Personal

Progress. "There are seven different Young Women values," she told me. "Faith, Divine Nature, Individual Worth, Knowledge, Choice and Accountability, Good Works, and Integrity. For each one, you'll get to complete six Experiences and a ten-hour project."

The idea caught my full attention. There were requirements to fulfill, boxes to check off, and a special prize at the end: a shiny necklace with a picture of the Salt Lake temple. I could wear it for the rest of my life and everyone would know I was a smashing spiritual success! I had until my 18th birthday to earn my Young Womanhood Recognition, but I decided then and there to finish by the time I turned 14.

I kept my eyes on the prize, but actually working through Personal Progress was a bit of a drag. Most of the Experiences involved reading a few scriptures and writing a personal response. Sometimes I was supposed to discuss a principle of the gospel with my parents. When I mustered the motivation to pull out my manual and work on Personal Progress, it was easy to finish four or five Experiences on a Sunday afternoon—read, reflect, check! read, reflect, check!—without really learning or feeling anything. Every few months, I'd remember to have my mom sign off on everything I'd done, and by then I could never quite remember doing any of it.

I never did a single extra thing for a ten-hour project. My leaders always figured out how to count whatever I was already doing. I practiced the piano all the time and I'd just started playing cello in the school orchestra (coincidentally the same instrument that Nate, my one true crush, played). My singing and dancing weren't up to snuff to make callbacks for any musicals, but I loved performing Shakespeare. My Knowledge Bowl co-captain (coincidentally also my charming crush, Nate) and I organized practices with our team. I was always trying out new sports, discovering new things that I couldn't do at all. On the bright side, I was getting pretty good at French, for an American eighth-grader.

Basically, my Young Women leaders had a lot of extracurriculars to work with and I checked off the Values quickly. Orchestra concert coming up? Knowledge. Church history tour with grandparents? Choice and Accountability. Played the part of a fairy/tree in A Midsummer Night's Dream? Good Works. "You'll be too busy in high school to prioritize Personal Progress," they always told me, but sometimes it felt like I was already too busy to do it properly.

I saw completing my Personal Progress as a moral necessity, practically a commandment. I plugged away at it because of that quote from President Ezra Taft Benson (my best friend Natalie's great-grandfather), where he listed all the qualities he believed a young woman should have and included "has earned her Young Womanhood Recognition and wears it with pride!" I needed to be that young woman "who will perform miracles for the Lord now and throughout eternity."

🐝 🐝 🐝

When I finished all the requirements, I looked forward to receiving my medallion as if it were a medal of honor, even though I knew the bishop would hand me my temple necklace and I'd sit right back down for a regular sacrament meeting. My family was going to a second cousin's mission farewell that day and, for the only time in my life, I asked my mom if I could attend our ward alone. I was somewhat surprised when she agreed.

I strutted the red carpet, posed for the photographers, was crowned, and delivered my tearful acceptance speech.

After church, my mom admired my major award. "Wow! That's a really nice necklace! They do something like that every two years?!"

"Um . . . no, Mom. This is it. It's like the Eagle Scout of Young Women."

My mom had signed off on all my Personal Progress requirements and was still surprised when I finished the program. Not surprised that I'd finished early—finishing stuff early was kind of my thing—but that it had fit so neatly into my life that she was scarcely aware of it. She'd seen other parents plan parties and place glowing newspaper announcements, so she was disappointed to have missed the hand-off. If I could earn the award without my mom noticing, I realized, maybe it wasn't that much like becoming an Eagle Scout after all.

🌸 🦋 🌼

I'd earned the necklace—now I just had to wear it with pride. Of course, there were still several years of "youth" before college. I got sick of decorating cookies and getting makeovers, yet I was at Mutual every week. The girls at church were always kind . . . but they weren't nerds, so we had nothing in common. Even the activities "we" chose were not my cup of cocoa. At girls' camp, I pretended to be asleep while the other girls talked about the boys they'd made out with and how hot Nate was. (I bristled silently. Nate wasn't hot, he was handsome, and these girls didn't even really know him.) Church activities always made me miss my weird, wonderful friends.

I could have cried with relief the day my mom finally let me skip Mutual to go to a friend's birthday party: "It'll be like Mutual," she reasoned, "but with people you actually like." And she had a point. Everyone I knew was a member of the Church of Jesus Christ of Latter-day Saints. Our church standards were a cultural norm in American Fork, Utah. Our stake dances and school dances were exactly the same. Surely some of my classmates drank or smoked pot or had sex, but I was oblivious: no one in my posse so much as dated before they turned sixteen. If any of us were gay, we were not aware. When there was a late-start day at school, we went to the temple together (including my sweet and spiritual crush, Nate).

For a long time, I wore my medallion every day. As I got older, though, and my peers' parents and leaders put increasing pressure on them to finish their Personal Progress, I started to feel uneasy about it. Did I earn the award so I could show it off? Or did I earn it to make progress in my personal spirituality? I knew that I never could have finished Personal Progress if I'd had to do it during high school. My medallion started to feel like a religious status signifier. I quietly stopped wearing it because I was "wary of pride."

Finally, I was off to college with a Relief Society basket of goodies to celebrate my graduation from Young Women. The baskets were so customized that each of the graduates got interest-specific magazines. My interest-specific magazine was a copy of *Crime and Punishment*. Apparently, somebody at church really did understand me.

WOMANHO

IT'S EARLY 2015 WHEN I ENCOUNTER an article in the New Era about the history of Personal Progress. The article describes an older program, a predecessor instituted in 1915 called Beehive Girls. The article only gives a few examples of requirements out of their manual, but they include "Care successfully for a hive of bees for one season and know their habits" and "During two weeks, keep the house free from flies, or destroy at least 25 flies daily." Wait, this is for Young Women? That's already two more insect-themed Experiences than I ever had.

The article quotes President James E. Faust, who says that when Beehive Girls was created, "the challenges of life involved an entirely different focus." Yeah, clearly more of a focus on bugs. "Modern conveniences grant us more free time to focus on spiritual needs." That makes sense, but I still have so many follow-up questions. It says here that girls could choose from among 300 requirements—what on earth were the rest of them?

"Nate, come check this out!" I read aloud to my husband about the flies and the bees.

"I've never heard of that either," he agrees. "Maybe it didn't last very long?"

Of course, it's right then that the baby wakes up, so we

spring into action to figure out what she needs. Jane is seven months old and whenever we think we understand exactly how to care for her, it changes.

Nate will be the one to figure out the next round of changes, though. I have a month to finish writing my dissertation. I've used a breast pump plenty of times before—so I could teach a class or check on the mice or run a western blot—but this week will be my first time staying away from my baby for so long that I have to use the breast pump at work. I never really stopped working when Jane was born—I wore her to her first graduate physiology class when she was two weeks old—but this feels like an entirely different thing.

Fortunately, Nate is an excellent homemaker. He bats away my insecurities and apologies with a smiling "It's your turn!" He finds so much joy in being with Jane. I've done this for him from time to time, but I never realized what an amazing gift it is until *I* was the one coming home to a safe, happy, fed, clean baby every night. My drawers refill themselves with fresh clothes and we have a real dinner every day.

Nate hikes all over with Jane in a pack on his back, which she loves except for the part where they get caught in the rain seemingly every day. She gets so excited and noisy and squirmy. She likes to hold new things in her hands. She can initiate her own game of peek-a-boo. She gives kisses when I ask for them and sometimes when I don't. I learn what it's like to work all day, get home, and have to remind myself to gather enough energy to interact with my sweet baby for the last couple of hours before bed. My head aches at all times.

The end is in sight—I'm going to be Dr. Thatcher two months from now—but then a whole new whirlwind begins. We're moving to Ann Arbor, Michigan for Nate to do grad school. I have no idea what's next for me. As a Latter-day Saint kid, I grew up preparing for the "decade of decision": obtaining an education, finding an eternal companion, and starting a family. I've already reached the end of the list. I can't call myself a student anymore. I should just be Mikayla, a fully-developed, grown-up person. But I'm not sure what that means.

So yeah, my work is painstaking and frustrating, I miss my little family, and my future is uncertain. My brain needs a break. One day, when my students are working on a lab and don't need much from me, I stop sleepily scrolling through Pinterest and instead surf my way to a scan of someone's entire Beehive Girls Handbook from 1915. It's full of stickers, stamps, and checks to mark fulfilled requirements, evidence that the program was *real* and really a century old. There was at least one Beehive Girl. I browse the handbook, enthralled.

It's so . . . old. The turn-of-the-century writing includes all the smug secret society trappings of the Masons and an award structure more complicated than Boy Scouts of America. This program has a watchword, and the watchword is "WOMANHO." Not sure how to pronounce that? Don't worry, it's all here and it is glorious: "The WATCH-WORD is Womanho (pronounced with a long o; the a as in father; and an accent on the second syllable). 'Wo' stands for work; 'man' for mankind; 'ho' for home; and the three taken together spell "Womanhood" except for the last two letters which are dropped." Yeah, this is way more fun than isolating lipids from mouse livers. (No offense to mouse livers.)

Each Beehive Girl was meant to select her own name and symbol and each group of six to eight girls was to choose a name and symbol for their "swarm." They could use flower names or qualities they wanted to develop: "One girl is desirous of having strength which will help her to be full of gladness—she might choose 'Strengla'." That sounds violent. But also hilarious. There's tacky, bee-themed poetry and sheet music for rousing, bee-themed anthems. The authors refer to a hike as "a long tramp" and are obsessed with the health benefits of sleeping outside.

I'm not just reading so that I can mock old-timers, though. I read through the 300 possible requirements, trying to understand what the program is all about. I'm amazed at the breadth. Whoever wrote this wanted Latter-day Saint women to know their way around both kitchens and mountains, to be able to take care of both sick people and automobiles, to contribute financially via both income and thrift. They directly challenged the girls to teach lessons, write hymns, and prepare to offer prayer in a variety of settings—not to be silent in church. While some requirements could be fulfilled in the context of daily routines, others would require significant planning and mentoring. "For several years past the idea has been growing that we need to make our work concrete," these leaders explained, "to give our members an opportunity to work with their hands, to show results from the training they receive." Why does this feel like the opposite of my Young Women experience? They were trying to embody their values in real ways. I had looked for ways (no matter how tenuous) to connect my own interests to a spiritual value.

I am surprised at the level of independence and productivity expected of my youthful forebears. I've always pictured womankind starting from pious submission, non-citizenship, and corsets and moving in a basically straight historical line to property ownership, college, and pants. But here I am, in the twenty-first century, with none of the confidence I would need to write a play or build my own furniture, or call the insurance company. (No, that last one isn't on the list.)

My generation, the millennials, has long been mocked for our seeming hesitancy to grow up. I would argue that we aren't refusing to grow up, but that our circumstances and values don't match those of our parents when they came of age. Growing up looks different. We are disillusioned and disconnected in our own ways. When I look at the Beehive Girls program, I see a grounding checklist. I see a set of diverse, concrete ways to develop and explore and become competent in everything required of an adult. I want to be the woman these early leaders envisioned.

And, in a lightning bolt of inspiration, I know I'm going to do it by earning the award the way it was laid out a hundred years ago.

WITHOUT ANY
VISIBLE EFFORT
AT SWALLOWING

"HERE YOU GO, DR. THATCHER! Congratulations!" The Office of Graduate Studies receptionist presents me with a king-size Symphony bar when I turn in my last piece of paperwork. I never realized that the reward for finishing this would be the same as the reward for going trick-or-treating in a wealthy neighborhood. I don't turn down the chocolate, though. "Don't forget to ring the graduate bell on your way out!"

I didn't know before this moment that the bell existed—I haven't been looking forward to ringing it—but now that I'm here? I look over my shoulders. It's summer and no one is around. I reach out and give the bell pull a quick tug. The clang is so loud and sudden that I'm almost embarrassed about disrupting the silence. This is so tacky.

Or maybe it's just too playful for what I'm actually feeling. I take a deep breath. I've finished it. Despite poor mentorship, a compressed timeline, scientific setbacks at every turn, pregnancy, delivery, and new parenthood, I finished.

Jane needs food, sleep, and fresh diapers with exhausting regularity, but at least I'm no longer a student. We go on long walks together, her baby carrier facing outward on my chest so she can see the things I'm pointing out to her. We visit the pet store, the art museum, and the park, even though she's too young to care. I'm the one who needs the variety.

One afternoon when she's napping, I print a copy of the Beehive Girls Handbook. The printing alone feels like a big commitment—the printer is wheezing and wringing out its last dregs of ink by the time I finish. I hole-punch it, put it in a binder, and start investigating what it's going to take to be a Beehive Girl. The requirements are called "cells," and the first few cells are the same for everybody.

First, I need to choose a name and a symbol. Strengla, obviously. Just kidding, but I'll come up with something.

Next, I have to "take one half-hour's daily exercise out of doors" daily for two months. Well, if it had to be vigorous exercise I'd be in trouble—my perpetual headache doesn't leave much space for jogging—but it doesn't say vigorous. My walks totally count.

I need to "sleep out of doors or with wide open windows" for two months. Those seem like *very* different things to me. But we don't have air conditioning, so I've certainly "accomplished" this.

It says I need to "know the vertical line test" for correct posture, but it doesn't say I have to use it, so that's no problem. It refers me to something called "The Young Woman's Journal" to learn more about posture—I wonder what the *Journal* is all about.

Apparently, I need to pull out our (only) tablecloth to set the table "tastefully" with "some simple seasonal decoration." Summer in Utah . . . I guess I could put a traffic cone on the table? I had such a vision for coordinating our dishes, tablecloth, and cloth napkins when I first put them in our wedding registry, but I think I've only put it all together twice in the last four years. The tablecloth gets so wrinkled in storage that I'd have to iron it, and that's a nonstarter. Right now, our "decoration" is Jane's Bumbo chair, where she sits in the middle of the table while we all eat together.

I need to pay my "dime fund" for the year. I have no idea what that means. Probably just my Beehive Girls dues . . . was it really only a dime?!

I'm supposed to mend my clothing every week, "not delaying it until ready to wear the article." Ouch. That hits a little close to home.

The last non-optional requirement is to do a good turn daily for a month. This handbook literally quotes the Boy Scout slogan. I'm so fascinated by these ladies'-finish-ing-school-style tasks presented right alongside outdoor sleeping and exercise and "good turns daily."

Now I'm getting into the elective stuff. There are seven fields of endeavor in Beehive Girls, just as there were in Personal Progress back in my day. It's a very different list of seven, though. The first field is "Religion" and that's the only churchy one. The others are Home, Health, Domestic Arts, Outdoor, Business, and Public Service. To earn the first award in Beehive Girls, called "Builder in the Hive," I need to choose 36 cells to complete. "At least two cells must be filled in each field and not more than ten in any one." I love that you can't completely skip any of the fields, but you can distribute the rest of your effort according to your interests. Kind of like college.

By virtue of being a grown-up, I've already filled a lot of the cells. I've planned plenty of meals and logged sooooo many hours caring for a baby. I don't mean to brag, but I *have* had a job where I earn "at least $10 weekly." These reg-ular efforts count toward making rank (the rank of Builder in the Hive), but I'm also choosing new cells for my check-list. I want to try some new things, *out* of my comfort zone, *not* part of my regular routine. I know right off the bat that I'll edit cell requirements to fit reasonably into my twenty-first-century life, but that doesn't bother me. It's not like I actually have a leader (a Beekeeper) or anyone to give me awards.

The fields of endeavor all include a broader, more cre-ative set of ideas than I expect.

For the Home field, I could learn about pediatric health, get to know in-season produce prices, explore literature, write a play, play an instrument, and throw a party with "social entertainment of a cultural value." Huh. Maybe I'm not as skillful a homemaker as I thought.

The field of Health suggests, "Propel yourself 440 yards in Great Salt Lake"—so Utah-centric and so oddly spe-cific—and urges, "For one month masticate your food so thoroughly that it slips down without any visible effort at swallowing." No, thank you.

As for Public Service, this manual has way more ideas than just yardwork and cookies. I could memorize coun-ty names, plan wholesome outings, write life sketches of great scientists, or learn about the cultures and needs of indigenous people in my area. If I were feeling *really* ambi-tious, I could try "co-operating with [my] town authorities in using water supply to the best advantage."

Even the Religion field is surprisingly hands-on. I can pay my tithing; I can learn about the history of the Young Women program; I can go to my church meetings. There is no "pondering" here, no journaling, nothing abstract. There are writing assignments, but they are *essays*. I doubt that most original Beehive Girls looked forward to writing life sketches, but to me it sounds like an amazing excuse to learn some history.

I put together a list of what I'm going to do. This is going to be incredibly time-consuming. I'm not sure how to do most of it, so I'm going to need a lot of mentors. But I'm eager to get started.

WITHOUT
HELP OR ADVICE

FIELD OF HEALTH, CELL 331: Without help or advice, operate and care for an automobile for five hundred miles during one season.

"CAN YOU TEACH ME HOW to change a tire sometime?" I'm on the phone with my go-to car guy: Nate's little brother Cole. Yes, I know that I'm defying the constraints of my very first Beehive Girls cell.

"Like, you just want to take it off and put it back on?"

"Yeah. My dad told me how to do it for driver's ed homework, but I don't think I'd really be able to figure it out in an emergency. . ."

"We can totally do that! When do you want to come over?"

"Tuesday morning?"

"Sure, I'm just helping Mom and Dad with projects, so I'm flexible. Hey, we could rotate the tires! Ten o'clock?" Isn't the whole point of tires to rotate? My tires are rotating just fine. I'll ask when I get there.

"Sounds perfect. I'll make sure Mom or Dad is available to take Jane while we're in the driveway."

"Oh, I'm *sure* they're available for that. You know they'd cancel anything for that."

❀ ℒ ❦

On Tuesday morning, Cole seems impressed that I've shown up. "A few of my girl friends have asked me to do this before," he tells me, "but they've never actually set up a time to follow through."

"Well, my motivation is a little weird," I explain. I tell him about the Beehive Girls and my plan to follow in their footsteps. "Driving an automobile five hundred miles 'in a season' is nothing new, but I want to learn how to do some regular maintenance and care for my own car properly."

"Cool. I can help you with that. Wait, Beehive Girls is from 1915? Teenagers didn't have cars in 1915, did they?" He's got a point. I'll need to look that up later.

My first lesson is that rotating tires just means taking all *four* of them off and shuffling their positions so that the wear-and-tear of driving affects all of them more equally and you can use the same tires longer. So . . . we're basically changing four tires instead of one. Good. I've been working in a lab for a long time and I know that verbal instructions alone don't get me very far—I have to do things to learn how to do them.

I chose Cole as my mentor because he loves cars. Cars are the one thing on earth that can throw off Nate's mood for a day—he considers them an expensive, stressful, necessary evil—but to Cole, every beater presents a series of exciting challenges. Something like Sudoku meets wilderness camping. He lives to tinker, to jury-rig, and to resurrect hopeless machines. And yes, I admire that he got a 36 on the ACT, but more importantly he's the most helpful person I know. He once came over to fix our digital piano (every composer needs an engineer for a sibling!) and made the mistake of asking what else he could do to help. In no time at all our air conditioner and ceiling fan were installed, too. Cole's parents and siblings jokingly shout, "Cole, make it go!" whenever they encounter a technical difficulty. Cole makes it go.

Cole takes off the first of the tires while I watch, and then it's *my* turn to make it go. I put in a second jack, with only a little stress about potentially tipping the car over. I encounter a problem immediately: my arm muscles are untrained and hypothetical. I can't loosen the lug nuts. I didn't expect to be foiled so easily.

Cole is over a foot taller than I am and much stronger, so he stands back for a moment, trying to imagine how someone like me would change a tire. "What if you stood on the lug wrench?"

I step up, willing to try. Nothing happens.

"Now bounce gently?" Cole suggests.

I bounce. Ever so slowly, the bolt begins to turn lefty-loosey. When it's time, I'll be able to get it out with my hands. I successfully remove my first tire.

Nate was with me the only time I've ever actually had a flat tire. He braved the coldest day of the year on the side of I-15 working to loosen a (very) stuck bolt while I stayed in the car to keep Jane calm. But if he hadn't been there? I wouldn't have had the luxury of trying things out. It would have been a problem that I've literally never handled car tools before. I couldn't have casually browsed the owner's manual for answers to all my questions. I would have had to wait for death or an embarrassing rescue. I'm so grateful to have this time now, with no one watching me except my little brother/coach.

Cole and I trade tires. "Okay, so now you just line the rim up with the lug bolts on the hub." Cole shows me on his tire, expecting me to do mine, but again I can't imitate his technique. I can't lift and guide the tire at that particular angle. Hm.

I prop the tire on my shoes to line it up without bearing its entire weight in my arms. I can't see what's going on, so I sit on the ground with the tire still balanced on my feet. I wiggle it onto the hub. Got it. From here, I can put the lug nuts on, tighten them, lower the car, and tighten again. On a hot, sunny day, with plenty of help and advice, I can change a tire on my own car.

"We should check the tire pressure," Cole reminds me. "Do you have one of these?" He holds out a small, pencil-shaped tool I have never seen before. So no. "Take this one! We have spares." The Thatcher garage is basically a mechanic shop.

He shows me how to stick the tire-pressure gauge into the valve stem of a tire. He does a double take and re-checks the standard pressure printed inside the driver's-side door. "Uh . . . I'm not really sure how you've been driving around on these."

I'm an optimist, but I have to admit that these tires are half empty. That explains a lot.

Cole and I are nerds, though, and it's time for us to set down our tools and go research whether teenagers were driving in 1915 Utah.

"Check this out!" I say when I find something. "In Enterprise, Utah, there were zero cars until 1912! Four years later, there were seven cars in town and local man Orson Huntsman reported 'automobiles are getting quite common now days.'" I'm cracking up. "SEVEN whole cars! Little did he know that within a hundred years most families wouldn't be able to function without one!"

"But isn't every new technology like that?" Cole points out. "First you hear about computers existing, and then your friend's dad and your neighbor have them, and then suddenly you have more computers in your home than family members?"

"And you need them *all!*" I agree. After years of holding out, Nate and I have finally made the switch to smartphones and, while we don't regret holding out, we wouldn't want to go back now. "I wonder which invention will spread like that next."

"3-D printers?"

"Self-driving cars?"

"Roombas?"

We learn that, fortunately for Utahns, cars didn't become popular here until *after* the invention of the stop sign, sparing a lot of lives. Those early cars were extremely unreliable, and if a teenage girl was going to be sent out in one, she would definitely have needed some troubleshooting skills. Beehive Girls was written quite early in the history of driving, and Cole and I conclude that it was somewhat bold for auxiliary leaders to picture teenage girls taking care of cars by themselves.

FIELD OF DOMESTIC ARTS, CELL 405: Make a piece of furniture.

I've deliberately scheduled the tune-up with Cole for the day before my second foray into Beehive Girls adventures: a solo road trip to Chubbuck, Idaho, to build a piece of furniture with my Aunt Andrea. (Technically, I'm not solo. Jane is coming with me, but she is nine months old and probably won't contribute too much "help or advice.")

I have never, ever been to Andrea's home. She's a favorite among my many relatives, but Chubbuck just isn't the geographical center of the family.

Andrea is my youngest aunt and the one who best understands Facebook. In fact, her Internet presence is the reason I feel close to her at all. She combines vulnerability and wit to admit that motherhood is hard, that moving is hard, and that some days even being nice to people is hard. She writes hilarious musings on school pick-up zones, creates the perfect Halloween costumes for her children, and builds her own cabinetry, and I've followed along with her life via her blog. Because of the Internet, she learned that I wanted to build a piece of furniture and generously invited me to come learn from her. This is apparently how intergenerational family connection works in the twenty-first century.

In preparation for our carpentry date, I try to envision what "piece of furniture" I can realistically make in a single afternoon. Jane will soon have a bedroom for the first time and it might be nice if there were something other than a pack-n-play set up in there. I'm picturing a large, simple toy box, lidded so that it can double as a bench. I sort of prepare, browsing toy chests on Pinterest and flinching at lumber prices on homedepot.com. I've helped Cub

Scouts build birdhouses before, so this won't be a big deal. We'll use heavier wood and bigger nails, but it's the same concept. Andrea seems to think we should have plans, so I send a couple of tutorials for her perusal.

Jane and I start by visiting my parents in American Fork, so we leave for Idaho later than planned. I blame my mom: she recommended that I pack myself a sandwich and she has proven that she is always right way too many times for me to ignore her. I also have to try four different gas stations before finding one with an air compressor to fill my floppy tires. I'm graceless with the nozzle, but Cole gave me solid instructions yesterday and I inflate the tires without using any lifelines.

My gas mileage improves dramatically. Jane sleeps, stares out the window, bobs to the music, cries. We pull over to nurse. She dozes some more. When she can't handle any more driving we stop at a reservoir and I dangle her feet into the water for a few happy, muddy minutes.

Google Maps autocorrects me to Kiersten Drive instead of Kristen and we end up on the wrong side of Chubbuck. We pull up 45 minutes later than even my "we're late" text said we were going to. We are behind, already crunched for time before Andrea has to go to work, but she doesn't say anything. I really should have eaten my sandwich earlier, but I don't say anything.

Andrea's kids—my cousins, but so much younger than me that we don't feel like part of the same generation— eagerly accept stewardship of Jane. Andrea and I look through the plans to decide what lumber we need to buy.

"I've been thinking about your toy box idea," Andrea tells me, after pleasantries. "And we can totally make that happen, but I wanted to . . . give you some options."

Her careful politeness makes me laugh. "It's okay, Andrea. I'm not married to the idea. Tell me what's wrong."

"Well, I've just had toy boxes before and little kids can't actually open them. They can only smash their fingers in them."

"Wow. Good point."

"And toys are always a mess, but they are *especially* a mess in a big box."

"Yeah, that makes sense. Let's do something else." But Andrea isn't done.

"Also, a big box would just be ridiculously expensive to make."

"You've already convinced me, but that would have been enough by itself! Okay. Um. Do you have a better idea?"

She shows me plans for a bench with three square cubbies. "I saw this and liked that it still fits your storage-plus-seating concept. It seems versatile enough to go anywhere and it'll be cheap to make."

"*Andrea.* This is perfect. Like, I know it doesn't matter, but it looks like this would fit the plastic bins we *already* use for Jane's toys." I'm so glad that my mentor for this project is an experienced woodworker *and* an experienced mother. She knows what I need to build and how to do it. I wonder what I would have undertaken on my own. I also wonder what the point of this project was supposed to be for the original Beehive Girls. Was woodwork a normal part of frontier womanhood? Surely not.

We drive to Home Depot in Andrea's minivan—for today's purpose, she refers to it as her "truck"—and as we walk in she pulls a pair of work gloves out of her purse. No employees assume we need help. I admire her purposeful walk and knowledge of the aisles. I would have been swarmed by helpers in seconds if I'd come in alone.

"The twelve-foot pine is out of stock. Shoot." We stand there, staring at the empty rack.

"I think we can just use two of these instead?" I haz-
ard a guess after some internal calculations. "I should have
looked more closely at the plans." I'm good at math, but
I guess I focused on the photos of the blogger's finished
product instead of on the measurements.

"I *think* you're right," Andrea agrees.

"Does it matter which ones we get?"

"Definitely. You're looking for planks with no holes, no
cracks, and no rough knots. Little imperfections will go
away as you sand and fill the bench, but you don't want the
wood to split while you're putting it together." I nod along.
I know what sanding is and I *think* I know what filling is. I
forgot about that part of the process. I kinda planned to
just nail it together and paint it. All the wood I examine has
knots—how big is too big?

"You also want to make sure the planks are straight."
She's showing me how, looking down the thickness of the
wood as though it's an extra-long spyglass.

I grab my own and try it out. "It seems reasonably
straight . . . ?" I conclude.

"Okay, look at a few more so you have something to
compare it to."

Oh, yeah, that first plank definitely wasn't straight.

Soon, I've obtained two solid planks and an abundance
of slivers.

"Oh, and I need to buy some screws and wood glue today, too." Andrea pretends that she needs them "anyway,"
and I know she's protecting me from the true cost of building something. Honestly, Nate and I are about to pay for a
cross-country move to pay out-of-state tuition for a master's degree in music, of all things, so I appreciate it. I wonder if the "dime fund" was enough to pay for Beehive Girls'
carpentry supplies. And what would they have built? And
who would have mentored them through it?

Soon we're in Andrea's big garage, measuring. "Look," she shows me, "if you sketch a little 'v' coming up from the measuring tape, you can cut more accurately . . . which is good because the segments have to be *perfect* for everything to look good in the end." Perfect? Oh no. As if perfection isn't intimidating enough, there's also the table saw—a whirling blade protruding from a table with no guides or supports. There's no limit to potential damage.

"You're not using that," Andrea states matter-of-factly. I momentarily feel indignant and infantilized . . . but who would let a Beehive Girl use a table saw her first day of carpentry? Andrea does trust me with the miter saw, the one that works more like a buzzing paper cutter, and I do a slow (but accurate!) job cutting long sticks into shorter sticks.

Once we have a pile of pencil-labeled pieces, I trust that we'll go into Cub Scout birdhouse mode and finish in about ten minutes, but apparently project complexity increases exponentially with project size. There are no nails to pound. To stick pieces of wood together we have to mark the wood, then glue it, drill holes for the screws, then put in the screws.

I lose my pencil every time I set it down.

I forget a step in switching the drill from righty-tighty to lefty-loosey every time.

It's like the first few times in any new kitchen. Like when you keep opening the wrong cupboard to find the trash or when you keep turning the oven off when you mean to stop the timer. New laboratories are the same way. This is my first time in a woodshop, but I'm familiar with being slightly lost in a new workspace.

My screws won't bite into the wood the way they should. It would help to be stronger and heavier.

"Let me try," Andrea offers. And then she does it. Even though she isn't any bigger than I am. Apparently, there's no need to think of myself as delicate and helpless. I just don't know what I'm doing.

We talk about how she learned to work with wood: she wanted to save money by building the bathroom vanity in this, the first home she and her husband Ty built. Ty was more experienced with wood—faster and far less nervous—so she forbade his interference and worked with a female mentor, who told her, "If you can make a vanity, you can make anything." Andrea laughs, looking back at her naiveté—"I thought I could do it myself cheaper!"— but she did learn a lot and did create a custom vanity that she loves.

I tell her about the Beehive Girls, about the remarkable breadth of skills and knowledge they were expected to acquire. "It reminds me of you," I tell her. "You sew, you cook, you write, you build, and you're basically an interior designer. Your house is amazing!"

"No, no," she insists. "I just know a little bit about a lot of things. My mom always just *knows* what to do, and I want to be like that." Bonnie Oscarson's April 2015 General Conference talk comes to mind: a mother needs to be "somewhat of an expert in medicine, psychology, religion, teaching, music, literature, art, finance, decorating, hair styling, chauffeuring, sports, culinary arts, and so much more." But where are we mothers supposed to gain any of this expertise? I guess that's basically why I'm becoming a Beehive Girl.

"Shall we take a break for lunch?" I don't know whether Andrea hears my stomach or sees the hopeless look in my eyes, but she's asked just in time. I try to pull out my sandwich, but she is appalled. "What? You think you're bringing your own food to my house? No. How about some tacos?"

She putters around her beautiful kitchen, pulling out taco ingredients. "I need to go to work soon, but all that's left is to add the framing and the legs. Then you'll need to fill in the holes and cracks with putty. Then sand it. Then fill and sand a few more times and you're ready to paint!" As Andrea teaches me about the intense steps of finishing a piece of furniture, it finally strikes me that chairs don't have visible screws or gaps between pieces of wood. Dressers don't. Desks don't. There's no obvious evidence that mortals built them; maybe they were just willed into being by some kind of furniture god. I must have known this before, but I've never considered the implications for creating a piece of furniture. I genuinely pictured myself walking out of here with a complete piece of furniture and my work is just beginning.

My visit with Andrea, though, is over. Jane has had a very happy afternoon of extremely positive attention from three big cousins. I load her up and gather our effects, including the bench. I hug and thank Andrea and the kids. Jane and I hit the road for my grandparents' house in Ogden, where we plan to eat dinner and spend the night before driving the last leg of the trip.

Jane is content, but not much of a conversationalist. When I get sleepy on the long, straight two-lane highway, I call Nate, who is leading band rehearsals for another composer in New York City. "Can I call you back in one minute?" he asks. "I need to wrap up this conversation politely and then I can give you all the company you need."

It's during that one minute that the car breaks down.

It is actually the perfect breakdown: the car just stops running. No one is around and I have time to coast to the shoulder before I run out of momentum. There's no explosion, no smoke. I have nightmares about car crashes all the time, so I really appreciate the lack of drama. I wait a few minutes, in case the engine will magically revive itself after a brief rest.

I try to call Nate, but there isn't any cell reception at this exact point on the Idaho range. He's going to think I fell asleep at the wheel and crashed. Sorry, Nate.

I dump some oil into the appropriate tank, since that's basically all I can do with what I have. For the first time in my life, I wish a tire were flat.

And that's how I end up standing on the side of the road with my baby. I pray aloud with Jane and appreciate her cheerful companionship even though she doesn't know that anything is amiss. We'll be fine. We have food and water. We can wait for a ride.

Somehow, though, I'm confident we won't have to wait long. I'm blessed with a feeling of peace so strong that I don't fully realize that what we are doing is hitchhiking. I know that a kind police officer is coming to pick us up soon. (I wish everyone could count on the police to be helpful.)

Someone does pull up within minutes, even if it's a regular pick-up truck instead of a police cruiser. Its occupants, Kevin and Pam, are fellow Latter-day Saints, they are grandparents, and they are on vacation: they were headed north toward Pocatello when Kevin saw me on the southbound shoulder and found the next possible place to turn around. They are exactly the kind of people we need right now.

Kevin inspects the car and helps me transfer the most necessary baby gear to the pickup while Pam offers her phone and her road trip food. Her phone works here. I can finally inform Nate that we were out of cell service, not dead, and tell Andrea that we're coming straight back to her house. Surprise!

Before we drive away, Kevin busies himself leaving a note for the police in my car's windshield so it won't get towed. "Don't worry," Pam tells me. "He knows exactly what to do. He's the chief of police in our county."

🌸 🐇 🦋

We have a forty-five-minute drive back to Chubbuck ahead of us, so we talk about their grandchildren, Nate's trip, their cabin, and what I was doing up here in the first place. I'm telling Kevin and Pam about the bench project when Kevin asks me, "Did you use period hand tools?"

"Heavens no," I clarify hastily. "I used a power drill." Then the specificity of his question really sinks in. "Wait . . . why do you ask?"

He tells me about the working heritage farm near Logan where he volunteers, reenacting as a carpenter in a pre-WWI woodshop. He builds furniture like it's 1915 and he invites me to visit the farm. If I didn't know I was living in a tender mercy before, I definitely know it now.

Kevin and Pam drop us off safely back at Andrea's home. My uncle Ty is already on the road with his brother to pick up my car and take it to "their mechanic." I didn't know until this moment that they run some kind of car lot. After their generosity with their time, I'm embarrassed to be depending on Ty and Andrea for an unexpected night while we wait for car news, but they seem unfazed. On the bright side, I was planning to spend the week away from home anyway and I'm equipped with plenty of diapers and clothes for Jane—even the good old pack-n-play she always sleeps in. We take over my cousin Saylor's room and everyone puts up with a lot of wailing while I try to get Jane to settle in for the night.

🌸 🐇 🦋

I start vomiting early in the morning, while the family is trying to sleep. Jane is fussy and I'm stressed and isolated,

trying to keep her quiet and cared for while fighting dizziness, weakness, and fever. I emerge at family breakfast
time and accidentally throw up on the floor because I don't
know how far away the nearest bathroom is. I feel like a
little kid.

Andrea takes Jane and orders me back to bed. I try to
insist on cleaning up after myself, but she won't hear of it.
I go to bed. I get up long enough to arrange for a friend to
teach my class in Provo tonight. Car or not, there's no way
I'm going to make it. I go back to bed. Ty staples the legs
onto my bench while I sleep.

My poor car's lifespan has officially come to an end. The
cubby bench is cute, but I don't think I would have traded
my car for it if I had gotten to choose. At least the stomach
bug is gone by the next morning. I move all of my stuff
from my car to Andrea's and say goodbye. With the help
of Andrea, my grandparents, and my parents, Jane and I
make it home.

I sand the bench and fill its seams in the driveway behind our Provo home, basically a round of each per day.
When I'm not working on the bench, it sits in the sunshine
and the putty sets hard. The daily task of finishing the
bench while Jane naps is completely different from washing the dishes while Jane naps: dishes are never ending and
cyclical, but as I sand and fill and sand and fill, the bench
becomes smooth and perfect. The screws disappear, along
with the irregularities in the wood. There is clear progress
every day. It is meditative and gratifying. I look forward
to painting it, coating it in perfectly smooth white paint. I
can't give Jane geographical stability for the next few years,

but I can give her a sturdy, serviceable set of cubbies that I made for her with my own two hands.

When the bench is perfectly smooth and ready to paint, it gets caught in a rare and unexpected downpour. It is unprotected. It warps. I sand and fill and sand and fill some more, but the perfection is lost. I've put a little too much feeling into the bench: I'm sad and embarrassed that I let it get ruined.

Finally, I paint it. It turns out looking homemade, but not in a bad way. It is as sturdy and serviceable as ever. It is fresh and simple and modest. My aunt helped me make it for my daughter. I'm proud to have finished it and excited to have it in our home forever.

SIMPLIFY AND UNIFY

FIELD OF RELIGION, CELL 16: Write an essay on the organization of the YLMIA.

THIS CELL REQUIRES SOME READING. Fortunately, someone named Susa Young Gates wrote a huge book in 1910 about the history of the YLMIA and I still have my BYU library card. Mwahahaha.

Susa starts by describing the "sudden influx of strangers" to the West resulting from the Gold Rush and the Transcontinental Railroad in the 1850s and 60s. Obviously, the Saints were stressed about potential persecution, but Susa says they dreaded even more "the spirit of folly and fashion, excitement and extravagance, which seems a necessary but sad accompaniment to all forms of high civilization." I wonder how many of Susa's contemporaries would actually agree with her. Just because she was stressed about excessive excitement and fashion doesn't mean everyone was!

As usual, there were big concerns about the youth. The rising generation had not found and joined the church in its infancy and they had never left their homes to follow a prophet into the great unknown. There was "no Primary Association, and practically no Sunday School." Some boys received focused spiritual and intellectual training when they were sent out on missions, but girls weren't invited.

According to Susa, the prophet/governor Brigham Young gathered his (large) family in the Lion House sometime in early 1869 or early 1870 and asked the (many) women of his household to "retrench" in their dress, cooking, speech, and behavior. This word is so old-fashioned that even Susa, writing in 1910, keeps calling it "quaint." To retrench means to "cut back": Brigham wanted more modesty and less consumption and competition among all Latter-day Saint women, with his own wives and daughters serving as model citizens.

I learn a lot from the transcript of President Young's speech about which women's fashions he considered "foolish and useless"—thanks for sharing, Brigham—but some of his message is downright timeless:

> I am weary of the manner in which our women seek to outdo each other. It is displeasing to the Lord, and the poor groan under the burden of trying to ape the customs of those who have more means . . .
>
> I want you to set your own fashions . . .
>
> I want my daughters to learn to work and to do it. Not to spend their time for naught.
>
> I wish our girls to obtain a knowledge of the Gospel for themselves . . .
>
> They might assist the older members of the church . . . in propagating, teaching and practicing the principles I have been so long teaching . . .
>
> Retrench in everything that is bad and worthless, and improve in everything that is good and beautiful. Not to make yourselves unhappy, but to live so that you may be truly happy in this life and the life to come.

Having been deputized, the young Young women had to decide how to respond to Brigham's instructions. They discussed recommending a uniform for women, but decided to allow each girl "to choose the style best adapted to her own taste and person." I wonder how much it would have impacted Latter-day Saint clothing culture if they had decided differently!

They did resolve to stop wearing all the fashions that Brigham told them were inappropriate, including "disgustingly short" skirts "extending no lower than the boot tops." They would not "disgrace" themselves by wearing a stylish silhouette called the Grecian bend—it was "a burlesque on the natural beauty and dignity of the human female form." Their revulsion reminds me of how I felt when edgy boys at BYU first started wearing fitted jeans or when women started wearing leggings as pants. Such a disgrace!

But I eventually bought leggings. These girls, on the other hand, made real changes in response to Brigham's counsel. One of the girls, Maria Y. Dougall, recalled fifty years later the "pathetic as well as humorous" aspects of that initial retrenchment. Overskirts, ruffles, "pinbacks," and "all kinds of trimmings were to be done away with. . . . Many of us cut rather sorry figures when we had removed the ruffles," Maria remembered, "as our skirts were of two distinct shades; at the bottom the material was bright and new-looking, the original colors, the upper part decidedly light and faded." Their next new dresses, though, were made in retrenched styles to begin with. The girls vowed to "exercise [their] united influence in rendering them fashionable." Trying to make a modest style fashionable by sheer force of numbers? That's a Mormon girlhood story if I ever heard one.

Around the same time, President Young asked a woman named Mary Isabella Horne to lead the Relief Society in retrenchment. The first official meeting was in May of 1870, with Junior and Senior divisions (and presidencies) of the Retrenchment Association. The official minutes reveal that Miss Susa Young was accepted as the general reporter of the society's meetings, so it's no wonder she was prepared to write this 516-page tome on the organization by 1910.

After the public organization of the Retrenchment Association, the adult presidency went from ward to ward in Salt Lake City and beyond, organizing Junior Associations wherever they went. Each new Junior Association came up with their own articles and resolutions, lovingly preserved in Susa's history. I have no idea whether the junior presidency ever did anything or why Mary Isabella Horne focused on the youth instead of the Relief Society . . . but Retrenchment Association became a movement for young ladies, led by older women. One of its names, the one I'm going to keep using, was the Young Ladies' Mutual Improvement Association: the YLMIA.

In tracing the story of the (eventual) Young Women program, Eliza R. Snow keeps popping out as an extremely important character. The retrenchment associations, the Relief Society, and the eventual Primary program for children were all under her ultimate authority until 1880, when they were organized as three separate entities with three separate presidencies for the first time. Eliza and her friends determined the scope of women's endeavors in early Utah (with large projects often prompted by a single comment from the prophet) and organized their sisters throughout the territory. I've heard of Eliza, of course, but mostly as a poet. I didn't realize that she was such a queen bee. Brigham Young understood her power. He said, "I may preach to the female portion of this community until I am as old as Methuselah; but when they, the sisters, themselves, take hold to reform they will wield an influence that will be successful."

❧ ✿ ❦

I flip through Susa's massive book, trying to figure out how an organization that was all about anti-materialism for adults became focused on hobbies for teenagers. Susa has recorded the detailed actions of every ward. It looks like for the first 20 years, each ward retrenchment association did its own thing. They met any time, any day but Sunday, with schedules shifting throughout the year to accommodate schooling and employment. The programs were unique to the ward. Sometimes the young men joined the young ladies, especially in rural areas for "strength of numbers, as well as the attraction afforded by the presence of the girls." The girls' leaders would have preferred to meet without the boys "because of the difficulty officers met in drawing girls to the front to stand before the public eye when there were young men to do the work." Why the reticence to fully participate when boys were present? Shyness? Laziness? Embarrassment? Distraction? Fear of harassment? I'm sure it depended on the specific girls and the specific boys involved. But yeah, it's easier to be fully engaged in something when you're not trying to impress anybody.

In 1892, Susa suggested writing a lesson manual "to simplify and unify the work done" . . . and also volunteered to write it. She had a lot of energy, apparently. The first year, her manual focused on church doctrine, church history, and human physiology. Physiology?! At church? It was such a big hit that Susa prepared another manual, this time for a year focused on housekeeping and physical education. By 1903 there was a course of literature, with an overview of "the most important of the world's classics," beginning with those written around 3000 B.C. What literature even existed that early? These were no ordinary church lesson manuals.

Hindsight is 20/20, and Susa is clearly embarrassed by how over-the-top her early manuals were, but she insists that the girls received them well: "When the girls undertook to teach the lessons in the Guide to each other, [. . .] their work became as play. . . . What the literary club did for the woman of the world, was accomplished through the M. I. A. for the simple-hearted Mormon girl."

I certainly never learned about classical literature or physiology in my Young Women classes and, because I'm a nerd, that sounds awesome to me. If all truth and beauty comes from the same source, why not study all of it at church? At the same time, I wonder what it felt like to the girls themselves. Was their work *really* as play? Did it just feel like more school? Wait, did teenagers even have school in the late 1800's? I go look it up.

As it turns out, the pioneers built their first schools in Utah (well, Deseret Territory) three months after arriving in the Salt Lake Valley. Ward schools proliferated quickly— wards came together to provide teachers and supplies to give children rudimentary education. By 1875, the Church was providing elementary and secondary education via academies in the Intermountain West, Canada, and Mexico. Unfortunately, having church education as the norm led to resentment and mistrust between members and their non-LDS neighbors.

Free public schools became more available beginning in 1890, perhaps not coincidentally around the same time as the Manifesto marked the beginning of the end of polygamy. The first public high school in Utah opened in 1890. More and more Latter-day Saint teenagers attended public high schools and the Church sought to supplement their education with on-site religious classes (seminary) starting in 1912. Seminary was gender-neutral from the beginning, which I think is cool. Scripture study for everybody!

So when Susa wrote her intense classroom lessons for Mutual, public high school was a brand-new concept. Her generation had received their secular education hand-in-hand with their religious education and she pictured a future where all topics still coexisted at church.

The part of YLMIA history that interests *me* most, though, is the story of Beehive Girls. Since it didn't exist in time for Susa's 1910 history, I find another history, from 1955. I keep looking for one written since, but as far as I can tell from BYU's catalog, none exists.

This is how it happened: Camp Fire Girls and Girl Guides were already popular Scouting-style programs in the United States when, in 1912, several Utah wards tested each of the programs. However, neither program was exactly what the YLMIA board was looking for. They needed something for just the summer, not year-round. The Boy Scouts of America had a fee compromise with the Church, but the girls' programs wouldn't budge on their annual fee of fifty cents per girl. Most importantly of all, there was no way for the YLMIA to retain any supervision or control over the programs at the stake or general level—each group of girls would report to the national organization.

Looking back, the general board's concerns were clearly valid and prescient. Scouting has long been, to quote my mother, "a cash cow," and there was often discord about how (and whether) the Church could exert the kind of control they wanted in the wards and stakes.

In the end it was the founder of the Camp Fire Girls, Dr. Luther H. Gulick, who encouraged the YLMIA to think outside the box and make their own program that "would fit [their] conditions even better than anything that [he had] done." He even looked it over for them when they'd finished. By 1915 Beehive Girls was being rolled out as "the uniform plan of summer MIA work" for all stakes.

I guess I knew a lot about the Joseph-Smith-era church and a lot about the modern church and *nothing* about how we got from there to here. I expected to learn new factoids, but I didn't expect to be surprised about every part of every process!

Things were so much smaller and more grassroots back then. Brigham Young didn't announce his ideas to the whole church: just to his family. There was no Church Office Building full of employees to create those early auxiliary programs: just Eliza Snow and her friends. There was no curriculum committee to make those early YLMIA manuals: just Susa Young Gates.

I didn't know that the Beehive Girl program was part of a bigger wave of scouting and recreation programs for kids. I didn't know that public high schools were part of preparing for statehood. I didn't know that stake leaders would try out ideas and send their results to Salt Lake City.

I love knowing that Beehive Girls was created to meet the unique needs of a specific audience. I love that there was change and collaboration at every level during the program's adoption. I love that it was women who saw what was needed and started trying out ways to make it happen. This is a cool story.

CATKINS

OUT DOOR FIELD, CELL 501: Identify any fifteen trees and describe them in a way to assure recognition in summer.

I'VE NEVER BEEN TO BYU's Botany Pond early on a Sunday morning. It's not quiet, technically, but the noise is all from the ducks. I'm the only one here, except for the steady procession of students heading up the stairs for church.

My friend Patti arrives on foot—she lives even closer to campus than I do. Her hair is pulled back into an amazingly long braid and she is smiling so warmly that I feel welcomed in as a beloved friend. I remember how good it is to be around her.

"Patti! Hey! How are you?!" We both know it's a ridiculous question. We have no way to catch up on the details of her mission, my marriage, her math education degree, my motherhood. We hug and try anyway.

Then it's down to business. "Ready to identify some trees?" I ask.

"Yes! I downloaded an app!"

It's a slow start. Neither of us is a botanist: Patti is my buddy here because I put out a call on Facebook and she volunteered. We aren't used to looking *closely* at trees, looking for their defining characteristics.

We stare up at trees and down at our phones, analyzing leaf shapes and seed types. We learn that the trees growing up out of the pond, supported by trunks with ridges like buttresses, are called bald cypress trees. We learn that the droopy seed things on weeping willows are called "catkins." We learn that the spongy white markings on the speckled alder are called "lenticels" and that they facilitate gas exchange like lungs do.

"Wait a second, Kayla. The alder has catkins *and* cones. Can deciduous trees have cones?"

"Maybe? But what are they for, if the seeds are in the catkins?" We do a lot of Googling to figure out what the adorable tiny cones are—it turns out that the male catkins are long (like a willow's) and the "tiny cones" are just the female catkins. But, in case you wondered, the general term for any cone-like structure is "strobile."

Now, I'm a trained scientist. I'm all about questions and hypotheses. Normally I have to read a great deal of highly specialized literature to find a tiny niche question about a single protein to pursue. So much research has been done that it's difficult to find a question no one has addressed yet. Like, there are still *many* important things we don't know, but they're so specific and so abstract that they're hard to get excited about. What does injected HMGB1 do to ceramide levels in murine gastrocnemius? No one cares. But as soon as we find tiny pine cones on leafy trees I am completely hooked. I ask questions at the pace of a 6-year-old and it feels good. Jane can't walk yet, but I suddenly look forward to making leaf rubbings and finding tadpoles with her.

Soon, it's time for us to part ways and go to church. "Thanks for meeting up with me like this. I know it isn't a normal way to hang out."

"I love it!" Patti says. "Sometimes it feels like I can only hang out with girlfriends if we're going out to eat or something."

"Seriously. I usually meet up with other moms so that our kids can play. Without kids, the approved activities are, like, exercising, crafting, eating sweets, or 'pampering' ourselves."

"I don't even like doing most of that with other people."

"Neither do I, but I care about having strong friendships with other women. . . ."

"Yeah, why does it feel like such a tricky thing to figure out as a 'grown-up?'"

Good question. She's not the only one asking it.

I think that the YLMIA general board, the creators of Beehive Girls, wrote this cell to be about trees. For us, though, this cell became about reconnecting with our innate curiosity and giving it some time to be giddy. It has also been about finding ways to socialize that are actually satisfying, with no materialism or "life optimization" involved. While developing friendships with other girls isn't a stated goal in the Beehive Girls manual, I think it must have been a key part of the plan from the beginning.

ASLEEP IN BEAVER

FIELD OF PUBLIC SERVICE, CELL 732: Know the genealogy of your grandparents and great-grandparents, including the maiden names of grandmothers and great-grandmothers; give homes and occupations.

I ALREADY KNOW THE FULL NAMES of my parents and grandparents, where they live, and how they make their livings (designer, farmer, institute teacher, homemakers). Another generation back, though, and my concept of my predecessors becomes a jumble of story fragments and old-fashioned names like Vernon, Alva, and the crown jewel of melodic-but-unbelievable family names: Clora Fontella Lay. I know that one of them coined the term "tater-tot" (really). I assume all of them were from Idaho? All eight of my great-grandparents were alive when I was born, but I was too young to figure out who was who. Someone had a really big ninetieth birthday party. Someone gave us grape juice made from his own grapes. Someone else pulled candy out of our ears.

Years ago, my maternal grandmother gave each of her grandchildren a huge book full of family stories and newspaper clippings from as far back as we have them, painstakingly typed and photocopied. This must have been so much work for her, especially with no computer involved. That might be useful right about now, but I haven't even brought it home from my parents' house. All of our dusty binders are languishing on the same shelf.

I imagine how this project would have gone a hundred years ago. A Beehive Girl would probably skip down the lane and consult her grandparents, learning heartwarming stories along the way. Should I drive half an hour to pick up the binder? Nah. I have FamilySearch and free access to everything on Ancestry.com. Even alone with a laptop, though, this detective work is pretty fun.

I've never looked through the census for anything specific before. Census records give me snapshots of my great-grandfathers' occupations at ten-year intervals, which is cool. When I see them like this, their careers look as variable and uncertain as careers are in my own generation. Not one of them scaled the corporate ladder and retired on pension, and it comforts me to realize that we all respect them anyway. Their struggles and employment gaps have, in effect, disappeared. One great-grandfather, though—Franklin Vernon Walker—seems to have evaporated from public records by the age of 23? I scour the internet for clues.

Wait a second. Franklin was my paternal grandmother's *dad*. To me, this is distant history, but she would know better than any census on earth what he did for a living. She doesn't live down the lane from me, but she does know how to text.

"Hey, Grandma! I'm having trouble finding Franklin Walker in the census. Can you tell me what he did for work?"

As I wait for my grandma to tell me all about her dad, I search for her mother, Erma Winn Walker, and discover the eulogy my grandma delivered at her funeral. I learn that Erma and Franklin met at an event called the "Civic

Operas" in Salt Lake City, when the boys and girls were lined up by height and paired for dancing. "She looked into those deep blue eyes" and she knew "she would never be the same again." Cute. Very cute. I knew already that I come from a family of happy marriages, but apparently that went farther back than I knew.

There's a photograph of Erma as a young mother and she looks just like me. I read on. Apparently newlywed Erma and Franklin had a really hard time starting a family. Erma gave birth extremely prematurely four times in a row. All four babies passed away. Doctors told them to stop trying. Erma refused. Her patriarchal blessing told her that her marriage would "result in a numerous, healthy, faithful, affectionate, and obedient posterity." And I know, with my view from her future, that the posterity exists. I didn't even know that there was a time when their hearts were broken and they didn't know how it was possible.

The key, for Erma, was a "sympathetic doctor who told them to try wheat germ." She carried a baby to term for the first time. Then she had eleven more babies. To me, that sounds like an excessive number of babies, but in the context of her story it's more like a miracle. I have so many great aunts and uncles that I hadn't even heard of all of them before this eulogy. I'm weeping for a great-grandmother who died when I was two.

This eulogy is scripture, if we think of scripture as the story of the Lord's dealings with my family. I wonder how many times my grandma, a middle child among the dozen, heard this story growing up. How did it feel to know you were so wanted? That your parents were so brave? That this family was all so important to them? Maybe the kids hardly noticed: it was the water they swam in. But I'm so grateful that my grandma wrote this all down so I could learn Erma's story. I want to learn the lullaby this eulogy says she sang to her many children so that I can sing it to my Jane.

The eulogy isn't all about fertility and infertility, though. The next anecdote I encounter is about the time Erma accidentally dropped a baby to catch a ball that another child threw to her. The baby was fine, so it's okay to laugh. I'm still laughing when my grandma responds to my texts: "My dad went by Vernon most of the time." That explains why I couldn't find Franklin in the census. "He was a farmer. Glad you enjoyed the tribute to my Mom. I wish you could have known her. She was a great lady. And a great musician. She would have longed to hear you play, I just know it."

I'm curious now about whether genealogy was popular in Utah when the Beehive Girls manual was written. I look up an article about the history of family history in the Church of Jesus Christ of Latter-day Saints and the short answer is, "Yes, because of Susa." Remember Susa Young Gates? She became passionate about genealogy after a near-death experience and a blessing of healing told her that "a council in heaven" had decided she would "live to perform temple work." She noticed that "there was practically no book of lessons in genealogy in existence" and no guidance for anybody trying to get started.

Susa strove to fill every need she saw. Soon there were classes, manuals, a weekly newspaper column, and even conventions—over the three days following each general conference—attended and conducted entirely by women. Sunday Relief Society meetings focused on the technical skills required for genealogy, though apparently the sisters hated it. Some wards "felt discouraged concerning the somewhat technical lessons given on Surnames for the past two years" and "felt almost justified in setting aside these lessons for the more attractive and really essential work" they were doing for the Red Cross. One report from the field read simply, "Everybody asleep in Beaver."

Anyway, since Susa was so strongly involved in the YL-MIA and in family history, it's no surprise that genealogy work made its way into the Beehive Girls program. I wonder how many of the Board members rolled their eyes at Susa's insistence. The year that the assigned visiting teaching message was about visiting teaching every month was hard enough—can you imagine two years of Relief Society lessons on *surnames*?

If she did have to insist, though, I'm glad that she did. I needed this connection to my ancestors. I needed to see them as people who lived long ago and, paradoxically, as people whose lives overlapped my own. I needed to see the ways that their lives were so different from and, somehow, so similar to mine. I'm going to get that binder from my parents' house, dust it off, and get to know all the stories that are my birthright.

THROUGH
AND THROUGH

FIELD OF PUBLIC SERVICE, CELL 711: Spend the equivalent of six afternoons in visiting the sick or entertaining some elderly persons.

I DON'T LIKE MAKING PHONE CALLS, and Provo Care Center for intellectually disabled adults is two blocks from home, so I drop in one day to learn about the volunteer process. Jane is with me, in her stroller instead of a front carrier. She's grown so much that long strolls with her on my chest have started to hurt my back.

In my imagination, Beehive Girls of 1915 visited homebound widows or sick children in their own wards, bringing lamb's foot jelly and hand-stitched quilts. Faced with this requirement, though, I don't know anyone who could use a visit. I have better sense than to show up on the doorstep of a sick stranger without a better excuse than, "I heard you were super lonely." (The lamb's foot jelly and quilt are also out of the question.)

"So you'll need to come in for an interview," an administrator is telling me, "and then there's a background check—oh no!"

I turn to see what she is reacting to and manage to catch Jane's toppling stroller before it hits the ground. A resident passing by in a wheelchair grabbed the handle and pulled while I wasn't looking. This was the perfect moment for me to exhibit jungle-cat reflexes. Janie doesn't even know that anything is wrong, but yikes, that was close.

"Good catch," the administrator continues, shaken, but professional. "Uh, where were we . . . oh, after your background check comes back, you can come and volunteer whenever you want. You just sign in here at the desk. But . . . you probably shouldn't bring your daughter."

No kidding.

The volunteer paperwork is more complicated than I expect, mostly because it includes a section where I need to write down every address I'd lived at in the last seven years. Since seven years brings me back to when I moved away from home, there are seven addresses to recall (or estimate). The main question seems to be whether I am here to abuse people who can't defend themselves. I'm not, though, so within the week I'm approved to volunteer.

❀ ☙ ❁

It's morning when I go to volunteer for the first time, but surely that can count as "the equivalent of" an afternoon. I'm nervous. This is not my first time visiting strangers as a service and I have some hangups.

I grew up near Utah's State Developmental Center, so we frequently volunteered at wheelchair dances for Mutual night or helped the residents (mentally and physically disabled adults) get to sacrament meeting. I remember these as distressing experiences. I was determined to see the personalities and spark of divinity in each of the people I met there, so I felt terribly guilty about not knowing what to say and not knowing where to look. The erratic shouting and grabbing disquieted me. I didn't know how to deal with drool. I could maybe have used some coaching.

In high school, I would go to a nursing home every Sunday evening with my friends to sing hymns for the elderly residents. I went for the friends, for the music, and for the service hours, but the residents wanted us to chat with them after the singing. I hated it. I could never figure out what to say or how to handle it.

Maybe seeing the same people more than once will help me get less awkward? Maybe it'll be easier now than it used to be? Today will probably be intimidating, but I'll probably get better as I go . . . ?

When I arrive, though, the place is mostly empty. The residents go to work every day. There are a few retirees to hang out with, but at my interview the staff certainly made it seem like I was going to be playing every game in the closet with the residents and instead they are wheeled out of their rooms every morning and pointed at the TV. I worry about their lazy, indifferent treatment. If the staff members aren't going to do anything, maybe I can be the one to brighten their lives.

I keep observing, though, and trying to engage with the residents. It becomes clear to me—quickly—that I am just an outsider here. The staff members know what the residents want and need, and for some of them that means not being bothered while they are trying to watch TV. Would I like someone to come pester me about playing a game while I'm watching something? Of course not.

There is a big kerfuffle about one resident's "whisper stick" (a soft, clean broom head), which I can't fetch for her because I am not allowed into her bedroom. One resident gets angry at me for not bringing her any printed pictures, even though I've never met her before. I feel useless, out of place, and bad at this.

I sit down with a resident named Susanna. Susanna is nonverbal and she usually holds her arms in a tight, defensive position up by her face—even though she can move them, they never seem relaxed. After I sit with her for a while, chatting softly, I figure out that she is reaching for my hand. When I give it to her she smiles and holds it against her face.

I think of when our close friends, Sean and Ana, became parents for the first time and I was confused about how they knew what the baby needed. She couldn't talk. She couldn't point or nod or otherwise gesture. How did they know when she was in pain, let alone whether it was an earache or a gassy tummy? How did they decide whether to feed her, rock her to sleep, or give her Tylenol? When our own daughter arrived, Nate and I realized how clearly we (usually) understood Jane's needs. Paying attention is required; words aren't. Now, holding Susanna's hands, I again feel the thrill of knowing exactly what I can do to show love for someone. In fact, one of Susanna's professional caregivers informs me, I've found the one thing on earth that Susanna wants from anybody.

🌼 🐚 🐚

One morning, I sit and read to a woman named Diana. She carries a board book with her name in it everywhere she goes: "I Love You Through and Through." It's a standard children's book about loving a child's fingers and toes, his silly side and mad side, but I find one line especially poignant in this context. "I love you running and walking, silent and talking."

"She can read that *to* you, you know," a passing caregiver points out. Oops. I haven't heard her say anything and assumed that meant she couldn't. I'm supposed to be helping Diana gain whatever independence she wants, not taking over her job. She speaks quietly and so slowly that it would be unintelligible if I weren't looking at the words, but she knows this book by heart.

"It's lunchtime!" another staffer calls. "Everyone to the dining room!"

When Diana gets up to begin her slow shuffle down the hall, I realize that she has wet her pants. I flag an employee down to help her change, but in the meantime I grab some paper towels and disinfectant and start scrubbing down the chair and the floor. Parenthood has definitely prepared me for this situation. I'm not grossed out or flustered the way I would have been as a teenager. In one way, at least, I can be useful here.

🐝 🐝 🐝

My sixth visit is my last, not because I insist on doing the bare minimum, but because I'm moving away. Six visits aren't enough to make me great at hanging out with the residents. Instead, the visits are enough to teach me that *no one* is great at hanging out with the residents. "The residents" aren't a monolith: each is an entirely separate, whole person. I think the value of this cell has been in realizing that it always takes time to get to know a new person. It's okay not to have it all figured out immediately. You *always* have to listen and watch someone over time to know how to love them. It's normal to start with basic respect and kindness and build from there.

A LONG TRAMP

FIELD OF HEALTH, CELL 327: Climb a mountain, attaining a point at least **2000 feet above starting point,** and return.

"IT'S NICE TO TALK OUTSIDE THE LAB," my friend Amy says. "There aren't, like, five different machines whirring and buzzing all day long."

"It's also nice to know that no one is going to walk through the room!" I agree. We've been subjected to a trendy new "open lab" design and it's impossible to have a private conversation anymore. On this drizzly Tuesday morning, life is quiet on Grandeur Peak and we can talk unrestrained the whole trip.

This cell is no big deal. I've climbed mountains before.

Okay, that's a bit of an exaggeration. I have summited exactly one mountain, Mount Timpanogos, in college. The only other girl in our party insisted—ignoring all our pleas—on hiking in flip-flops, so we were on the mountain for 14 hours. I thought my bladder would burst. I didn't know how to pee outside and I certainly wasn't going to ask for help from the random neighbor boy who had invited me. The worst part, though, was encountering other groups (always passing us) who applauded the girl in the flip-flops.

Nate and I have a dream of climbing the seven peaks around Utah Valley, but we have attempted and failed to climb the shortest of them, Loafer Peak, three times. The first time we visited, we thought we could just ramble up while listening to General Conference live on our radios. I was in sneakers and it was muddy and we decided minutes in that we needed to come back with hiking boots at the very least.

The second time, it was January. Payson Canyon was closed for the winter, so we couldn't access the regular trail, but we slogged through thigh-deep snow all the way to the top of one of the foothills anyway. We thought we were within reach of the summit when we discovered that we were not even on the right foothill.

The third time, we planned for a short, casual birthday hike of just a few miles and prepared accordingly. But Nate *cannot handle* going back the way he came, so we chose a detour that looked like it would take us to the top without much effort. The "detour" ended up turning the day into a 14-miler with five miles of hitchhiking back to our car at the end (Don't worry, I knew how to pee outside by the time this happened). I think we pretty much survived because there was some snow to melt to refill our water bottles and Nate found a wrapped Slim Jim on the ground. We did come within about half a mile of the summit, but we knew by then that we were in big, exhausted, dehydrated, sun-setting trouble, so we kept moving. I will mention, because it's funny, that I was five months pregnant at the time.

I have requested that next time we remember that even short little Loafer is a mountain, not a grassy knoll. But there may not be a next time. We're a little sick of dealing with that peak.

Anyway, regardless of my number of summited mountains, hiking is among my favorite hobbies—certainly the closest thing I have to a sport. I love being in spaces without air pollution or noise pollution. I love flora and fauna. I love pushing through a climb I don't think I can do. I love long conversations and long silences and I love how delectable a squashed sandwich can be after hours of slow ascent. I also appreciate that hiking is cheap and sustainable and, in Utah, extremely accessible.

Most of all, though, I love hiking because it has always meant time with Nate. We have hiked together since high school—we're especially proud of our weekly hiking adventures during pregnancy. That kind of alpine waddling, though, is nothing compared to the backpacking trips Nate grew up taking—some in Scouts, but even more with his dad, who was born to be a forest ranger.

Because Nate has spent a week at a time in the wilderness with nothing but a heavy pack and a mountain, he serves as my expert guide whenever we take an excursion. My role is to say, "Hey, let's go for a hike!" and buy some granola bars. His is to choose a destination, learn the route, make all preparations, drive us there, and carry the majority of the weight (except the fetus, where applicable). In general, this is a good division of labor for us.

Planning my Beehive Girls hike, though, makes me aware that I've never been on a hike *not* led by men. Whether my dad, my bishop, my guy friends, or my husband "presided," it was men, men, men. Thus, I determine to hike—just this once—with a female mentor and no men at all.

Amy was in my grad school cohort. She's a diligent and creative scientist, but she also has a formidable amount of running, rock-climbing, and camping experience and she readily agreed when I asked her to climb a mountain with me. I assigned her to choose the mountain so that she would have some control over how much of a free day to spend away from her fiancé: she picked a short one.

But even a short mountain takes some time to climb. We've never gotten to hang out socially before and it's wonderful. We talk about how we ended up becoming scientists, our aspirations and concerns for our futures in our field. We talk about our families, our dating experiences, our favorite books, our developing politics, lingerie and her upcoming marriage. We talk about church and the gospel and our faith. I think we could have been intimate friends all along, but we couldn't converse nearly this well when any of our professors or colleagues could walk through the open doorway at any time. We had to stay reasonably professional.

When the path is especially steep and we focus on breathing, I think about the other women in my life I talk to like this. My sisters, a little bit—I think we'll relate more as they get older. My mom, with the exception of politics. The other PhD student in my lab, Melissa, particularly when we've shared a hotel room during conferences. Lately it has been my friend Christina, who has a talent for open and deep conversations in small moments, patched together over days, with no need for a special occasion to foster community. We've taken our daughters to the park together, but we've also sat in her kitchen peeling peaches that were going bad too quickly. We've never gone out for pedicures or ice cream or a movie. A night out would be fun, of course, but I'm grateful to have a friend who doesn't *require* that kind of planning. I have absolutely texted Christina to ask if I could come over just because I was feeling lonely.

Most of my female friends from before I was married are very distant now. Marriage and motherhood make my social needs and preferences different than they were in college and I'm not sure what the intervening years have done to my old friends' social lives. In my head, everyone has classes all day every weekday, schoolwork every week-night, and dates every weekend. I know from experience that that isn't true, that many people could pencil me in for Sunday morning tree identification or a lunchtime video chat or *dinner* (who doesn't want to be fed dinner?), but I use my assumptions as an excuse not to call.

"I just realized that I've never talked about most of this stuff with my best friend!" I remark to Amy.

"Why not?"

"I don't know. I guess . . . we've been friends for so long that Natalie and Nate are tight too, so she's like a family friend? And then once she started dating her husband, it just made sense to hang out as couples."

"Yeah, I can see how you wouldn't talk much about sex when you're hanging out as couples . . ."

"Well, and we're in constant 'catching up' mode, so I barely know the surface-level details of her life, let alone what keeps her up at night or what she's reading or how it's changing her."

"I mean, at least you're still friends. I keep seeing people just, like, disappear from their friends as soon as they get engaged."

"Yeah, it was really important to me and Nate *not* to do that. We love our friends. But maybe we also don't know them very well anymore . . ."

We've made it to the top of the mountain. We take a sweaty selfie at the summit and sit for a while, munching on snacks. Even a three-mile hike deserves a lunch break. From the top of this mountain, I can see the Salt Lake Valley and, turning, rolling green foothills and other peaks. The rocky mountains aren't just a wall of the major peaks you see from the valley with flat ground on the other side—the range is a wide belt, with so many layers that from here I can't see any sign of their ending.

You know the feeling of connecting with a stranger on a flight? You walk away in a rush of fresh understanding, re-invigorated by the sharing and fresh perspective, but with the knowledge that you'll never see this friendship go further. Well, my friends Pete and Jess married after meeting on a plane, but *usually* you'll never see this friendship go further. It's exciting and sad. Amy and I make our final descent from Grandeur Peak with newfound closeness, but without making plans for another hike. I won't even show up for her wedding reception. I'm moving to Ann Arbor in two weeks.

I've never been to Michigan. Truthfully, I'd never heard of Ann Arbor until we chose a school, and then it turned out that everyone else in the world had a connection to the college town to talk about. Everyone insists that it's extremely beautiful. I believe them, of course, but it seems a little pretentious now to leave behind these mountains.

Nate and I both grew up "in the shadow of the everlasting hills." When Nate was a missionary, far away from the mountains, his weekly letters still came to me here. We courted here, married here, brought Jane home to a little Provo apartment just like so many Latter-day Saint families before us. Even though we've been planning for this our whole marriage, looking forward to the parting moment, this is our home. Leaving it is a massively big deal.

EDGES

"WHAT ON EARTH IS A FIRELESS COOKER?" Nate asks. I'm reading the Beehive Girls manual aloud to him while he drives. Sweet Jane is snoozing in the back seat.

"I have no idea. It's not like microwaves existed yet. And it says you can use 'modern labor-saving devices' to do laundry, but I don't know what those would have been back then."

We're on our way to the American West Heritage Center. It's where Kevin, my rescuer from The Infamous Chubbock Expedition, volunteers as a reenactor. He told me I should go and I'm running with it.

"So I still have no idea what cells this is going to fulfill . . . if any," I admit.

"Yeah, but we obviously have a lot of questions about life in rural Utah in 1915, so it'll be good regardless." Nate is always encouraging. "Like, what did people eat regularly?"

"What is bluing? The manual says to 'take care of milk' . . . what does that mean?"

"What is the *point* of airing a bed?"

"Oh, and I don't need to use period hand tools for carpentry, but it would be cool to know what they were. I'm also supposed to learn about twelve different kinds of lace and their uses, but . . ."

"There are uses for lace? I think of it as purely decorative."

"Yeah, exactly. What else is there to say about it? Also, I still haven't chosen a name or symbol for myself."

"Right! You can keep your eyes open for ideas today."

We're excited to quietly enjoy the historic 1917 farm this morning. Our calendar is filling up, logistically and emotionally, as we prepare for our move next week, so a family day-trip is a breath of fresh air. This is all we have on our schedule until dinner, when we have to say goodbye to Natalie and her husband. We bask in the absence of pressure. We have time to pull off the road to investigate an interesting building we see (it turns out to be the Wellsville Tabernacle). With our little Janie napping, Nate and I actually get to talk without constant distraction.

After we arrive and buy tickets, our first stop is the woodworking shop. The two grandpas there are delighted to have an audience. The walls are hung with real vintage tools, so they can demonstrate each when I ask about them.

"What's that one?"

"That's a lathe. You keep it going by pumping the pedal, like an old sewing machine, and it just rotates a chair leg or a wagon spoke or something like that so you can sand or cut it evenly all around."

"Oh, like a potter's wheel, but for wood! Cool. What about that one?" I ask, gesturing to a pointy spike with a handle.

"That's an awl. It's for puncturing or marking wood."

"What's he using to make that spoon?" It looks like a chisel with a curved blade—they have all different sizes in the shop.

"That's a gouge." Well, that makes sense. It's interesting to connect so many familiar words with unfamiliar tools. I feel like I've always known the words lathe and awl without knowing quite what they are for. I get to try out a plane, a big block with a cutting edge that smooths out a large flat surface. The plane is a little too heavy and too high for me, but the satisfaction of making a pile of curling wood shavings distracts me from worries about looking silly. Jane is delighted to sit on a wooden rocking horse.

I think of pioneer woodwork I've seen—the tabernacle organ, the curved banisters in the Manti temple, the ornate mantelpiece in our apartment (with lion's heads, fleurs de lis, *and* caryatids)—and I'm awestruck to realize what went into making even the simplest chairs. There was no power saw. There was no power sander. There was no electric lathe or factory. Oh, and a lot of the time these craftsmen joined wood pieces *without screws or nails*. I think every tour guide at every church history site I've ever seen (and I've seen plenty) has pointed this out to me. Now that I've built the most basic piece of furniture and looked around this shop, I finally get it.

"Carpenters in this shop would have thought I was *so lazy*," I joke to the reenactors.

"Oh, no," one corrects me. "They would have used power tools if they'd had them. They jumped onto whatever new technology came out. They would have wanted to work faster."

He has a point. While my generation looks longingly back at the zen-like hours of carving in the life of a chair-maker, the chair-maker would gladly have taken a break from intense physical labor. Those who revisit his methods do it as a hobby, not as a family-sustaining career. They can afford extra hours of lovingly handling fresh-smelling cedar.

After the woodshop, we visit the big barn. I could have come today by myself, for research, but I have a 10-month-old baby who loves animals and I didn't want her to miss this. We watch someone milk a cow, but there's a crowd and I don't ask to try it. When the crowd disperses a little, I ask the reenactor what it means to "take care of milk."

"You basically just pour it through a filter into a milk can. The filter gets the dirt and grass out. Then you have to put it on ice to keep it cool."

"And what else?" I ask, expecting it to be more complicated.

"Um . . ." I've thrown him off. "That's . . . pretty much it." Oh. Well. There you have it.

There are big, beautiful horses, the kind that could definitely pull wagons. There are pigs basking in the sun. The goats keep Jane's attention longest: they are endlessly noisy and in motion. She laughs and laughs at their antics. The chickens are briefly endangered by a badger, who is understandably confused and terrified by all the humans. Everyone backs off and watches as some of the workers help steer the poor badger back to the wild.

Once the chickens and badgers are all feeling more at ease, we board a little train on its loop around the farm. It's a perfectly Instagrammable family activity, though Jane doesn't seem to notice the train. She would be just as pleased to suck on a rock.

🪻 🐚 🦋

The crown jewel of the heritage farm is a restored farmhouse from 1917, with appropriate furnishings in place and in full working order: the re-enactors here have cows and goats to milk, eggs to gather, animals to feed, and children helping. One of the staff members, Rosie, cooks an authentic lunch for her crew every day using an original wood-burning stove and introduces me and Nate to her "baby" by sharing some freshly-baked snickerdoodles.

"Everything tastes better when it's cooked in one of these," she tells us and, with cookies in our mouths as evidence, we wholeheartedly believe her. I would never *choose* to spend an hour and a half preheating an oven to 350 degrees, especially with no way but experience to know whether it was the right temperature, but Rosie clearly takes great pride in her intimate knowledge of her particular stove. "Women used to spend so much time with their stoves, learning all of their quirks and how to work with them, that the stove was like a member of the family," she tells us. "A husband would try to surprise his wife with a new electric stove and she would completely freak out and demand that her old stove be put back in its place."

Leftovers from lunch are resting on the sideboard— cornbread, plus macaroni and cheese that I wish she offered to share. "The other crews just order pizza or sandwiches and it drives me crazy. That's not authentic!" Rosie chuckles ruefully at her coworkers' antics, but I can tell it's a real pet peeve. I ask what *is* authentic—what would people have been eating on the farm in 1917. "A lot of noodles," she tells me (I'm surprised). "A lot of dairy, always some meat."

Nate is delighted to find an old-fashioned electric toaster on the counter—the "fireless cooker" we've wondered so much about. There's also an ice chest to keep milk and butter cold: it's an insulated box that would have been stocked daily with a large block of ice dragged from the ice shed, where it was stored in sawdust after purchase from the ice man. There are some "leather britches," an evocative term for dried string beans. The resourcefulness and effort that it would take to keep a family fed year-round are astounding.

Rosie has plenty to do in the kitchen, and a twelve-year-old volunteer takes over as our tour guide. Her name is Parker and she comes here with her parents and siblings one day of every week. She looks like my baby sister and I like her immediately. She is a stereotypical oldest child: a confident leader who sees herself as having real responsibilities in helping her parents and the guests.

There's a laundry display set up in the "summer kitchen," a structure separate from the house. Since I, too, live in a home without air conditioning, I understand the wisdom of such an arrangement. Parker shows us how to scrub clothes on a washboard, but we also get to see some of the "modern labor-saving devices" mentioned in the Handbook, including a hand-crank washing machine. Parker's little brother is eager to carve soap shavings into the wash water—the same lye soap that they would have used for everything else. Among the laundry artifacts are various types of heavy, stove-heated irons, and different brands of starch, soap, and bluing. The old-timey box of bluing teaches me that it's a blue dye that, when used properly, makes white clothing look whiter.

Parker starts telling us about milking cows and I decide to ask my question again: "how do you take care of milk after milking?

Her answer is the same: "Oh, you just run it through a filter and put it in the ice chest. We have a butter churn too! We've never finished making butter, though . . . because we're lazy."

She shows us through the house. We see straw mattresses and lace doilies and (my favorite) kerosene lamps with the kerosene dyed red, just to be pretty. They look like lava lamps. The small touches lovingly added for beauty catch my attention, but there's something else too. I hear a strong pattern from Parker:

"This is the little girls' room. I would have slept in the big girls' room."

"The little boys whittled these clothespins."

"I would have been in charge of making butter."

"My brother would have been in the big boys' room and he would have been in charge of helping dad out on the farm."

Parker sees herself clearly when she looks at the farm. She knows what she and each of her siblings would have been doing to help the farm succeed based solely on their ages and genders. She knows where they would sleep and what toys they would play with. I've never thought of my place in the household being pre-determined by my gender and birth order, but it absolutely was. I was a girl and the oldest of six children. You could probably guess most of the details of my childhood from that alone.

There's one other thought-provoking thing about the house: 1917 doesn't really qualify as "frontier Utah." Latter-day Saints had been in Utah for seventy years. Seventy! The farmhouse was built during World War I, when there were already electric refrigerators, electric irons, electric lights, indoor bathrooms, cars, and airplanes. Many people worked in factories and in offices instead of on farms. Utah had been a state for a while by then and the population was slowly diversifying—not everyone was of northern European ancestry anymore. I guess I subconsciously lump together the era of the early church (the 1830s) with everything up until my parents were born at the tail end of David O. McKay's presidency. Things had changed considerably by the time the farmhouse was built, if you lived in a city and had money. (The same principle applies now, of course: there are *still* many people in the world without plumbing or electricity.)

After we visit the farmhouse, we wander across a bridge and past an old-timey store, currently closed. There's a Shoshone teepee across the field that might be interesting . . . but then I see a couple of reenactors bent over some kind of needlework. Whatever they're working on is probably something I'm supposed to learn about. "Let's go check it out!" Nate suggests.

I hesitate. In the bright sunshine, my daily headache is encroaching on my ability to think. "I don't know if I feel well enough to talk to strangers . . ."

"I'm here. I'll help." Nate assures me. It's enough to get me to try.

We approach and admire the display boards bedecked with the women's extensive portfolios: butterflies, flowers, doilies, jewelry, all kinds of beautiful thread and yarn creations. I don't know how to classify what I'm looking at, but they tell me it's all lace. "Lace just means 'edges,'" one explains (her name is Chris and she's married to one of the woodworkers, apparently). "If it decorates the edge of something, it's lace." I restrain myself from questioning her concise definition—she's displaying art that is *entirely* lace, with no edges involved.

FIELD OF DOMESTIC ARTS, CELL 428: Identify twelve kinds of lace and tell reasonable price and appropriate use of each.

Chris sets me up with a pillow tied to some beaded stick things (she calls them bobbins) and teaches me how to move them to create stitches for a lace bookmark. I imitate her and get a few stitches in before she corrects me: "No, that bobbin needs to stay in the right hand, this string in the left."

Her way doesn't come naturally to me, and she has to correct me more than once, more harshly than I think is appropriate. "Does it matter, as long as the strings are crossing the right way?" I ask, trying not to sound argumentative. It's important to me to keep only rules that make sense. I consider any other rules a power trip.

"Yes, it matters," she tells me, without offering any explanation or data.

We talk while we work. "People have been decorating with lace since at *least* the late fifteenth century," Chris tells me, "but the techniques came from weaving and making nets and tying knots, so we have fishing communities to thank!"

I think of lace as basically white and delicate and frilly—I never knew that lace could be knitted. It can also be crocheted, tatted, embroidered, woven using a pillow and bobbins (as I'm doing now), or crafted using a variety of other methods. That must be what the cell means by "twelve kinds of lace." I think of the white, temple dedication handkerchief my great-grandmother tatted for me before she passed away. That's lace.

"So, I'm supposed to learn about appropriate uses for different kinds of lace. Do you have any idea what that might mean?"

"I mean . . . one of the original uses for lace was to cover worn cuffs on shirts and coats, hiding the rough edges with something pretty and making the clothes last longer. But other than that, I can't think of any *uses*." Oh, that's a beautiful concept. It reminds me of Kintsugi, the Japanese art of repairing broken pottery with gold.

After a few minutes of slow, thoughtful bobbin movement, I'm picking up speed. Chris was right to scold me before: having the correct bobbins in the right and left hands is essential to getting into the rhythm I'm finally reaching. A little fish is beginning to take shape on my pillow.

Chris's companion, Rosala, is excited to hear about my Beehive Girls project. "I'm not surprised that lace is in there! Lacemaking was a really big deal in early Utah, especially since St. George was such an important silk town." Huh. Silk in frontier Utah is news to me. "Pioneer women brought lace and patterns across the plains with them." As they left their established homes behind for the great unknown, they valued the way lace connected them to their old lives. "Even today, a lot of altar cloths in the temple are handmade gifts from volunteers. An altar cloth takes hundreds of hours to make. It's an amazing gift." I wonder how many of these cloths I've seen without really admiring them or feeling their impact—lace can be made by machine now, and I've never tried to tell the commonplace from the truly remarkable.

Today, Chris is pleased to tell me, there are groups of "lacers" who meet all over Utah to make lace together and to keep the tradition alive. In the town where Chris lives, the lacers meet at the senior citizen center every week and one woman brings her five-year-old daughter along.

Rosala mentions one of her current projects, a lace jacket to go over her temple dress, but Chris laughs when I ask about whether her clothes are all lace. "I don't wear it!" she tells me. "I'm a tomboy."

Jane is delighted with the little fish I made her, so apparently "fish bookmark" is one appropriate use of lace.

I'm glad that we came today. So much has changed in

the last hundred years—in how people cook, keep animals, do laundry, build furniture, make clothes, and raise their children. Beehive Girls was invented during an intense period of transition to modernity. Many of the Beehive Girls would have lived on farms like this, while many others would have been surrounded by trappings of modern, industrialized, urban life. It feels like the Board was trying to create a program that would bring some progress and modernity to the farm girl and some practical, hands-on living to the city girl.

I'm also glad that we came today because I've come to a decision: I'm going to use lace as my personal Beehive Girl symbol. Just as pioneer women used lace and other folk art to "blend the old and the new by preserving the past and welcoming the future," this Beehive Girls project will come with me across the plains, connecting me to Utah and my ancestors as I leave what I know and make a new home in Ann Arbor.

GIRL QUERIES

FIELD OF HEALTH, CELL 307: Every time you can remember it, during one month, assume and maintain correct posture of body as tested by the vertical line test. Learn knee-chest position: during three months put into practice some simple home treatment for prevention of pain during menstrual period. (See Young Woman's Journal, Vol. 23, pages 62–4. Read entire article.)

I'VE NEVER HEARD OF THE Young Woman's Journal, so I'm glad the instructions are so specific. It turns out to be a monthly periodical and the whole thing is available on archive.org. The issues are listed by publication date rather than by number, but I do manage to find the required pages.

It's a practical course in bodily cleanliness, beginning with an introduction to the physiology of the skin and the concept that preserving the health of the entire body is the key to great skin. Make-up is dismissed as unnecessary, expensive, and potentially dangerous—simple, at-home washing and moisturizing are recommended.

I'm already impressed. Maybe I would have spent less of my adolescence layering on acne treatments and orange foundation if anyone had taught me this.

Then there's the keeping of hair. "Brushing the hair thoroughly with a stiff brush (not a wire one, which breaks it), will keep the hair glossy," due to the "wholesome secretion of oil which is nature's own dressing." As for cleaning, "drugstore concoctions should be avoided," in favor of castile soap or egg yolks. My guess is that these instructions were out of fashion when they were written. Drugstore concoctions must have been the hip new thing. Also, this can't be how curly-haired people were supposed to care for their hair . . . right?

The lesson describes care of nails, teeth, and eyes, then finishes up with a reminder that taking care of your whole body is what matters. I resolve to try a few days without my regular shampoo, conditioner, mousse routine—as a curly girl, I don't generally brush my hair and I'm brimming with curiosity about how it will behave without my "drugstore concoctions."

I'm far *more* interested, though, in looking through the rest of this magazine! Poetry, short stories, and informative articles all appear together, with a variety I need to list to fully convey. There's a literary analysis of Edgar Allen Poe's evolving understanding of religiosity, as evidenced by his early, middle, and late work. There's a plea to help the Red Cross provide warm clothing for devastated areas of Europe during this war, which no one yet knew history would classify as World War I.

There's a piece on how ladies should stop wearing enormous, fashionable plumage on their hats out of ethical disgust for the mistreatment of birds, and another contrasting New Year celebrations in the United States and China. Two exciting articles tout the modern miracles of vaccination and cement, whole worlds of newly-opened possibility. There are recipes, finally what I'd expect from an early-twentieth-century magazine for girls, but they're in a lesson titled "Carbohydrates" and are supported by some impressive chemistry and culinary science.

As for the fiction, I have to hush my mind—accustomed to faster-paced entertainment—as I slog through what is known as a "short story." The stories feature surprisingly spunky heroines, slow and sentimental though the action might be. The first story I read, "Jim's Speech," is a teenage romance—it ends with a kiss!—but Lucy catches Jim's eye because she is a generous, resourceful, determined friend who trudges through snow for hours to save him embarrassment.

"The Featherweight," in a subversive twist, features no hint of romance. It's the story of a girl who is valued at work by her male colleagues. When she comes down with typhoid, the office misses her terribly for her humor, her diligence, her selflessness, and persistent good cheer. Fortunately, she recovers. The plot is . . . not quite a plot . . . but it's still fun writing and a positive message.

My favorite part of the magazine by far, though, is the advice column: "Girl Queries." With the whole 40-year corpus of the periodical at my fingertips, I can't help flipping through months of Queries, imagining the stories and people behind them. Sometimes the questions are included, more often only the answers.

"Inez" simply wonders what wisteria is, while "Vida" wants to know when Charles Dickens was born, highlighting how revolutionary the internet has been in accessing information. "Blue Eyes," "Jessie," and "Olga" write in regarding their "love affairs," and are promised answers in private letters if they'll send self-addressed envelopes. In a jarring tone shift, "Cecil" asks how to keep her ribbons fresh while "Mother" asks about her guardianship rights in Utah. The responder, Catherine Hurst, replies to each in the same matter-of-fact tone. I learn from their exchange that Utah was one of the first states to give mothers legal guardianship equal to that of fathers and I hope the best for "Mother" as though she is a contemporary friend. One entry reads shortly, "No, we do *not* approve of such a low cut gown," and I long to see the original submission.

The best entries, though, concern the girls and their beaux.

> Young girls should not accept rings from gentlemen friends unless they be engagement rings.
>
> There are many ways of entertaining boy friends. If you are a good conversationalist—that is a good listener as well as talker—well informed on several subjects, there should be no difficulty in passing an hour or two very pleasantly.
>
> [Your parents'] consent is necessary before a [marriage] license can be secured. Under ordinary conditions the age you mention is rather young.
>
> If you do not love the young man, or if he is not necessary to your happiness, do not marry him. Marriage without love is generally a failure.
>
> Girls should not permit young men to kiss them good-night at the gate.
>
> If you do not wish to go out with the young man, it is certainly proper to refuse.
>
> There are some cases on record where two persons have been mutually attracted at first sight and succeeding acquaintance has ripened into love that proved enduring, a happy marriage following. More often, however, this love at 'first sight,' is only a delusion and girls would do well to avoid such an allurement, fancying it to be fate.

Who is this wise guru, anyway? Who are any of these authors? Whose vision were they building? This magazine was clearly intended to nurture wise, capable, thoughtful women, solidly prepared for their disparate life roles, but it looks nothing like church publications I grew up with. I want to know how the Young Woman Journal happened.

So I take a detour. I need to know this more than I need to know "knee-chest position."

By the late 1880s, literary culture throughout the United States centered on periodicals. Latter-day Saints were no exception, with a whole fleet of their own magazines: Woman's Exponent, Juvenile Instructor, and Contributor (publications of the Relief Society, Sunday School, and Young Men, respectively).

Woman's Exponent (1872–1914) was the first newspaper by and for women in Utah. It was not an official church publication but its first editor, Lula Greene Richards, was set apart as a missionary and blessed in the undertaking by Brigham Young at her request: editors and contributors were always fiercely loyal to their church and to their Priesthood leaders. Exponent was widely circulated and far more widely discussed, giving Latter-day Saint women a voice and a wide audience.

Woman's Exponent is best known for its intense support of women's suffrage, women's education, and—paradoxically, from an outside perspective— polygamy. (It's worth noting that all of these were mainstream positions for Latter-day Saints at the time.) From the beginning Exponent promised "to discuss every subject interesting and valuable to women" and it was never a one-track publication. Exponent was full of local and national news, reports of Relief Society work, short fiction, poetry, humor, and domestic advice alongside its activist editorials and essays. Distinctly Latter-day Saint fiction was a new movement, and women were seen as especially virtuous: the perfect authors to imaginatively influence the Saints toward moral living.

But Susa Young Gates—Susa again!—thought the Exponent's tabloid style was shabby and felt called to create "a perfect woman's magazine," modeled after her favorite secular publications.

When Susa announced *The Young Woman's Journal*, everyone was excited to read "the highest thoughts, brightest fancies, and the most elevating ideas of the Daughters of Zion." But Susa had a more motherly angle in mind. In her first editorial, she invited submissions without mentioning a desired age group, then specifically asked the young women to donate money and submit questions for the advice column. The *Journal* carried only occasional written offerings from teenage girls themselves.

The other things I need from the Journal are the "vertical line test" for posture and some home remedies for menstrual pain—the requirement says to "learn knee-chest position," which makes it sound like the plan is to spend Shark Week curled up in a ball.

The vertical line test just says to stand up straight and sit up straight. Nothing new there.

The title of the menstruation article is "Optional Studies. IV. THE WOMAN.", so I'm already laughing. Studying THE WOMAN is *not* optional.

The introduction is all about the beautiful gift of motherhood to womankind. It contains classic warnings about how "God never intended woman to be a competitor of man." It encourages women to emulate their own mothers and Mary the mother of Jesus.

And then, abruptly, the article changes into an anatomy lesson: "Woman differs from man in the organs which rest in the small pelvic cavity." I'm shocked to see a sketched sagittal view of the female abdominal and pelvic cavities, as though this is one of my textbooks. It's true that the idea of intercourse is neatly avoided by referencing "marriage" as what leads to conception, but there is still a frank discussion of puberty, the menstrual cycle, pregnancy, and infertility (which is unfortunately labeled "the curse of barrenness"). Periods are identified as indicators of overall health and a short, light, painless period is suggested as "the end [that should be] sought by all women." I'm fascinated by the discussion of the latest scientific question: are ovulation and menstruation connected events or do they just happen to occur in coinciding cycles? Today the connection between them is extremely basic reproductive physiology, but a hundred years ago no one knew for sure.

The author insists that a girl should not be allowed to attend parties, plays, or dances during her years of sexual maturation, as they might interfere with her nine hours of nightly sleep. So . . . who is going to go to the parties, plays, and dances? Restrictive admonitions like "Excessive nervous and mental exertions are detrimental to pelvic health" are placed right next to more modern ideas: "As girls, we have been taken from our out-door sports, and put in long clothes and made 'ladylike' at this very period when we needed these activities most. . . . Keep the girl young and a tom-boy as long as possible."

Did two different people write this article? I'm concerned about the pelvis preserver's uncited statements. "Don't socialize and don't think too hard so that someday you can have babies" is one heck of a take. Like, I believe in adolescents getting the rest they need, but it feels wrong to me for a young girl to design her whole life around providing an accommodating womb. Reproductive anatomy and physiology is my favorite subject to teach, and I was excited that there were diagrams in the *Journal*, but it's almost worse to have these restrictions in here, mixed up with the science as though it's all equally valid.

Anyway, the instructions for knee-chest position are to "kneel on your bed and lie on folded arms, bringing your chest as near the knees as possible. This brings the organs, through gravity, in proper position." Wait, do the organs generally move out of proper position? A quick search leads to plenty of health websites that say yes and nothing in scientific literature to support the idea. Phew.

For cramps, I read, "take a hot sitz bath for ten minutes and get right into bed with a hot cloth on the abdomen and hot water bottle at the back, and remain quiet for one to three days." One to three *days*? As appealing as it sounds to sit in bed for three days, I'd probably better just swallow some ibuprofen and continue taking care of my child and going to work. At my house, ibuprofen is considered a "simple home remedy," not a "drugstore concoction."

ANN ARBOR

NATE AND I SKIP OUR RESPECTIVE graduation cer-emonies to pack up our possessions for the big move to Michigan. My parents and siblings come to help us load the trailer with everything we own. Our kitchen chairs are so bulky and irregularly shaped that they don't get to come with us and we gleefully give away our fans to make more space. We've spent this summer huddled around the win-dow AC unit or with our fans pointed directly at our faces, dreaming of moving day and the wonders of central air at our Michigan apartment. We've handled all the heat we're emotionally prepared to handle. Good riddance, fans.

It is always the cleaning that stresses me out the most on a moving day: it feels impossible after endless hours of dismantling a home. I'm grateful that my mom is there to help scrub. Jane plays with my baby brother, her proud 11-year-old uncle, out of the way. The cleaning is done by the time the trailer is loaded. My family has brought lunches for everybody.

It's on days like today that I understand exactly why people leave their hometowns for a couple of years and then hurry back to move in next to their parents. We plan to live out of state for the rest of our lives, but as we hug my family goodbye I can certainly picture my resolve revers-ing. I don't even know when we'll see them next.

We're not alone yet, though. Nate's family is escorting us to Michigan, by way of a move-cation to the family cabin in Minnesota. It's my first time joining them in the place Nate visited every summer as a kid, his grandparents' summer home. From the conversations I've heard concerning the Thatcher family cabin at Little Moss Lake, I expect a tiny shack, covered in insects.

So I'm surprised and pleased to discover that the cabin is a beyond-magical haven in the woods that the Thatchers just take for granted. After two days of driving, we get to spend two day swimming, kayaking, canoeing, and biking our way from lake to lake. We eat fish and crayfish Nate's uncles catch and set off fireworks over the lake. We're surrounded by family—Nate and I can leave for a romantic boat ride at a moment's notice because someone is always willing to care for our Jane.

We're sad to leave, but anxious to get to Ann Arbor, unload our trailer, and start building a new life. After fifty hours in the car with my in-laws, I thought I'd be relieved as I watched them drive away. And I am, a little. But I'm also viscerally aware that when they cross the state line, I will know zero people in Michigan outside the walls of my own home.

Fortunately, we belong to the Church of Jesus Christ of Latter-day Saints. So on Sunday morning, we go to church certain that we will be able to make new friends (and probably find someone we already know).

Sure enough—a friend I tutored through Advanced Physiology is now a dad and a med student and lives a

block away from us. Two other ward members are older sisters of our good friends in Utah. In Sunday School,
we single out someone named Justin as a potential friend
simply because we like his comments during the lesson. I
make sure to talk with him in the hall and sit by his wife,
Shelby, in Relief Society. They are at our place for cookies
and milk by nightfall. They have a daughter, Noelle, just
two months older than our Jane and we love all three of
them immediately. With homemade chocolate chip cookies and newfound friends in the house, can we really be
said to be "just moving in"?

By now we've discovered, to our dismay, that we did *not*
get the central air we requested. It is our old apartment all
over again, but without a window AC unit or ceiling fans or
the standing fans we left behind. There is no escape from
the sweat and stagnation and general warm dampness.
I've been a desert girl for a long time and I can't cope. My
headaches are having a hayday. My heroic husband takes
Jane out with him to buy some fans while I lie very still on
the basement floor and wait.

Once we get the air in our house moving, there is plenty to
love about Michigan. We live in student family housing, in
one of hundreds of townhouses with dark wood siding and
surrounded by so many trees that it will always look like a
summer camp. There are trees everywhere in this town,
and the spaces between the trees are full of native plants.
The lawn of our summer camp complex is mowed occasionally, but otherwise uncultivated—no sprinklers and no
spraying. The patches of clover and dandelions feel like a
healthy part of the natural landscape rather than enemies
to be vanquished, and the many children in the neighbor-

hood can eat the dirt without worrying too much about what's in it. Utah may blossom like a rose, but Michigan blossoms like a wildflower. Driving ten minutes in most directions will bring us to a gorgeous, wooded park or to the bank of the meandering Huron.

We prioritize locating the public library and learn that it has five entire branches, one of them less than half a mile from our apartment. They have a story time just for babies, which is how I meet Autumn and Isaac our first Friday in the state.

They're a young couple, bringing their very young daughter to story time together because they've also just moved in. They've come from Oregon for Autumn's master's in social work. We chat for a few minutes and then, when it's time to walk home, realize that we live about 200 feet apart.

"Wait, are you in my *ward?!*" I blurt out. And then I'm mortified. Yes, they live in my ward boundaries, but they aren't members of the Church and there was no reason to think that they were . . . except that they're young to be married and parents, haven't used any expletives in our brief conversation, and have no visible tattoos or piercings. I clearly haven't been out of the Utah bubble enough lately.

I'm lucky. They shake off my weird question more easily than I do and within the week they come over for cookies too.

When I stop to think about it, our chocolate chip cookie recipe is "lace" for us: it's knowledge that we brought on our reverse journey across the plains. It connects us to Nate's family, to our courtship, to Utah. Now, we use it to start making a new home in Michigan.

LITTLE BLACK SPECKS

OUT DOOR FIELD, CELL 529: Care successfully for a hive of bees for one season; know their habits.

I'VE JUST WALKED INTO an unexpected potluck. Shoot. The website for Ann Arbor Backyard Beekeepers just said that there was a meeting the second Tuesday of every month: an informal Q&A followed by a "formal presentation of a bee-related topic." But this is the most beautiful potluck I've ever seen and everyone is feasting and I didn't bring anything.

Is it less awkward to eat without contributing or to sit down without food? I'm not sure. I opt to sit down at a table of strangers, all women, with nothing in my hands but a notebook and pen. Nope. This was definitely the wrong choice. I'm such a pro at casual mingling.

"How long have you been keeping bees?" a friendly stranger asks me.

"I . . . don't keep bees," I tell her "but I need to visit some hives for a writing project."

"Oooh, wonderful! Tell us all about your writing project!"

I do my best, but it's difficult to explain to someone who is completely unfamiliar with the Church of Jesus Christ of

Latter-day Saints. I mention Utah and the Mormons and the Boy Scouts and the Girl Scouts and home economics and bees. My audience nods along absently.

When I finish, the woman nearest me hands me a business card that says she's a "bee educator."

"Hi! My name is Rebecca. I have four hives and an extra suit and I'd love to take you out for a hive check." We make plans right away.

Is this what it feels like to *network*? I've found what I needed in the first five minutes of my first beekeeper meeting! I get to sit back and relax through a lovely talk on how to make neighborhoods safe for bees and planting vegetables that double as great sources of nectar.

I meet up with Rebecca a couple weeks later, on what is quite possibly the worst day of the year to be outside in a heavy beekeeper suit and thick gloves: it's the hottest week of summer, with rain promised later this afternoon. The bees know about the storm and have already retreated comb-ward. They won't be able to fly if their wings get wet.

Not only do we suit up, we get a fire going in a "smoker": basically a large tin can with a funnel to direct the smoke and a little bellows to drive it out. "We can burn anything in there to calm the bees, but my favorite is dried sumac flowers," Rebecca tells me. She hands me a flat metal tool, a miniature ice-scraper-qua-back-scratcher that turns out to be called a "hive tool," used for prying, nudging, lifting, and scraping.

Beekeeping isn't something you can jump into for a single season. The initial monetary investment is large, and you hope that in a couple of years, with enough care and luck, you will receive a return on your investment. I have no intention of making that kind of a commitment. But this is Beehive Girls and I can't call this project complete without at least coming into contact with a hive of bees.

"Okay, so, the goal for today is to put in a new frame. We give them one at a time and the last one is almost full." The bees are supposed to use frames to build straight, regular, easily harvested honeycomb.

But when we open up the cone, Rebecca sighs. "We're a week too late." The bees have already run out of space and started building comb every which way. It's unusable, a sad waste of energy (and since bees eat honey, their wasted energy means wasted honey). I hope for a moment that I can take a piece of the skiwampus comb home, but Rebecca carefully scrapes it off and packs it away to be made into candles.

The bees are everywhere, sleepy and unthreatening, even as we get right in and rearrange their living rooms. "Excuse me, ladies," Rebecca chats to them as she carefully nudges them out of the way, gently blowing air at them when needed. She loves her "girls" fiercely.

Before we insert the new frame, Rebecca lifts some of the others, showing me what's happening on each. The hive is somehow both more and less uniform than I ever imagined: the cells are so perfect, so tiny and hexagonal, but some are filled with honey and some are "brood cells," where eggs are incubating or larvae maturing. "There's a greater concentration of brood cells in the frames closest to the middle of the hive—maybe for safety? or temperature control?— but I don't really see a pattern beyond that," Rebecca explains. She shows me how the wax isn't all the same, either—some of the comb has been used through multiple seasons, stiffening and darkening from white to amber.

When we insert the new frame there isn't a lot of space between layers for the bees to move, but for bees the gold standard is 5/16ths of an inch. "Any bigger than that and they'll fill it in with rogue comb!" Rebecca warns, obviously from experience. Any smaller and they'll just fill it in with a glue-like secretion. "They like to be very tightly crowded in there."

Our last step in the first hive is to put the lid back on. I do it myself, ever so carefully. I still end up squishing a bee by accident. Shoot. Shoot. Shoot. I meant to look at the bees, not kill them.

Rebecca doesn't say anything. She loves her bees, but in the end, her "girls" are tiny insects. She can't get too attached to them as individuals.

🌸 🐝 🐝

Rebecca and I spend most of our time together driving between hive locations, so I get to chat with her. I find out that she teaches a culinary class at the local community college, coordinates meals at an assisted living facility, and plays poker professionally. While she has a business degree, her honey business won't go beyond breaking even for quite some time. She could make money sooner, but she refuses to take shortcuts or cut costs with her bees.

"Okay, so it doesn't pay the bills," I summarize, "Why do you love it?"

"Well, I got into it in the first place because it's something my boyfriend loves . . . even though he's super allergic to bee stings . . . and now we include my son too, so it's a whole family thing."

"And it seems like you've found other community too."

"Yes! It's so fun to learn from other beekeepers and

hang out. Oh! And this year we won the hive contest! I'll show you pictures when I'm not driving. Basically, you get a hive and you can decorate it however you want with your team and then it gets judged."

Even though beekeeping isn't a moneymaker for Rebecca, I'm impressed by how many of her other needs it meets. Beekeeping has given Rebecca a community of people with shared interests. It has given her hands-on outdoor work, an excuse to get outside. It has given her something to bond over with her boyfriend and son. It has given her something to nurture, like a garden or a pet. It has given her an outlet for business creativity and, to my surprise, an outlet for artistic creativity too. It has given her outreach and teaching opportunities. I guess for me, church ends up filling all of those needs, so I've never really looked around at how everyone else finds their people and their place.

When we reach the next hive, we have to stop to look at pictures of the hive contest. It's like a lineup of parade floats, except less expensive and more practical. Then we suit up again and light up more sumac.

"Look! They're festooning!" Rebecca points into the hive. There are bees hanging together in a kind of chain. "No one knows exactly why they do this. Some people think that they're surveying the space, using their bodies and gravity to get a straight up-and-down line to start from. Some people think they just can't make wax unless they're festooning or that maybe the chains of bees are a kind of scaffolding. It's so cool." She's right. I mean, I don't know which *explanation* is right, but this is so cool. Something very organized and collaborative is going on, even though I don't understand what it is.

Here, too, we're too late in bringing a new frame. The bees have already built rogue honeycomb and they've already filled it with honey. Rebecca can't even salvage the wax for candles.

Instead, Rebecca hands the comb to me and tells me to taste. I take a bite of honey and wax together, like an all-natural Gusher. I taste the fresh, local honey as I chew—it's too sweet to eat all at once like this, but I'm doing it anyway—until the wax consolidates into a tasteless ball and I spit it out. I rarely experience anything so rustic, so obviously fresh and straight from its source. It's energizing.

Somehow, Rebecca and I forgot to discuss honey as a motivating factor for beekeeping. But the honey is everyone's reason.

After my outing with Rebecca, I have a big question: Why is this whole Beehive Girls program bee-themed, anyway? Is it just because Utah is the Beehive State? In the Handbook, the leaders go on and on about the beautiful symbolism of bees and hives, so there must be something more to the story.

I find my answer in a celebratory Beehive Girl Anniversary edition of the Improvement Era. When the YLMIA general board began designing their own summer recreation program for girls, the first thing they all agreed on was the name. From there, they found every book they could on bees and assigned them to various board members to scour for guiding ideas.

"As they read, the first feeling was one akin to despair" because bees were all about self-sacrifice and labor. Self-sacrifice and labor are worthwhile things, but not a great cornerstone for a fun program for kids: "to be attractive to girls it must contain something else."

Then, someone on the committee ran across the 1911 winner of the Nobel Prize for Literature: The Life of the Bee, by Maurice Maeterlinck. It changed everything for the board members. Apparently, it isn't just a book about bees.

Reading Maeterlinck's bee book is technically a requirement for the second rank of Beehive Girls (called "Gatherer of Honey") rather than "Builder in the Hive," but it *is* a Nobel Prize winner and the foundational text for this whole program. I sign into the University of Michigan's library with Nate's account and reserve a copy.

When it arrives, I haul Jane on the blue shuttle to north campus to pick it up from the (very cool) architecture library in the Duderstadt Center. I take her to the park so that I can get a little reading time in. She's getting old enough to enjoy more than just the swings—she crawls up and down stairs and throws wood chips. She can go down slides if someone helps. While she focuses on pulling herself to standing with the rung of a ladder—the serious work of her life—I start reading, looking for the layers of symbolism the original general board members saw.

The book is structured as the story of one year in a beehive, and its table of contents sounds like a list of movements in a Stravinsky ballet: On the Threshold of the Hive, The Swarm, The Foundation of the City, The Young Queens, The Massacre of the Males, and The Progress of the Race. The writing is lofty, flowery—Utah women were apparently not the only people writing like that at the turn of the century.

The beehive in the story is only active from April to September, just like the original Beehive Girl swarms. The hive is made up entirely of female bees for much of the year. The queen bee mates once in her life, but other than that everyone in the hive is celibate—in a "state of perpetual chastity"—much as the leaders would have hoped their young women were. Interesting. I wasn't expecting there to be so many literal connections.

The bees are industrious and good team players, obviously. I assumed from the get-go that the General Board members wanted to draw parallels to the bees mainly because of bees' diligent work for the common good. Now that I'm reading the book, though, I suspect that they had deeper, more compelling reasons. Here's an excerpt about making a new hive that must have stood out to those who had crossed the plains and those whose mothers had crossed the plains.

> Here, in the new abode, there is nothing; not a drop of honey, not a morsel of wax, neither guiding-mark nor point of support. There is only the dreary emptiness of an enormous monument that has nothing but sides and roof. Within the smooth and rounded walls there only is darkness; and the enormous arch above rears itself over nothingness. But useless regrets are unknown to the bee; or in any event it does not allow them to hinder its action. Far from being cast down by an ordeal before which every other courage would succumb, it displays greater ardor than ever.

The Saints left everything behind, moved, and rebuilt in an empty bog or desert so many times. Sometimes I forget. YLMIA leaders probably wondered how each successive generation would re-connect to their resilient, faithful roots. As Maeterlinck said of the bees, "Break their comb twenty times in succession, take twenty times from them their young and their food, you still shall never succeed in making them doubt of the future." The bees may not bring lace patterns with them, but they carry the knowledge of how to build a new hive.

The Board members probably saw themselves, too, in the ways bees sacrifice themselves to "a Law superior to [their] own happiness." The workers will die of starvation to keep their queen fed. The queen will see the light of day only once. The workers will never be mothers. "For the sake of [the] future, each one renounces more than half of her rights and her joys."

This book is sort of about bees and sort of about the meaning of life. I can see how it inspired my foremothers to design an entire recreation program based on fields and flowers, cells and swarms, hives and keepers. Everything came together quickly once they'd found this source material. The board felt even more guided when, a year after publishing the handbook, they realized that they'd used "seals" and "chains" in their award structure without even realizing that those are bee-related words. The symbolism lingered for decades in the Young Women program, where the youngest girls were called "Beehives," and never just "Bees."

One passage from "The Life of the Bee" seems specifically relevant to me right now, as an inhabitant of 2015 looking back on the inhabitants of 1915. Maeterlinck asks the reader to imagine being an alien watching human civilization from such a high point that the people look like "little black specks" as they go about their lives. What would you notice? What conclusions would you reach? They would probably be "no less erroneous, no less uncertain, than those we choose to form concerning the bee."

With all my reading history and earning cells, I know that I'm scraping the surface. I've been watching little black specks go about their tasks with very limited knowledge of how they felt about them or what deeper motives drove them.

BLESSING HER
ALL OVER:
THE STORY OF
ELMINA S. TAYLOR

FIELD OF RELIGION, CELL 8: Give brief account of the life and labors of Elmina S. Taylor and Martha H. Tingey, presidents of the YLMIA.

I CAN SEE THIS BEING an exceptionally boring requirement for 1915 Beehive Girls, but I've had so much fun getting to know Susa already that I'm sincerely excited to "meet" a couple of her peers. Besides, I've spent so much Sunday School time learning about the lives of the prophets, and zero Young Women time learning about Young Women leaders. I'm into this.

Elmina Shepard was born to devout New York Methodists in 1830, just a few months after the Church of Jesus Christ of Latter-day Saints was organized. She received her teaching diploma at age sixteen and taught school in rural areas where she was paid in room and board. Then her cousin Kate invited Mina to join her in Haverstraw, 200 miles from home, teaching in a bigger school with wealthier patrons. Mina boarded a train to begin a life-changing adventure.

At her new job, Mina met a trustee of the school, John Druce, who gave her a copy of the Book of Mormon. She joined the church in 1856, at the age of 25. While there was some muttering among her higher-ups about her joining the controversial young church, she was saved from dismissal because "she had kept the best school they had ever had in that district."

Meanwhile, John Druce also taught the gospel to his young boarder, a copper engraver named George Hamilton Taylor, who "soon became very much interested in [Mina]." George later wrote, "I thought that I would be supremely happy if I could get her for a wife. But I was of such a timid, bashful disposition, and so fearful of being refused, that when in the company of both of them, I paid nearly all my attention to [Kate]. And I carried this to such a length that [Mina] thought that I did not care anything for her, while her cousin thought that I was in earnest in giving her seemingly the preference." Is this a romantic comedy? I love this.

Kate went home to visit her family for a few weeks, giving George time alone with Elmina to express his true feelings. (Kate felt completely betrayed when she returned to find them engaged, and was so angry that she left her post at Haverstraw and never spoke to Mina again, but that is hardly the important part of the story.) I probably shouldn't focus so much on the how-they-met part of the story, but that's always my favorite.

After two years of marriage, George and Elmina made the five-month trip to join the saints in Salt Lake City by train, steamboat, and covered wagon. Winter Quarters was where George made his first forays into handling oxen and a wagon and where Mina first tried her hand at housekeeping (not that they had a house), but they were reasonably proficient by the time their wagon rolled into the valley. They watched other members of their wagon train being met by family and friends. They knew no one and had nowhere to go. I'd never thought about that part of the journey before—the part where you've been walking for weeks and now you're just standing there.

Elder John Taylor and his wife, Maggie, invited them to supper. From there, they found work and a place to live and began to build a life in Utah. Over the years Mina gave birth to seven children, four of whom survived to adulthood.

I'm inspired by the way this balanced and deeply affectionate couple handled the difficult issue of polygamy. George wrote, "We had rather it were not a principle of our religion, yet we knew the principles we had embraced were true, and as that came from the same source we could not reject it." Since no one was asking them to live in polygamy at the moment, George and Mina decided "We would go forward, live our religion, keep the commandments of God, and strive to do right in all things, as far as we knew how, trusting that if the time ever came when we should embrace that principle and practice it, that we should know it and be prepared for it."

The time to practice polygamy did come, after George and Mina had been married for twenty years. When George was called on a mission to England, Mina was left to care for the lumber business and her own four children, plus her new sister wife Louie and her baby. Oh man, sending away husbands and fathers as missionaries for random amounts of time was *the worst*. Mina recorded days and nights of loneliness and longing for her husband in her diary, including this one that made me cry:

"Someone sang *Maggie Dear*[.] Immediately was I carried back to Haverstraw and the tears sprang to my eyes and my heart gave a great throb. I was sitting by your side, riding up the long Clove and you were singing it to me with a *slight* change in words and a heart full of love." Did he sing it as *Mina Dear*? I know I don't get to be in on their inside jokes, but I must know. "While my mind was thus busy Mae looked up in my face and whispered, 'Papa sings that.' So you see every slight event brings to mind our absent loved one."

After three years of missionary service, George sailed to New York City, where Mina surprised him at the dock. They crossed the plains together again, but this time toward the comfort of home and this time by train. I can't imagine looking out the window and seeing hundreds of miles you *walked* over just whiz by.

In 1885, George took a third wife and was sent to prison for six months as punishment. His ward threw him a farewell party before he reported for his sentence, which I think tells us something important about the time period.

Meanwhile, Mina served faithfully in the presidencies of her ward's Relief Society and Young Ladies' Retrenchment Association, concurrent with a role in the stake Relief Society presidency. At this point, the three women's auxiliaries hadn't been divided, so Eliza R. Snow was in charge of everything. She noticed Mina's diligence, once telling Mina that she "always felt like blessing her all over, because [she was] such a faithful worker in the Kingdom." The mental image of blessing someone all over makes me smile.

When general presidencies and boards were officially organized at a conference in 1880, Sister Snow informed Mina during lunch (between sessions) that she needed to choose her counselors because she was going to be made president of all the Young Ladies' associations. Mina's protests were ignored. She was sustained in the afternoon session. Sheesh, Eliza!

For her callings, Mina overcame her natural reluctance to speak publicly and she encouraged all young women to do the same. She was asked to "find new and surprising ways . . . to teach girls how to develop every gift and grace of true womanhood." This was the first time the various retrenchment associations and mutual improvement associations had been brought together in unified programs and procedures . . . and it's not like wards had phone trees set up yet. Elmina made hundreds of visits to wards and stakes during the first ten years of her presidency, traveling thousands of miles before the age of the automobile, organizing new associations and holding conferences, giving instructions but also bringing ideas and input back from the field. This is making me realize that I don't know exactly what the Young Women General Presidency does now.

Over the twenty-four years of Mina's tenure, the YLMIA grew enormously in size and scope. There were the *Young Woman's Journal*, united courses of study, traveling libraries, annual general conferences of the youth, the initiation of "Mutual" nights on Tuesdays (a tradition that continues with the same name today), and activity with the National Council of Women. Already, she'd created something that looked impossibly different from Brigham's family meeting about the pitfalls of fashionable clothing.

BOLDNESS, BUT
NOT OVERBEARANCE

NATE'S FIRST SEMESTER OF GRAD SCHOOL is the first time I have been "primarily responsible for the nurture of my child." So many people would give anything to be a stay-at-home parent, but I have trouble embracing this remarkable privilege for a couple of reasons.

First, I'm unemployed. It's not just that I'm not working, it's that I've been actively looking for work since spring and haven't found it yet. My mentorship at BYU was haphazard, to say the least, and I don't know how to build a career now that I have my degree. I really just want to teach college classes, but for a while I apply for research jobs, post-doctoral fellowships, because (1) there are so many at the University of Michigan and because (2) they are full-time jobs with benefits. I'll absolutely do a job I don't really want to do for two years to give my family that kind of stability. Nate's scholarship is huge (or we wouldn't have come), but tuition here is even huger, and we're just running down our savings as I follow lead after lead.

Usually, I know that my graduate advisor was being preposterously sexist when he said that he didn't know how to work with "someone getting a PhD just for fun." Right now, I'm discouraged enough to think he might have been right about me. Maybe I'll never work in my field again.

The week before school starts, I finally admit to myself that any work I get won't start until next semester. Nate applies to be a server at a few downtown restaurants and is hired on the spot at a nice Italian place.

The second reason I'm struggling is that I'm sick. The daily headaches that started just before Jane was born have morphed into a constant . . . migraine? I'm not sure what to call it. It's not like the blindingly painful, classic migraines I experience about once a year, but I have some combination of brain fog, head pain, fatigue, dizziness, and nausea at all times. Sometimes I can't speak. Sometimes I can't drive. I can take care of Jane in a basic way, but Nate and I have always envisioned balanced teamwork in breadwinning, child rearing, and homemaking and instead things are swinging wildly out of balance. The combination of joblessness and chronic illness is depressing, especially since it leaves Nate scrambling to do everything that we used to do together. Everything plus grad school.

In the midst of this, it's the little things that help. My new friend Shelby keeps me company the nights Nate is working: each of us is tethered to a sleeping baby, but we send Facebook messages back and forth. Natalie mails us a "Michigan Winter Care Package" with a gift for each family member. My visiting teacher Nycole, whom I've met only once, babysits Jane so that Nate and I can go on a date when we desperately need it. My neighbor Autumn takes care of Jane while I go to a job interview. Shelby picks me and Jane up for playgroup on a day I can't drive so we can still get out of the house. I'm sick, but I'm also supported.

Beehive Girls helps too. When I can't think, but want to do something healthier than staring into the oblivion, I turn to my checklist. I can make concrete progress toward something and I have some degree of control.

Within weeks of moving in, I accept a calling to teach the Laurels in our ward. I don't tell the bishop why this means a lot to me right now, and I don't tell the girls either, but I'm so excited to get to observe today's Young Women while studying their predecessors.

OUT DOOR FIELD, CELL 514: Build and supply a lunch counter for birds; at close of season, report how many kinds of birds you have seen use it.

As a little kid, I had this book full of 365 things to do with your kids instead of watching TV. It was definitely not meant to be read by the children in question. Whenever I picked it up, I learned about a dozen new crafts that I wanted to make *immediately*. It was like reading a cookbook all at once.

One of the crafts from the book was a pinecone bird feeder and, when I see this lunch counter cell, my deeply-rooted desire to roll a pine cone in peanut butter and birdseed comes rushing back. Plus, it's exactly the right kind of thing to do with a migraine and a baby.

Now that I'm paying for my own peanut butter, I understand why my mom was never enthused about slathering it all over a pinecone . . . plus, Jane is allergic. I think that a simple syrup of sugar and water could stick the birdseed on just fine. It's worth a shot. I have never in my life purchased anything at a pet store, so I'm pleased to discover that we can get all the birdseed we need for under a dollar. I can finally fulfill my long-suppressed dream of making a sticky mess. For the birds.

It takes something like two minutes to make the mess. I planned to let Jane help, but I can only stand spilling so much bird seed. I let the syrup dry overnight and hang them up on a wall just outside our sliding glass door, where there are already some random nails jutting out. I mentally check "lunch counter" off my to-do list as though making it was all the cell required.

Then the birds show up. My daughter takes up residence at the window, pointing and shouting her excitement about the birds eating outside. Her bird imitation is not a "peep" or a "cheep" or, indeed, anything audible: she just cocks her head from side to side and tries really hard to whistle. She dances from foot to foot and smacks the glass with her tiny palms. The birds are unfazed: they've lived in the neighborhood long enough to know all about small children.

I watch the birds, too. I think our lunch counter increases bird traffic just a little bit: the rest of the magic comes from our increased attention to the grand stage behind our sliding door. I've sketched chickadees before, but from a book. Now, they're real. There's a woodpecker in our tree at any given moment. The bright cardinals and bluejays probably aren't rare in an ecological sense, but they amaze me every time. This campus has the biggest, brashest squirrels I have ever seen and I love watching them strategize to get at the birdseed. The geese party on the lawn at all hours, though I'm not sure what they snack on. Occasionally, at night, a skunk ambles by our window, close enough to be bathed in living room lamplight.

I don't think there was this much animal life in Provo. Or maybe there was, and I never slowed down enough to pay attention. Knowing all of our tiniest neighbors attaches me to this place, makes me *care* that we're precisely here. I notice the weather, the shifting season, anticipating a winter unlike any in my memory. Once, Nate and I watch a silent lightning storm through our observation window. There's no rain and no thunder—just lightning and lightning and lightning. We've never seen anything like it.

The particularities of life in Utah, my motherland, become more distinct in my head as I have something to compare them to. I hope that as Jane grows, I'll be able to share with her this new sense of home. Watching her watch the birds, I feel like we have a solid start.

FIELD OF DOMESTIC ARTS, CELL 413: Make a water-color, charcoal, pen and ink, or oil sketch from nature.

Jane's room is pretty empty. A thoughtful ward member— not even mine, but my *parents'*—passed their cute crib along to us and we have my state-of-the-art cubby bench . . . but that's it. The floors are hardwood, so it echoes. To quote Maeterlinck, "There is only the dreary emptiness of an enormous monument that has nothing but sides and roof." It doesn't feel right for a baby.

Oh, and there aren't any ceiling lights. I'm worried that Jane would tip over a floor lamp, but if we get a small lamp we'll need a bookshelf or something to put it on . . .

My brainstorming and problem-solving is pointless. Under the financial circumstances, we shouldn't buy nursery decor. Nate and I made one trip to Ikea the week we arrived, on a quest to find Michigan's four cheapest dining room chairs, averting our eyes from everything else. My mantra was, "It will be fun to come here when we have an income." That was when I still hoped that I'd have a full-time job.

But here's what I do have: ten small canvases Nate gave me last Christmas, some acrylic paint, and a Beehive Girls commission to paint from nature. I decide to use the canvases to paint her a menagerie—nine cute little animals on her wall. Animals count as "art from nature", right? I have to choose animals that are distinctive enough in shape or coloring that they are recognizable after a non-artist paints them. (If I painted a woodchuck and a beaver, no one would be able to tell them apart.) I start with a fox, with its trademark colors and simple lines. There are plenty of images on Pinterest to consult.

I paint my fox in bright acrylics after Jane's bedtime, while Nate is working at the restaurant. I'm proud of it, especially because I pulled together multiple ideas from the Internet instead of just imitating one person's work.

But a fox is a common image for nursery walls and now that it's done, I'm feeling more contrarian. For the other eight, I want more obscure animals. The next time Nate works late, I paint a musk ox and a mandrill. They both turn out kind of hideous. They are difficult animals to translate from a photo to a cartoon when you don't have any skills. I can see why foxes are so popular.

I only have mammal paintings so far and I want a broader selection from phylum chordata. Plus something from each continent. Plus multiple ecosystems. Since I'm only planning for nine paintings, this is getting complicated. I paint an iguana and a Moorish Idol (a gorgeous fish). I paint a dik-dik (an adorably tiny African antelope) and a puffin. Yes, I admit that I'm prioritizing cute animals over cartilaginous fish. Some biologist I am. I look at many pictures of indigenous Australian birds before choosing the colorful but deadly cassowary (I've never heard of it before, so I'm shocked when Nate sees the painting and knows exactly what it is). It turns into a biology project as much as an art project as I try to properly represent the world of cool animals. With interior design and Beehive Girls in mind, I can treat my painting as "productive." I've never been able to prioritize painting above cleaning before.

By the time I get to my last painting, I've had some practice. I paint the most adorable little anteater I've ever seen. I've arrived.

Then I show them to Jane and it gets even better. Jane is over the moon. She doesn't talk yet, but she runs from canvas to canvas, picking each up and hugging it. When I hang them on her wall—with velcro Command strips because we're in a student apartment—she begins each morning by saying hello to each of them and ends each night by waving goodbye. If we read a book with one of her nine animals in it, she widens her eyes and points upstairs. She knows she has a musk ox on her wall.

Jane loves her animals. Her menagerie quickly becomes the most worthwhile creative project I have ever done. I feel like part of the long tradition of women finding a way to make their homes welcoming and beautiful without spending any money. Some people have dyed their kerosine red, some have turned their rags into quilts, and I've painted nine cute animals.

The dumpster provides everything else we need for Jane's room. Technically the space right *next* to our dumpster, where people "donate" things to the neighborhood at large. Our complex (judging by the cars in the parking lot, since most people don't go outside) comprises mostly poor student families and extremely wealthy expats. When the latter move home, they basically provide for all of the former's furniture needs. The night before Jane's first birth-day, I find three things by the dumpster: a cheerful rug, a small lamp, and a small bookcase. I feel watched over by the universe.

FIELD OF BUSINESS, CELL 617C: At a regular Bee-Hive meeting, write the following: An application for a position

---

When my poor, migrainous brain is still functioning after Jane's bedtime, I work on job applications. I've been do-ing this since spring, when we found out where we were moving. I apply for post-doc positions, writing a new cover letter for each one to try to make my research experience sound sufficiently relevant. I apply to teach at every college within forty-five minutes of my apartment, even though each biology department keeps a pool of applicants and I have no way to know if any humans have even seen my resume. I post Craigslist ads that are only ever answered by scammers. I start browsing janitorial jobs and receptionist jobs, but I know that I shouldn't give up on my doctor-al field four months after graduating. There's a commu-nity college where I have particularly wanted to work all along—I email the department head to try to draw atten-tion to my application, but she never responds.

One night, I'm reading the Book of Mormon when I feel a sudden connection to the text. Alma the Younger is giving advice to his son, Shiblon, and says, "And now, as ye have begun to teach the word even so I would that ye should continue to teach; and I would that ye would be diligent and temperate in all things. See that ye are not lifted up unto pride; yea, see that ye do not boast in your own wisdom, nor of your much strength. Use boldness, but not overbearance; and also see that ye bridle all your passions, that ye may be filled with love; see that ye refrain from idleness." I'm not usually one to take the scriptures very literally, but what stands out to me is "I would that ye should continue to teach" and "use boldness."

The next day I call the biology department head at the community college one more time, even though she already has my application, even though she already has an introductory voicemail from me, and even though calling strangers on the phone is petrifying. For me, this requires a great deal of boldness. I am rewarded by getting to leave another message and, later, getting one in return: she is currently looking for anatomy and physiology lab instructors with experience teaching from cadavers.

I don't have experience teaching from cadavers. My only anatomy experience is taking one class at BYU. But I have a lot of physiology experience and I know I could teach this class no problem if given the chance.

So, encouraged by Alma the Younger and the Holy Ghost, I write the boldest email of my life.

Dear Anne,

Thank you so much for returning my call yesterday. I was glad to learn more about your department's hiring process and current needs.

I have not yet taught in a cadaver lab. If your ideal candidate is not in your applicant pool, please know that I would like nothing better than to refresh my anatomy skills in your lab and prepare to teach this winter. I'm definitely running into the paradox of needing experience to get experience, but I know I could be an asset.

Attached is an updated resume that doesn't represent me as a student in Utah.

Thanks again for calling back,

Mikayla Thatcher

Within an hour and a half, Anne invites me in for an interview.

She loves my teaching demo. She hires me. I'm still home with Jane, but in January I know I'll have work.

I was never getting a PhD just for fun. Now, the knowledge and skills that I carry with me are going to help me take care of my family. I never thought of my education as "lace" before, but it's something that connects my old life to a bright future in a new place.

WOMAN HERSELF IS BEGINNING TO FEEL THAT SHE IS AN INTELLIGENCE: THE STORY OF MARTHA H. TINGEY

FIELD OF RELIGION, CELL 8 (PART 2): Give brief account of the life and labors of Elmina S. Taylor and Martha H. Tingey, presidents of the YLMIA.

AFTER THE JOY OF GETTING TO KNOW MINA, I am pumped to read about Sister Tingey. Her life overlaps Mina's, but she's basically a generation later. I wonder how Utah and the Church were different for her than they were for Mina.

Martha Horne (Mattie) was born to Latter-day Saint parents already settled in Salt Lake City. She was the fourteenth of fifteen children and still managed to stand out

academically, winning awards for reading, spelling, arith-
metic, and speech. She would recite enormous passages
of scripture in her Sunday School class, as many as forty
consecutive verses at a time, and was always praised for her
eloquence. She was singing with the Tabernacle Choir by
the age of twenty. Few would have suspected the shyness
and timidity that were a constant challenge for her.

When she was sixteen, President Brigham Young invited Mattie and five other young ladies to learn typesetting,
a job reserved for boys up to that point. Susa Young Gates
wrote that it was "a departure, even for the progressive
Mormons, and much was said to discourage the innova-
tion." Cool! I wish I knew more about what dissenters were
worried about. Mattie was trained by working at the *Deseret
News*, where her foreman praised her as one of his best
compositors. There she met a young man called Joseph S.
Tingey, and though his duties were in another part of the
newspaper office he made a point of finding opportunities to visit her. By 1880 they were good friends. Then, of
course, he was called away to serve a mission. I've been
there, and it's not fun. But at least Mattie and Joseph (and
Nate and I) were born after the time when married *dads*
left their families to go on missions.

While he was gone, Mattie was called as a counselor to
Elmina Shepard Taylor, the general president of the Young
Ladies' Mutual Improvement Association (Mina, remember?). She was only twenty-two, serving with women her
mother's age to care for girls closer to her own age and
situation. While this occasionally put her into awkward
situations (she would have preferred not to ban waltzing
at stake dances), her youthful perspective had a valuable
influence on the other leaders.

When Joseph returned from his mission, the pair courted for two years and were married in the Salt Lake Temple.

Joseph continued to work as a printer, but after an entire decade of typesetting experience Mattie left her job to rear their children. The birth of their first child brought on major complications for Mattie's hips and knees and the doctor warned her that she might never recover the ability to walk. Joseph attentively nursed her back to health and, though the rest of her life was marked by a limp and frequent relapses into poor health, she eventually resumed her responsibilities at home and at church. She had a strong testimony of the gift of healing through priesthood blessings. All in all, Mattie and Joseph raised four children, though they grieved the loss of twins in infancy.

Mattie and Joseph were known for a well-matched marriage that was "very congenial and one of mutual helpfulness." Susa Young Gates praised Brother Tingey as "an example of what a man can do, as a husband, father and Elder in Israel, without in any way hindering the development of a gifted wife." In a speech at the Congress of Women at the 1893 World's Fair, Mattie spoke about the expanded vision of women she and Joseph believed in:

> "Let woman prepare herself to stand side by side, shoulder to shoulder with her husband in all the affairs of life. . . . Woman herself is beginning to feel that she is an intelligence, with talents that it is her duty to develop. This feeling is gradually but steadily growing . . . and it will continue to grow until it becomes a power in the earth."

This quote tells me so much about their marriage and about Mattie, but also about the time period. There's a sense of awakening and preparation there, a sense that big things are coming. It's an exciting zeitgeist.

Mattie had served in the general YLMIA presidency for 24 years when President Mina Taylor passed away. Mattie's own mother, President Mary Horne of the general Relief

Society, passed away only four months later and the loss of these two great mentors surely weighed heavily on Mattie. She was called as general president of the YLMIA and in turn called Mina's daughter Mae to serve as her counselor.

In spite of her health challenges, President Tingey's first item of business was to "visit every stake in the Church and to look upon the inspiring faces of the young women wherever they are gathered under the Mutual banner." By this time period (1905–1910) this meant traveling far beyond Utah—to Oregon, Wyoming, Idaho, Canada, and Mexico. At first, the general board met every three months in a borrowed space, but as the pace of the work sped up the officers of all three women's auxiliaries transitioned to weekly board meetings and days spent in their own offices. During Mattie's 48 years of service in YLMIA, membership exploded from 4,000 to 50,000. Wow, yeah, that would change the job quite a bit.

Mattie was president when the Beehive Girls program was developed and implemented! Roadshows became popular. Girls camps were established throughout the church—in fact, the First Presidency handed responsibility for the church's entire recreation program over to the MIA. The young women focused on service projects during World War I and the YLMIA began renovating Brigham Young's Salt Lake home, the Beehive House, turning it into safe and appropriate lodgings for single women coming into the city to work. I love that this former working girl headed up a project to help other working girls.

President Tingey was released to take care of her health when she was seventy-two and dedicated her remaining energy to her children and grandchildren. They always remembered her as a fun grandmother who sang to them and didn't scold them for sliding down her curved banister. The YLMIA became the Young *Women's* Mutual

Improvement Association in 1934, four years before she passed away, in spite of her specifically asking her successors to make the change over her dead body. Oof, I hope she was being playful.

HEAD SPACE

FIELD OF HOME, CELL 112: **Can or preserve three different kinds of fruit, at least two quarts of each.**

THE BARE BONES OF Catherine's apartment are identical to mine, but it feels completely different. While I've tried to convince myself that the bareness of just moving in is Classy and Minimalist, Catherine has filled her home with cheerfully-colored furniture and wall hangings she embroidered with her own hands. Every item I compliment turns out to be a Catherine original. Her space is so homey. It's my third time here, but my first time outside my official capacity as Catherine's visiting teacher.

"Hey, come on in!" Catherine welcomes me. "Have you met Jesse?" I exchange pleasantries with her husband. "Jesse is here to care for the kids and keep them out of the kitchen."

"I can take Jane, too," Jesse assures me.

"Oh my goodness, *thank you.*" Jesse has just become my favorite person. Nate had to go straight from school to work today, so I have been extremely on my own with our (sweet) one-year-old all day. My parenting certainly wasn't going to improve over the course of hours in a hot kitchen with a (wonderful) baby pulling on my pants, but I didn't have a better plan. Jane will be so much happier with new faces and attention.

Catherine places me on peeling duty while she explains the sequence of events today: slicing apples, boiling in light syrup, filling a jar, cleaning the jar, putting the lid on, boiling, and cooling. She introduces me to all the terms and tools. "Head space" is the space you leave empty at the top of the jar, measured with a little plastic tool. The little magnet is to pick up the newly-sterilized lids so your hands don't re-contaminate them. Catherine has an enormous canner on the stove—well, maybe it's a regular size for a canner, but I'm in awe of this pot big enough to cover *two* gas burners—to which she adds water from an electric kettle. "This is so many gallons of water that the burners would have to work for hours to bring it to a rolling boil. If I just keep adding water that's already boiling, everything goes faster."

I've been peeling apples throughout her tutorial and quite enjoying myself. Catherine soon remarks, "You don't look like you're enjoying yourself," and maybe it's because I wasn't smiling (I often forget, especially with migraine), but it's probably because she's too kind to say "You're slow and clumsy with the peeler."

My next assignment is to use an apple slicer and corer to turn six apples per jar into slices, then cut each of those in half to make thinner slices. "I just realized that the recipe says quarter-inch slices," Catherine explains. "I haven't done it that way before, but I think they'll cook well and fit better into the jars." I'm a little too short to center my weight well on the slicer, but I manage to keep up. Catherine removes an apple's entire peel in one long strip. My hair frizzes in the steam.

My parents don't can, but we always had plenty of beautifully bottled peaches, pears, and jams growing up because my mom's sister loved to create and share them. My dad would do graphic design work in exchange for Gwen's raspberry jam, which he insisted he wouldn't share with me and always shared anyway. It was a tradition. We carefully saved the empty jars to return for refilling the next year. My in-laws consider homegrown salsa an absolute necessity in their food storage (along with semi-sweet chocolate chips, which they simply purchase in bulk). Given the culture I'm from, I'm not entirely sure how I've gotten this far without learning to preserve anything.

"How did you learn to can?" I ask, when we've fallen into a rhythm.

"I learned to can from my mother-in-law, who learned from *her* mother-in-law," Catherine chuckles. This is a skill that I really could learn in adulthood, I guess. I'm not too late. I don't think I'm very interested beyond Beehive Girls, though. "I kind of want to try a pressure canner sometime, so I could do foods that are staples instead of 'just for fun,'" she adds, "but it sounds expensive and complicated. This is already a lot of work."

From what I know of her life, though, I can see that hard work isn't enough to dissuade her from doing anything. She's starting her master's degree while her husband does a master's degree and law school *simultaneously*. They have a three-year-old and a six-month-old. She swaps childcare with another family, so she has extra kids at her house often. She plays in a local orchestra for fun. And every fall, apparently, she makes time to can her own apples. Catherine amazes me.

After an hour or so of apples in light syrup, we transition to making apple pie filling. The syrup is heavy with sugar and thick with cornstarch and we put fewer apples in each jar, but everything else about the process is the same. I consult the recipe to remember the new proportions and

I notice that it was printed from the Internet—Catherine may have learned the *principles* of canning from Jesse's mom, but that doesn't mean she is limited to procedures she has been guided through. In today's world, endless canning recipes and tips are available to her at the click of her mouse. I can't imagine the troubleshooting these resources have saved her. She can be an expert her first time with a new fruit or vegetable.

"You know what I wonder?" she asks. "How long has canning been a thing?"

". . . Yeah, I have no idea. It feels like an old-fashioned tradition at this point, but it's not like medieval peasants had canners . . . I'm looking it up right now. Can I have your wi-fi password?"

I step outside the galley kitchen and the temperature drops fifteen degrees. "Wikipedia says that a French brewer named Nicolas Appert first developed a method for preserving food in glass jars in 1809. It was fifty years before Louis Pasteur figured out the whole bacteria thing, so Appert didn't even know why his method worked!"

"Oh my goodness, 1809?! So, was drying the only way to preserve food before that?" Wow, I can tell already that this woman and I are going to be great friends. She wants to go down this rabbit hole with me.

"Drying . . . pickling? I'll check. Drying, pickling, sugaring, cooling—in, like, a river? Or the snow?—jellying, lye, jugging, burial, confit, and fermentation." I'm trying to read and summarize at the same time. "Wow. Some of these sound pretty gross, but humans are *amazing.*"

She laughs. "No wonder people got so excited about canned food!"

"Oh, totally. Canned pears don't taste like regular pears, but they're a heck of a lot closer than pickled pears! It looks like canned food became really important in the United

States for the first time during World War I and World War II. Everyone was supposed to preserve produce from their Victory Gardens in an effort to divert other food to the troops."

"So is that when it became such a classic 'Mormon' thing?"

"I guess? The older generations right now either lived through World War II or had parents who did, so that's got to have an influence. And the prophets have been encouraging us to have food storage ever since."

To me, canning is a routine element of harvest time (for people with harvests), so I'm surprised to see that canning is having a trendy moment right now. There's an article making fun of millennials (of course) for buying expensive farmer's market vegetables and turning them into insta-grammable condiments. There's a rebuttal article pointing out that aesthetics, flavor, and self-determination have *always* been reasons people love canning food, even where "not starving" is the main goal. Apparently I'm not the only one unsure of canning's place in the modern world.

"This would all feel different," I muse, "if we *only* got to eat fruits and vegetables when they're in season."

Catherine agrees. "Yeah, it feels like a lot of what we've done with technology is just make every season more similar. We cool the house, we heat the house, we ship in all the produce . . ."

"So the fruits and veggies are all vaguely mediocre, but available year-round. And yeah, we expect to find everything on our grocery lists every time we go shopping."

"Which is honestly pretty important when we're expected to show up for our jobs eight hours a day regardless of the season!"

"Good point. Most people don't get to have shorter days in the office to make time for harvesting and preserving food from their garden."

"I mean, wasn't that literally why school used to be a winter thing?"

"Yeah, the kids weren't needed at home!"

Obviously, the availability of fresh fruit year-round is a new (and environmentally destructive) development in human history, as is the existence of canning factories. These innovations shift the pros and cons of canning dramatically. I don't need to do any of this to eat apples in winter. This is hot, sweaty work to create things that I could almost-but-not-quite buy at the grocery store and I, for one, don't ever want to do it again.

I like the *idea* of being closer to the land, of knowing where my food comes from, of growing, harvesting, and preserving it myself . . . but doing it like this doesn't make sense. If you have to buy the apples, home-canned fruit costs considerably more money than factory-canned fruit or fresh fruit—even before considering all the work involved.

It would be different, though, if I had my own garden or fruit trees. It *will* be different someday.

In this student family galley exactly like mine, in the middle of canning, I finally consider learning to can—on my own, not just for Beehive Girls. With the guidance of Catherine and Youtube, I could definitely figure it out. What if we had homemade salsa year-round from our own garden tomatoes like my parents-in-law? What if I learned how to make my aunt Gwen's raspberry jam or something else outlandishly good? It could be our family tradition to make it in the summer or fall and bring it out on special occasions in the middle of winter . . . our traditions could follow the cycle of the seasons where we live.

For now, I'm content to join in Catherine's and Jesse's tradition. They send me home with three jars of apples. Apple crisp is Nate's favorite food, and I can feel in advance our cozy contentment and gratitude as the house fills with the smell of apple crisp in a Michigan February.

PURE FRUIT FLAVORS

FIELD OF HOME, CELL 109: Make four desserts—jellied, boiled, baked, frozen.

"OKAY, JANIE, WE'RE BUYING marshmallow fluff today. Get excited, because we've never bought this before and we probably never will again." As always, I'm giving a quiet, bizarre narration of our grocery trip to my shopping buddy, Jane. "We're going to use the marshmallow fluff to make ice cream, of all things. And we're getting Jell-O, too. Daddy hates this stuff sooooo much. It's comical. Orange Jell-O to make Maple Mousse. Yeah, I know, Janie—I have my doubts too."

I was shocked and betrayed when I looked up what "jellied" desserts are and realized that they were Jell-O. I thought that pre-WWI desserts were so unadulterated— just flour and sugar and butter, the way I like to make them today—and now I learn that powdered gelatin dessert has existed *under the same trademark* since 1897!?

I can't blame the Board for including Jell-O in the handbook, though. It was part of the zeitgeist. Salesmen for "America's most famous dessert" swarmed the states in the early 1900s, handing out free Jell-O cookbooks touting the virtues of Jell-O in all seven of "the pure fruit flavors" (including chocolate). The propaganda made it very clear: everyone loves Jell-O, it takes one minute to prepare, it will *never* cost more than ten cents, and an inexperienced housewife on a budget can prepare it just as beautifully as can a trained chef.

"Well, Janie, the propaganda was wrong. This definitely costs more than ten cents. I wonder what on earth chocolate Jell-O was like. Ew is right, Janie." The Maple Mousse recipe is actually straight out of one of the old sales pamphlets. My other options were Paradise Pudding, Peach Delight, Raspberry Jell-O Supreme, Russian Sponge, and Mrs. Rorer's Bavarian Cream. There's no way that Maple Mousse is going to work, but . . . it sounds delicious. "Maybe it'll work, right, Janie? Maybe it will be our new favorite food."

I'm more hopeful about the boiled dessert I've chosen. A boiled dessert means pudding. I looked through a lot of old British recipes for weird boiled cakes that required a pudding cloth, a lot of alcohol, and a month or two of aging before realizing that that wasn't what the Board meant at all. In the United States, a pudding was always "a sweet, milk-based dessert." I've chosen a caramel pudding recipe from the kitchen of Mrs. G. A. McIntosh in a 1913 Civic League Cookbook. Caramel pudding sounds unironically delicious.

While I'm in the baking aisle, I stock up on chocolate chips and feel like a real Mormon mother with a line-up of dessert ingredients (including Jell-O!) ready to go at the drop of a hat.

I get the groceries home and text Shelby: "Want to come make some potentially disastrous 1915 recipes with me?"

She demonstrates her undying coolness by getting onboard immediately. "Ummm, of COURSE I want to! When?!"

"Okay, so this is called Maple Mousse and it's basically orange Jell-O with maple syrup and whipping cream blended in."

"Orange and maple, huh? Let's do this."

We start pouring and mixing and making one big mess. Jane and Noelle are more productive, making a series of three large messes with books, cheerios, and grocery bags. It's hard to explain how two one-year-olds can be best friends when they are barely figuring out parallel play, but these two are thick as thieves.

". . . Is it supposed to fluff up?" Shelby finally voices the question that has been gnawing at us for the last five minutes of beating.

"I really thought so, but it's not going to happen."

"Maybe we were supposed to whip the cream before we added the Jell-O?

"Yeah, probably. The recipe is really ambiguous. Sorry."

"I came here knowing it was potentially disastrous, remember? This is fun."

"I was planning to, like, pour it into pretty glasses to set up, like a real mousse. But now . . . I guess we just set it aside?"

"Let's at least stick it in the fridge. There's still a chance it will set up."

We leave the Maple Mousse for dead and turn our attention to Frozen Marshmallow Pudding.

Shelby deciphers the recipe. "There's a cup of marshmallow fluff *and* a cup of sugar in this?"

"Holy cow. I wonder if marshmallow fluff used to have less sugar in it."

"Yeah, I thought modern Americans were the ones who use way more sugar per person than anyone else ever has . . .

oh my goodness, there are *four tablespoons* of cornstarch."

"I mean, I guess I won't struggle to get the liquid to thicken, for once. Four tablespoons?!"

It becomes very clear that this is not 1915 when I pull my beloved ice cream maker out of the freezer and plug it in: no hand crank, no rock salt, no ice, and only 20 minutes to ice cream.

We sit down and watch our babies while it churns. They're ready for some attention—fresh diapers, snacks, kisses—but we try to chat anyway. It's during this lull that I realize something.

"Shelby! Jell-O and marshmallow both have gelatin in them! None of this is vegetarian!"

She's not surprised. "Oh, I know."

"You weren't going to speak up?"

"Heavens no. It's all good! It's not like it's meat. And you've done your due diligence with taking good care of vegetarians lately."

"I'm glad that you feel that way." Nate and I didn't know a single vegetarian when we lived in Utah. Now, it's most of our close friends. We both grew up thinking that meat was the center of the meal, so we've had a lot to learn. We had to figure out one meatless meal at a time if we wanted to have friends over.

"It's getting easier, by the way," I reassure her. "I've started planning almost all vegetarian meals so we always have leftovers to share with you and Noelle if you're over through lunchtime." Feeding people stresses me out to no end, but we're with Shelby and Noelle a lot. We need to be able to feed each other. We need to be able to feel at home together.

"Thanks." Shelby talks as though this is some kind of favor I'm doing for her.

"Ha! You're welcome. Thanks for all the amazing pastas."

I didn't need Shelby to come over to do this cell with me: I can follow a recipe just as well as she can. But we spend more than half our days together and it's so much more fun this way. When you're in school, you can rely on your schedule to force you to see the same people over and over, enough times to be friends. When you have a job, you usually have some kind of coworker to see and/or talk to frequently. When you're a stay-at-home parent, you have to carve that out for yourself.

 Shelby has been a lifesaver. We're both introverted and pretty private, but I'm starting to lay off the cleaning before she comes over. I can fold laundry while she's here. She is welcome to see my basement. I don't get frazzled when Jane melts down in front of her. She knows without asking when my headache is particularly bad and she doesn't have to hide her real moods around me. We don't have meals together only when it's a special occasion or when we have something presentable. We can use the last of what's in the fridge.

Our Frozen Marshmallow Pudding has frozen. I pull Nate out of his basement homework lair to join us for a treat. He's been down there so long that Jane and Noelle are surprised to see him.

Our bowls are smooth, deep-turquoise stoneware and they were made for this moment, for this exact contrast with a bright white confection. We all take our first bites, our spoons clinking almost in unison. We taste. We pause.

"Holy moly, that is sweet," Shelby acknowledges.

"Yeah, it definitely didn't need that extra *cup* of sugar," I agree. It's overwhelmingly sweet. Cloying.

"It's delicious." Nate is a great cook and completely un-picky. Kind of the perfect combination in a spouse, now that I think about it.

Shelby eats half her serving, then wisely stops.

I finish most of mine, but with deep regret.

Nate downs his with full compliments to the chefs.

I probably didn't need Beehive Girls to get me to eat more sugar.

STRONGER:
THE STORY OF
JANE MANNING JAMES

FIELD OF RELIGION, CELL 9: Give brief account of the life and labors of four other local women who have done much good in Church service.

THIS IS MY FIRST CHANCE to choose whom to write about and I'm excited to find more stories. I'm going to ignore the word "local." I know there are great Latter-day Saint women around me, but there's just a lot of Church *history* I still need to figure out. The first person I want to learn about is Jane Manning James. She's represented in the 2005 movie "Joseph Smith: The Prophet of the Restoration" and it feels like the audience is already supposed to know who she is. I don't know her story beyond what's shown in that movie . . . and she seems cool . . . so here I go!

Jane Elizabeth Manning was born around 1822 to Isaac and Phyllis Manning, a free Black couple in Connecticut. She heard the message of Latter-day Saint missionaries as a young adult and felt that it was true. (I wish we knew more about her early life, but she was interviewed by people who mostly cared about her Joseph Smith stories.) She joined the Church in about 1842 and brought many family members with her. Soon after her baptism, she experienced the gift of tongues and a vision of the prophet Joseph Smith, giving her confidence in her decision.

Jane and her young son joined a group headed for Nauvoo via boat, planning to unite with the Saints, but the group was divided in Buffalo, New York: the white members continued their voyage while someone (the crew?) denied Jane and her family passage. Oh, and stole their luggage. Racist jerks.

So, without their boat fare and without their luggage, they had 800 miles to travel on foot. Along the way, Jane healed her companions' bloody feet and healed a baby so sick that everyone else had given up hope.

In Nauvoo, each family member found work in a different household. In the interview where Jane dictated her life story, she recalled being welcomed to Nauvoo with love, but it was not insignificant for this group of Black saints to leave behind their homes and communities to move in with a bunch of white strangers. They were exceptionally brave.

Jane worked in the home of Joseph and Emma Smith, so she observed some of Church history's most interesting characters and events up close. While doing the laundry on her first day, Jane encountered Joseph's temple clothing. She later described her experience: "I looked at them and wondered—I had never seen any before, and I pondered over them and thought about them so earnestly that the spirit made manifest to me that they pertained to the new name that is given the saints that the world knows not of."

Lucy Mack Smith, Joseph's mother, told Jane stories of the bringing forth of the Book of Mormon and allowed her to handle the wrapped Urim and Thummim. Four of Joseph's wives confided in her about their polygamous situation. Jane didn't converse much with the prophet himself, but recalled that he "never passed me without shaking hands with me." Emma asked Jane if she'd like to be sealed to the Smiths as a child, but Jane wasn't their child and she turned the offer down, probably hoping to be sealed to her own family members.

After Joseph's death, Jane went to work in Brigham Young's home. She met and married a man named Isaac James, another free black convert, and they crossed the plains (with Jane's young son) among the earliest pioneers in 1847. Isaac and Jane had their first of at least six children together on the trek to Salt Lake City. They began farming together. They were thriving financially until around 1869, when Isaac "sold his portion of the family's property" to Jane and left.

Jane was married again, briefly, but overall she was alone and the main breadwinner for a large family. She moved to a cheaper home, rented out her land, and went back to working as a domestic. She lost several children. All but one of her family members left the church.

Jane participated diligently in the Relief Society in Utah. I hope that her spiritual gifts were embraced there and that her sisters helped her resist loneliness and recover from setbacks. But she was obviously going through some things that her white peers couldn't have understood. There had been no restrictions on worthy men holding the priesthood when Jane joined the church, but by the late 1870's the brethren had fully solidified a "priesthood ban," meaning not only that Jane's male family members couldn't be ordained to the priesthood, but also that no one of African descent could be endowed, sealed, or sent on a mission. Proselytizing to African Americans was now discouraged, furthering the isolation of the few Black saints in Utah.

Jane, already cut off from so many loved ones by apostasy, distance, or death, feared being cut off in the eternities. She wanted to receive her temple ordinances, even if she had to receive them by proxy. She petitioned church leaders: visiting them in their homes, writing letters, and having prominent white women write letters on her behalf. Jane asked to be sealed to her ex-husband, Isaac James. She asked to be sealed to a deceased Black man who *did* hold the priesthood, Walker Lewis, if that was more acceptable. Finally, she asked to be sealed to Joseph and Emma as their child, as Emma had offered so long ago.

In 13 years of pleading, the best Jane was ever given was to be sealed by proxy to Joseph and Emma as their servant. Their *servant?!* It is the only sealing in history of its kind, designed specifically for her . . . which sort of sounds special and sort of emphasizes what a disappointment it was. The brethren, thinking they'd solved everything, may have been surprised that Jane continued to petition until her death in 1908 to receive her endowment.

Zandra Vranes, a Black Latter-day Saint author and activist, wrote in 2016 about how important learning about Jane was to her: "Jane's story is not just, 'if she can stay and her life was so hard, then I can stay too.' It should inspire us to think about what we each have to contribute to the Gospel and what legacy we will leave for those who come after us."

Jane left a legacy of love, faith, and courage. She led her family across the plains. She healed the sick. She watched over Isaac when he returned, dying, after twenty years away. She once saved a neighbor from starvation by sharing half of her flour. Surrounded by church members who believed her entire race to be cursed or stunted, she showed grace and generosity. She fought with great persistence for inclusion in rituals she held sacred, insistent on her own equality before God. In spite of her exclusion, she shared her kind memories of the Prophet Joseph Smith with her fellow saints when they asked.

When she dictated her story, Jane concluded thus: "I want to say right here, that my faith in the Gospel of Jesus Christ as taught by the Church of Jesus Christ of Latter-day Saints, is as strong today, nay, it is if possible stronger than it was the day I was first baptized. I pay my tithes and offerings, keep the word of wisdom, I go to bed early and rise early, I try in my feeble way to set a good example to all."

Not feeble at all, Jane. Your example is still helping me, over a hundred years later. Did that sealing ever get fixed? I pull her up on Family Search to see what I can learn. There are recorded ordinances in 1979, probably because the temple and priesthood ban was finally lifted. Jane received her endowments, and was sealed to her children and to Isaac. The Smiths are mentioned nowhere. That's a relief.

SIMPLE, EASY, QUICK

FIELD OF DOMESTIC ARTS, CELL 418: **Make a dress.**

"OKAY, SO YOU'VE CUT OUT your fabric already, but we definitely need to step back and iron this before we go any further."

Shoot. I was trying to ignore the ironing and Shelby isn't going to let me.

"Then we'll need to match the fabric back up to the pattern to cut the notches because you don't have any of those yet . . . and then we need to sew the darts."

Shelby cares about *all* the tiny details I was trying to ignore. I've been working through making this dress on my own, trying not to inspect anything too closely, but Shelby sees and evaluates everything.

This isn't Shelby's first time helping with Beehive Girls, but it's my first time tapping into her professional skills. Shelby is a product designer with a background in bags and a future in children's clothing. She sews, she drafts patterns, she tests patterns for others. She can browse Pinterest *productively*. The dress pattern said things like "simple," "easy," and "quick" all over it. Shelby is so skilled that when

I asked for her help making a dress, I was sure it would take an hour, two hours tops.

I'm not so sure anymore.

Shelby pulls out her iron. Do I even know where my iron is? The back of the closet, probably. I iron the pieces. I cut the notches. I sew the darts. Because I don't know what I'm doing and because we are simultaneously caring for two toddlers, it takes a million years. The kids start to get a little whiny, obviously ready for naps.

It's time to go home. We haven't sewn a single stitch and all of the pieces of fabric are still entirely separate.

We find a time to work at night, without the girls. We re-cut the neck binding.

"Now we finally attach some pieces together, right?"

"Yes." Shelby hesitates. "Do you want to sew the seams the quick way? Or the right way?"

What a question. "The right way . . . ?" I choose, without conviction. I should at least *try* to learn something from this.

I mean, I have learned a few things. Don't go to JoAnn's and buy quilting fabric when you're trying to make a dress. Don't buy a dress pattern if you don't know how to sew. Sure, the pattern you used to make a pillowcase in eighth grade sewing was just a posterboard rectangle, but most patterns contain a lot of information and instructions that *you are supposed to read.*

I bought this dress pattern in the first place on a WalMart errand with my little sister, Emily. I was Nineteen, she was fourteen. I'd just graduated from college and moved back home, so I was eager to rebuild my relationship with her. We thought the dress on the pattern package was cute and it was clearly labeled as "simple"—I pictured making it with Emily. We were going to have so much fun. No matter that Emily was in that phase of life where one cares dramatically more about stake dances than about sisterly bonding. No matter that Nate was about to get home from his mission and my life was going to change rapidly. No matter that I had never sewn anything more complicated than a pillowcase. This dress looked basically like a pillowcase anyway.

That was five years ago. The pattern and the (completely wrong) fabric I bought for it cost money, so I've felt obligated to keep them. They've moved with me into all four apartments I've shared with Nate, an albatross around my neck.

Tonight, though, the dress is finally getting its first stitches. Shelby and I make good progress putting together the basic outline of the dress.

"We can almost attach the sleeves!" Shelby congratulates me. "That will be the hardest part. First, you just need to press a couple more seams." She starts explaining a complicated bit of ironing to me.

"I'm so sorry, can you say all of that again?"

"Of course." She re-explains. I still don't understand what she's saying.

She sees the blank look on my face. "How's your head?"

"I guess it's pretty bad. I'm not really processing any new information." Not even ironing. For Shelby, it's "only 11 o'clock," but for me, it is very late at night.

"You should go to bed. We'll finish another time."

"Thanks. I wasn't planning for this to take so much of your time."

"The more you sew, the more you'll know that every project takes longer than you expect. There's always something. You're not the only person to feel like you're slow."

"You did it! Your first sleeve! Let's start pinning the other one."

"But . . . this is going to be way too small for me." It's really obvious now that the sleeve is on. "I thought it was going to be too big for me!"

"What size did you cut?"

"Well, the smallest size you can make with this pattern is a six, so I went with that. I thought it could at least be a nightgown or something."

Shelby, admirably, doesn't laugh in my face. She gently explains, "Well, um, home sewing patterns are standardized, but they are completely different from ready-made clothing sizes. So they're smaller than what you're used to."

I laugh, but unenthusiastically. I'm truly disappointed. Like, I don't think I can even fit *into* this, let alone wear it for real. Do I still finish it just for Beehive Girls? Why finish something no one will ever wear?

I think about all the ways I could have prevented this. If I had ever worked with a real pattern before, or read the pattern instructions, or asked for help before cutting the pieces, I would have known.

Whoops.

I do finish the dress. Well, except for the button. This would be a great time to learn to sew a buttonhole, but I just can't bear it.

I squeeze into the dress for a "nailed it" photo shoot—photo evidence of my great embarrassment—and try to throw it away.

"Wait, don't throw it away!" Nate stops me.

"Why not?"

"I don't know—it's special, you made it. Maybe Jane could wear it as a dress-up someday?" We both look at the sad, yellow pillowcase dubiously. Then Nate folds it up and packs it away.

❀ ✿ ❁

Sometimes I feel like I don't know the best questions to ask to get to know my fellow adult women—when I ask what someone does, she automatically tells me about her occupation . . . and if her occupation is stay-at-home motherhood, she always sounds apologetic. I'm not trying to define anybody by how she makes a living, but most people don't know what to say if you jump straight to deeper questions: What are your hopes and dreams? What occupies your thoughts most of the time (other than your children, where applicable)? What do you most love to create? What do you find most difficult about being a parent? What's something you'd like to learn how to do? What kinds of things do you read every day and what do you *wish* you had more time to read about? What is something you're looking forward to?

Beehive Girls has shaped my first months in Michigan by giving me concrete goals when I was sick and unemployed, but it has also helped me make friends and tap into the power of the women around me. Most of my time with fellow young moms is spent parenting side-by-side at the park, but Beehive Girls gives me an excuse to ask my new friends questions that aren't about baby milestones or diapers. I look at each of my mentors as an expert in something, even if our project together had nothing to do with her daily work. Outside of this project, I didn't really need to make Jell-O or sew the world's worst dress, but Beehive Girls again helped me find meaningful ways to build three-dimensional friendships with the women around me.

🐝 🐛 🦋

BUILDER IN THE HIVE FOUNDATION CELL 7: Mend at least one piece of her own clothing each week for two months, not delaying it until ready to wear the article.

Mending, to me, is something that women do to pass the time in romantic period films. I thought this requirement was one that I couldn't do because I didn't have anything to mend. Then I found a hole under the arm of one of my favorite blouses. A button came off my sleeve while I was teaching one day. If both of my slacks' legs had come un-hemmed, I probably would have ignored it, but I can't wear my favorite slacks with one leg two inches longer than the other. Gradually, I've built up a pile of things that need mending.

But that's not what the requirement says to do. The point is to mend the things. One of Nate's shirts is missing a button, too. "I've learned to sew a button back on before, but it never stays put," he tells me. "Do you know how?"

"I mean, I think so, but I've had the same issue. Let's fig-ure this out." We sit down with a YouTube tutorial to teach us how to sew on a button. Our instructor uses a button the size of a dessert plate to demonstrate.

"Wait, she's starting with a threaded needle and a knot already?!" Nate needs to back up a few steps. We pause the video to thread our needles and tie our knots. "Okay, let's do this."

We pull our needles up through the fabric and back down like a dolphin—"Dolphin up! Dolphin down!" Our instructor is full of colorful similes. She speaks to us like five year olds but, to be fair, we're the fully-grown adults trying to make buttons stay on our shirts.

"These are good instructions," I remark, as though I'm an expert. "This is turning out looking much less . . . desperate . . . than my usual attempts."

"Yeah, this is way better. The buttons are going to stay on this time." We high-five.

🌼 🐝 🌸

"And then the buttons fell off as soon as we wore the shirts again!" I'm telling my sad tale to Shelby. "We're missing something. Thanks for helping me learn how to mend all of this."

Shelby is still somehow undeterred by my ineptitude with a needle. Nate is playing with our kids, so I'm crossing my fingers that this feels like a welcome break for her. She refers to each of my blouses and pants as a "garment." I know she can sew, but I am impressed by her teaching ability: she lets me fumble every step. It's the only way I can learn.

"You've got to be so bored," I remark while I struggle. She laughs in reply. "Can you remind me why I'm trying to get *four* threads through a needle?"

"Well, the serger stitches left four loose threads. Right now, they're on the outside of the hem, but everything will stay together a lot better if they're tucked away inside, hidden and safe."

"I guess I thought that running each hole through the machine would be the *only* step. And four threads is too many." I wasn't expecting so much of mending to involve tucking threads away. I've let two slip back out of the needle, so I'm back to square one.

"Yeah, your blouses are made of delicate fabrics. In a perfect world, they would have been made with a French seam."

"What's that?"

"Well, wrong sides are sewn together first so that the edges prone to fraying can then be folded and sewn again with right sides together, producing a neat seam that leaves nothing exposed, so it doesn't wear out or get caught so easily."

"But my clothes were all produced in the most exploitative way possible, so no time for nice seams?"

"Exactly." In her former life, Shelby toured a lot of Chinese factories and is always teaching me about ethics and fast-fashion.

When I finally manage to take care of the serger threads, she helps me hem the bottom of my slacks. "This is called a hand hem. You do it by hand so you can make really small, spread-out stitches that really aren't going to show, even to you when you're standing."

Cool. I totally expected to do this with a machine, but you learn something new every day. "How did the original hem experience enough stress to fall apart in the first place?" I ask.

"Uh, you know how when you put your pants on, there's a point where your toes catch slightly?"

"Oh! Yeah, that makes sense."

Then there are the buttons. Shelby is confident that she knows what we're missing. "You've seen buttons with holes in them and buttons with a little loop on the back, right?

The little loop creates enough space between the button and the fabric for you to, you know, button it."

"Oh, right. Another layer of fabric has to fit in there!"

"Right. When you sew a button with holes, though, you have to create your own shank to give the button space to function. A perfectly tight button isn't the goal: if you can use the button at all, you're going to be putting some serious strain on it, especially if you're dealing with thick fabric." She teaches me how to make a thread shank. It isn't even hard. We just didn't know. Once I pass this magic along to Nate, we'll be set for life.

As I sew up a tiny hole in a sweater, I think about the day I bought it. It was, perhaps, the only shopping-for-fun trip of my life, the week before Nate returned from his mission. My friend Pete was with me, hyping up my sweater choice ("That sweater will go great with your Nate!") and I appreciated his celebrating with me. Now that I think about it, why was I buying a sweater in June . . . ?

The newly-mended slacks were a gift from my mother-in-law my first semester of teaching my own class at BYU. I'd never had professional pants that were actually stylish before and I felt so loved and supported.

I first wore this vertical-striped "pirate shirt" very recently, at our first Thanksgiving away from home—a friends-and-neighbors meal that was surprisingly delicious considering the huge list of allergens we needed to avoid. There was no pressure for us to drink, but the wine made everyone else more relaxed and turned the scene cozy and familial. I loved it.

The feelings and memories evoked as I handle these clothes are not "stories" exactly. They don't have a beginning, middle, or end and I can't think of a way to tell them to Shelby. But I certainly feel connected to the past via these clothes. I'm happy to be saving them.

In several clumsy hours, I repair four blouses and a pair of slacks. I feel the rush of walking away with a whole new professional wardrobe. An actual shopping spree couldn't be any more thrilling. In these hours my humble clothes have been elevated by the time and work I put into them. I think about how I can better maintain my clothes in the future, washing and drying them more gently and hanging them more carefully. They are garments now. Each has become a "piece" rather than just part of the pile.

SOME PLACE
WHERE AMBITIOUS
GIRLS MIGHT BUY
EXPERIENCE

FIELD OF BUSINESS, CELL 614: Write a paper of from 1500 to 2000 words on vocations for women, and read it at a Bee-Hive meeting.

I DELVE INTO THE *Young Woman's Journal* to find something about jobs for girls and the rhetoric around jobs for girls. I find a ten-part series from 1927. Hmmmm . . . that's a little later than most of my Beehive Girls study. I'll read the first installment to see if it's any good.

Part one is the introduction, so the author, Agnes, says all the usual things. You're looking forward to marriage and children, of course, but pursuing a career is valuable for several reasons, even if it just ends up being for a few years after high school. First, you don't know what the future holds. You might not get married, you might not have children, or you might end up needing to support the family that you create. This is the reason I heard constantly in my own Young Women classes; got it. Second, your practice in managing your own money will bless your family when you transition to managing your husband's income. Okay, yep, the "your skills will make you a better mom" thing; got it. And then Agnes makes a bolder claim: "Every girl has the right to the joy and independence which earning her own living brings."

That one stops me in my tracks. I guess I didn't realize I was bringing a bunch of pent-up angst to the table on this cell, but no one has ever told me that I had a right to joy and independence in my work. I was taught that working, for women, was a last resort—if you *couldn't* get married, if your spouse *couldn't* support you, if you *couldn't* have children. I was taught to "obtain as much education as possible," but basically just in case.

In my circumstances, "as much education as possible" has turned out to be quite a bit of education. And somewhere along the way, I stopped seeing my education as a backup plan, as a way to get a job in an emergency. I started enjoying my work—enjoying the stretching and learning, enjoying my students, enjoying dividing my day between home and work, and enjoying imagining a future of continuing work and motherhood (even though I still only have a semester of adjunct teaching under my belt). That deviation from my upbringing has been something to work out between me and God. I would never have asserted a right to that joy. But as a motivation to go to work, "joy" sure feels different than "fear of widowhood."

Maybe Agnes wouldn't have said every *woman* has a right to joy and independence. But still. I feel like she captured something I've learned about myself and couldn't articulate.

Obviously, this is a very privileged and optimistic way to look at work. Women have always worked, and they haven't always had a joyful time of it. For some women, liberation has meant the ability to get jobs outside the home, while for others liberation has meant the opportunity to be home with their own children. It's complicated—tied up with industrialization, capitalism, race, and birth control at the very least. But for *me*, it is important to work outside my home at something I actually care about.

With that right to joy and independence in mind, let's dive into Agnes' ten occupations for girls.

THE NURSE

I've taught classes of nursing students at BYU and the pressure on them is intense. Their grades have to be basically perfect to get into the program and once they're in it's a pile of science classes and early morning clinical shifts.

It was a little easier to become a nurse in 1927. You could go directly from high school to three years of on-the-job training, which would prepare you for licensing exams. Agnes points out that "No patient wants to be fumbled with": nursing requires medical knowledge, dexterity, physical energy, professionalism, cheerfulness, and never-ending kindness. Nothing about this has changed.

I remember my first time really working with nurses, when Jane was born. A nurse had been with me all day during labor and stayed past the end of her shift because she didn't want to miss meeting the baby by fifteen minutes. She cared. Throughout my hospital stay, I was amazed that every nurse was willing to bring me water, examine my still-puffy uterus, teach me how to breastfeed, and help me walk to the restroom. As Agnes wrote, "Hers is the kind of work of which the Master spoke when He said, 'If you do it unto the least of these, you have done it unto me.'"

THE TEACHER

Even in 1927, a bachelor's degree was a prerequisite to public school teaching, but a high labor turnover rate made it easy to find a position once you were qualified. Agnes mentions teachers leaving for marriage or to continue their educations, but motherhood is conspicuously absent. I know that women used to have to quit their jobs when they got married, but was that still happening in 1927?

I look it up. A law or policy that excludes married women from the workplace—either by firing or not hiring—is called a "marriage bar" and they were common in Utah until the 1970s. The seventies?! One of the stated ideas behind marriage bars was to give more households a shot at an income, and the rules did relax during wars, but occasionally widows were still considered married and were barred from employment to support themselves and their children. That . . . doesn't make any sense.

But as long as you were single, there were real benefits to being a teacher. There were opportunities for advancement and entire summers to spend studying or traveling. There were co-workers who were "likable, cultured, and worth knowing." There were even pensions.

Agnes does warn that while a love for children is the first requirement for teaching, you'll also need patience with their parents as "it is sometimes difficult to make parents realize that perhaps it is not partiality on the part of the teacher which makes their children's report cards come home marked in red."

THE SALESGIRL

I pictured something like a cashier, but Agnes is all about upward mobility in the sales world. She writes about how you can gain seniority and lead your department, but "of course this is not the limit of [your] progress." You could be a buyer for a department store, managing thousands of dollars. You could get raises and business trips East. You could head up a training department. You could be an executive. So Agnes definitely isn't talking about a temporary, emergency job here.

How did one get a job in retail? Agnes interviewed the superintendent of a large department store to find out what he looked for. First of all, "Slouching or half lying down in a chair while waiting never got anyone a job yet." You had to look neat and business-like, not sloppy and not ready for a party. Well, obviously.

When it came right down to it, though, the girl with the most education would most likely end up with the job. "Usually, this superintendent says, girls can obtain an education nowadays if they have ambition enough to do so. Poverty used to prevent them sometimes, but now if a girl wants to work her way through school, there are usually opportunities to be arranged for her." To me this illustrates the time period beautifully. For the first time, education and a small career were part of society's *expectations* for privileged young women.

THE MUSICIAN

I think Agnes gave the people what they wanted when she wrote about music careers, but she sounds like a worried parent whose child wants to be a rock star. She begins by talking about Utah's unique musical culture: "Nowhere is there greater opportunity for young girls and boys to develop their musical talents. The cultural value of the music which we enjoy so abundantly is beyond price." The subtext is, of course, that everyone enjoys making music and thinks they're going to be a musician. Agnes recommends expressing your love for music at church meetings and talent shows. "It would be splendid if we could follow the inclination of our talent without having to worry where the bread and butter were to come from, wouldn't it?" I get it, Agnes. I'm married to a composer.

So what could a musician do to make money? Teaching in a school was an option, but "the positions are few and the requirements many." Church dances paid players five dollars a gig, but it was hard to string enough gigs together to make a living. Orchestras at summer resorts were paid well, "but these are usually composed entirely of men and boys." As for the radio, it was "only just in its infancy. . . . Performers over the radio are usually paid, but no definite sum has been fixed." So private teaching was about as good an option as existed.

DOMESTIC ART AND SCIENCE

What could a girl do with special training in cooking or sewing? She could teach at a high school, as long as she was also a qualified teacher. She could teach cooking classes offered by stove and oven companies. She could work for the government, traveling and teaching underprivileged "women to improve their home conditions, and teaching them better ways of cooking and sewing, giving them instruction in nutritious, balanced diet and the other scientific things mothers have to know nowadays."

She could work for a company that sold clothing patterns, training customers in how to use the commercial patterns. She could design dresses, but Agnes is skeptical: "Doesn't that give you a thrill? I think most girls would like to do that. And there is where the trouble lies." Some things never change. Agnes warns that correspondence schools for this field are generally scams and that there are no factories in the American West for clothes or hats. So good luck.

Agnes bemoans the change in clothing culture—factories could create new styles so quickly and cheaply that consumerism was rampant. I didn't realize that fast fashion was already an issue in the twenties. Anyway, dressmaking was no longer a clear option.

Agnes suggests a catering business or restaurant, with the caveat that businesses are complicated. Selling embroidery was an option too, but "The profit for you in this work will usually be very small, as you can never get the prices you should for the exquisite stitches which take so much time." I'm reminded of my many friends with Etsy shops.

In spite of limited career potential, Agnes acknowledges that domestic arts are a great field because "You may never have any use for typewriting or shorthand after marriage, but you will always have use for sewing and cooking."

THE BEAUTY OPERATOR

Agnes begins this article with a delightful history of beauty, describing the colorful hairstyles of Marie Antoinette's court and the elaborate up-dos of the 1890s Gibson Girl. Then came the twentieth century and the liberal application of scissors. Agnes shows clear disapproval for "boyishly short" cuts and worries that the scissors don't know where to stop—she obviously never had a pixie cut. I myself have shorn "my crowning glory" this year and it has been so freeing that I'll probably never go back. Her point is, though, that ordinary people suddenly needed frequent haircuts and the beauty business had become a big deal.

An apprenticeship was no longer enough to become a beauty operator, though. Scientific knowledge of the skin, scalp, hair, muscles of the face, and sanitation were vital for customer safety. Licensure exams (both theoretical and practical) were tough. An aspiring beautician would have to go to beauty school. Agnes recommends that a beauty student build up her own clientele during school so that she will have experience and customers to bring to the table when she starts looking for work.

Here, the oddest 1927 detail comes in a comment about pay in barber shops: "Girls do not usually desire these positions, and the salary has to be higher to counteract her natural reluctance to work in a place frequented mostly by men." I wonder whether that explanation was accurate. Did girls really avoid being around men? Did stylists get harassed by male customers? Or was pay higher in barber shops because men needed haircuts (and shaves) more frequently than women? Or even because men tipped girls more?

In the end, the greatest advantage of beauty work was the possibility of opening your own salon, at home or otherwise, and running your own business. I appreciate that Agnes encouraged Latter-day Saint girls to get trained, build up experience, and then become entrepreneurs.

THE STENOGRAPHER

Agnes admits right away that "the value of making funny scrawls on paper which nobody else can read, and pecking away at a little machine, lies not in being a stenographer, but in making stenography a stepping-stone to something greater." My first thought is that she's going to talk about marrying the rich boss. I've seen the musical "Thoroughly Modern Millie" twice, so I have a certain set of assumptions in mind about stenographers.

It turns out that she's not talking about marrying the boss. Agnes shares her own experience as a stenographer. She had a master's degree when she became a stenographer and it allowed her to rise through the ranks of the business world rapidly. "I will quite cheerfully admit that any girl fresh from business college with no other education above the eighth grade, could have done much more accurate typing than I, and as for shorthand, I did not know a single stroke!" But she was a stenographer for only one fiscal quarter before moving on to better things.

Not all girls, of course, could wait to finish graduate school before picking up a career. Business college could train you well in typing and shorthand in six to nine months. If a girl chose this route, Agnes advised, "Study as you go along—night school, correspondence school, reading—and never allow yourself to stop growing mentally."

It was difficult, even then, to turn a degree into a first job when a girl had no experience. Agnes muses, "And . . . how will you ever get experience? If there were only some place where ambitious girls might *buy* experience at so much a pound or so much a bushel!" I think everyone in my generation hears you there, Agnes.

THE ARTIST

"The stories they tell of artists in garrets aren't all based on fancy." Thus Agnes delves into another area of endeavor that should, for the majority of people, remain a hobby. On the bright side, there were plenty of opportunities to create commercial art. "Folks won't pay for real art," she says, but they would pay for comics and art for advertisements. Much of the space in newspapers and magazines now filled by photography was filled with sketches in the twenties. "Art service" companies produced images of every new dress and handbag and china set: department stores could then purchase the rights to use these images in their advertising.

But the angle that surprised me was crafts. "Go into the art department of any store and you will see women and girls grouped around a table busily painting linen lamp shades with wood alcohol and wax, making paper flowers, painting frocks and scarfs, and decorating screens." Women wanted to make things to beautify their own homes, but they needed teachers up to date on the latest decorating fads.

For those who intend to be "real" artists, Agnes doesn't offer precise advice, but she points out that there is a growing demand for fine art in Utah. There are two art shows in the state every year, one by the Utah Art Institute and one at Springville High School, "which has taken the lead in the state in the encouragement of a knowledge of real art values." Little did she know that Springville would remain "Art City," with a fabulous, free art museum to this day.

THE DOCTOR

"If you like to do difficult things that few others are able to do, you might choose to be a doctor." How's that for a challenge? As a teenager I planned to become a medical doctor and I think that Agnes just summed up my entire reason. Fortunately, I realized in time that that wasn't enough motivation: becoming a doctor is "like Jacob who worked seven years for Rachel and got Leah, and then worked seven years more for Rachel because he loved her so." The path from college to medical school to residency looked about the same in 1927 as it does now, plus about seven years to build up a profitable practice.

But for a woman, building up a practice could be nearly impossible. Men wouldn't go to women doctors and women wouldn't go to women doctors if there was a serious illness. Women were still uncommon in medicine and not seen as skilled or trustworthy in the same way as male doctors. Agnes does not for a second agree that women are less capable, but she urges patience. "It is a new field for women, and it always takes the world quite a long period of time to get used to new ideas." By "quite a long period of time," she apparently meant "at least 200 years," since this issue persists today, two centuries after Elizabeth Blackwell became the first American woman to graduate from medical school. "So if you become a doctor, you are being a true pioneer, and you are blazing the way so that more women may enter this profession with less difficulty."

The very inclusion of doctor among the options for Latter-day Saint girls is remarkable to me. I live in a ward full of medical students at a prestigious school and all of them are male. I do know Latter-day Saint women who are medical doctors, but they have not proliferated much since the twenties, perhaps in part because practicing medicine has only gotten more demanding over time.

To cope with the prejudice against women doctors, Agnes suggests going into the specialties surrounding women and children: gynecology, obstetrics, and pediatrics. Women still cluster in these areas, and while they favor these fields for their relative flexibility, these have also become the specialties that pay the least and have the lowest prestige.

THE WRITER

"We want to write for magazines. That the notion is almost universal is proved by the steady stream of manuscripts which pour into every editor's office." I read this, of course, just after submitting my own first magazine essay and while writing this book. I'm in this picture and I don't like it.

But Agnes isn't trying to shut down young authors so much as direct them to the more likely places they can build careers with their writing talents. Newspapers, for example, where you can either beat sexism by being undeniably extraordinary or by writing special women's features, such as advice columns. (The two she mentions are called "Heartitorium" and "Heart's Haven." Holy mackerel, those sound insipid.)

And then there's advertising. Agnes asserts that women get hired in advertising because they are the purchasing agents for most homes. They could look at a product and know what its best selling points were to appeal to other women.

Finally, Agnes warns against correspondence schools for writing. She says they'll send you fliers, ask for a writing sample ("merely a little plot"), and then write back to tell you that you have talent and all you need is their six-month course to be a great writer. "Don't believe it! There isn't any royal road to authorship, or men and women would be streaming along it by the millions."

A CONTEMPLATIVE
TRADITION OF
GOODNESS,
QUALITY, BEAUTY

FIELD OF HOME, CELL 125: Take care of milk and make two pounds of butter a week for two months.

IN DECEMBER, I CONTACT TAMMY, the manager of the goat herd at White Lotus Farm, to ask if she can teach me how to milk a goat and take care of the milk. "Oh, I'd love to do that!" she agrees immediately, even though I am a complete stranger. "Do you want to come milk this Thursday morning?" She stops and reconsiders. "Wait, I guess that's Christmas Eve, sorry . . ."

I appreciate her thoughtfulness about the holiday she doesn't celebrate. The farm is a Buddhist collective, so Thursday is just a regular milking day for her. Honestly, though, Jane is one year old and doesn't know it's Christmas. We have no traditions for Christmas Eve *morning*. "I could totally do Thursday morning. If my husband comes along, can our toddler come too? She loves goats."

"Yes! It's so good to have kids here, learning about the animals."

And that's how we end up joining the Christmas Eve traffic out of Ann Arbor even though we have no aunts or grandparents in the suburbs. People snug in their houses might be sad there's no snow, but it sure makes driving easier. We haven't seen any of the −40° F temperatures we've heard other Michiganders reminisce about, or even anything near zero, but it's chilly when we pull up to the farm—the kind of day where you don't realize until too late that you should have brought gloves.

The farm feels so different than it did on our first visit, on a warm Saturday in September. It was the first of our Saturday Family Outings, the weekly drives and exploration that Nate and I lived for during his intense first semester. The description on White Lotus Farm's website sounded like tacky advertising copy to us ("a contemplative tradition of goodness, quality, beauty") but it didn't take long *on* the farm to realize that the description was earnest. These Buddhist farmers are dedicated to mindfully caring for the land and the animals and sharing the fruits of their labors with the world. They sell the most beautiful produce, eggs, breads, and cheeses that I have ever seen. They keep goats and chickens on the small farm so they have full control over how the animals are treated, what they eat, and how their milk is cared for on its way to cheesemaking. On summer weekends, they open their market and grounds to the public. Jane was delighted by the livestock and the koi in their peaceful pond, while Nate and I were taken with the variety of gourds and the flavors of the pizza we ordered—sopressata with farm-fresh mozzarella and spicy wild honey.

Today, though, it's too cold for "the public." No one is outside to meet us and we aren't sure where to go. Jane is not a fan. I should definitely have brought her some mittens. I try shouting "Tammy?" once, but the wind snatches my call away. Finally, she pops out (wait, was she behind a truck?) and for a few moments we converse only in misunderstandings, as the wind fills our ears. Finally, Tammy guides us to the shelter of the goat barn, where we can hear one another.

Tammy greets Jane warmly, but is undistracted: after brief introductions and zero small talk, she's ready to begin the task at hand. We can see the thirty-ish goats out in their pen, and Tammy starts pointing to individual goats and introducing them by name. "Cinnamon is the queen bee—right there, with the white tail—and her sister is in the far corner, with the bigger horns." She's distinguishing goats by characteristics I can't even see. "It's a matriarchy," she tells us. "If the queen's sister doesn't get milked right after the queen, she gets grumpy and uncooperative. You figure out the pecking order fast."

Tammy has *had* to figure out the pecking order fast. The herd is only a few years old. "This year, we've started using a small pump so I can milk three goats at a time, but before that I was doing all of them by hand twice a day. I really needed the update. The herd is growing so quickly—we had forty new kids last spring!" Even though I know what a "kid" is, I momentarily picture forty newborn humans in my house. A goat kid is probably easier to care for than a human kid, but forty is still a *lot* to deal with. I realize that I have a clueless question about livestock.

"Okay, I have a really clueless question about livestock."

"Go for it. I'm here to answer questions," Tammy encourages me.

"So if the goats are here so that you can milk them, but the goats are nursing baby goats . . . how do you get any milk?" I, like the goats, am lactating. I've finally "weaned" Jane down to nursing only four times a day, but when she was younger it was never-ending.

"No, that's an excellent question. It's something we wrestle with all the time because we want to treat the goats well. The normal way is just to take the kids away from the dams after a few weeks and make them eat hard food, but that really stresses out the kids because they've imprinted on their mamas."

"Can they even *eat* goat feed that young?"

"They can, but if they were left to themselves they'd keep nursing for four months or so. Plus, if we wean them really early, they have to be kept in a separate pen from the adults, which is a weird way to grow up."

"So what do you do?"

"Well, what matters for the newborn kids is milk and, like, snuggling. Warmth and contact. Later, what matters is being part of a regular flock. So—this sounds bad—but we take the kids away *immediately,* before they imprint on their mothers. We have volunteers come in to hold them, cuddle them, and bottle feed them when they're really little. Then they can rejoin the herd much earlier and they don't notice the separation. It's counter-intuitive, but it's working really well."

Yeah, wow, that is counter-intuitive. I would never have guessed that it's kinder to take the kids away from the dams even earlier. I appreciate that she has thought through the needs of the farm *and* the needs of the kids and found a way to meet both, even if it is a way that requires maximum work from human caregivers. How does one sign up to bottle-feed and snuggle brand-new goats?

Tammy ushers us and a single black-and-white goat into the milking shed, a white and sterile place that wouldn't normally be called a shed. It's more like the inside of a spaceship. "This is Iris. I milked her enough to keep her comfortable this morning, but I left some for you to practice on." There's a raised platform in the middle of the shed, with gates and troughs to encourage the goats to hold still while they're being milked. Iris is eager to get to the top of the platform—she knows there is a treat in store for her. Jane is also eager to get to the top of the platform. Nate takes her out to visit the other goats up close.

Like many of her peers, Iris has curvy, black horns. "Sometimes farmers shave down the horns on goats, but we don't do that here. Goats have true horns, which means there's living bone in there."

"So taking off their horns hurts them?"

"Yes. Some farms have problems with aggression from the goats and between the goats, but we haven't really seen any of that . . . so we leave the horns alone." I touch Iris's smooth horns and find them warm to the touch. It's amazing. There really is blood flow there. "You'll notice that Iris needs to have her hooves trimmed. She also has very small teats." No, Tammy, I would never have noticed. I'm still picking up on obvious differences between goats and cows: up close, I can count that goats have two teats. I didn't know.

We wash our hands and Iris's teats in preparation for milking. "It's because we're dirty, not because she is," Tammy clarifies. From there, I just squeeze out milk, alternating teats, gripping the top of a teat and then sliding down. Why do I mentally know how to do this? Did someone verbally rehearse it with me as a kid? I know I've accompanied my grandma to milk her beloved cow, Nike, before, but I don't think I ever helped.

Except for the sterile white-and-steel environment, the process is exactly as I expect, complete with a metal bowl that sings as streams of milk hit the sides. It's difficult to keep the milk in the bowl because a) I'm clumsy with it and b) Iris kicks it over. Apparently that's a real thing. We don't cry over the spilled milk, but if I were dealing with more than a quarter cup of it? I might. Tammy did this twice a day for *how many goats?!*

"Okay, great. I'll just make sure you got all of it and then I'll show you how we make cheese!" Tammy takes over, quicker and stronger and so much more assured. I expected to milk for a long time, long enough to have a meditative moment and sore wrists, but I think she's done watching me milk innocent Iris poorly.

"So Tammy, if the goat herd is only a few years old, what did you do before this?" I ask while she cleans up.

"Oh, I'm a microbiologist," Tammy tells me, as though I shouldn't be surprised to hear that. Maybe I shouldn't be, but I am. Since I'm figuring out my career, it's exciting to find a fellow scientist doing something so far from stereotypes.

I would have figured out her background myself, though, listening to her for another two minutes: she chats during our transition into the cheese room, palpably enchanted with the microbiology of milk and cheese. "Milk is full of sugar and protein, right? So it's a party for bacteria. If you leave milk on the counter for a week, bacteria *will* come to the party and you *will* get cheese. It will just be disgusting." She teaches me that making cheese that tastes good requires deliberately introducing the *right* bacteria, so good cheese requires clean milk as a starting point. This particular farm has an exceptionally good track record for clean milk. The inspector always measures bacteria levels a small fraction of what is allowed in commercial milk.

I picture my own experience in a corporate genetics laboratory. There were endless checklists to initial, processes we had to "witness" for each other, a push to make every process more efficient, rules cinched tighter whenever someone made a mistake. I don't see any of those factory trappings here. Things seem clean, but simple. "What do you do if there *is* a problem?" I ask.

"Well, we have a protocol that works really well. We trust our protocol. If there's a problem, it's because someone is doing their chores mindlessly—they're not being present. That's when the mistakes happen. So when our numbers don't look good, we just re-commit to focusing on the protocols when we're in here."

Here it is. Here's my takeaway from milking the goats. When I am in a slump—when I have a rough parenting day (or week) with Jane, when I feel distant from Nate, when I haven't felt close to God in a while, when I'm lonely—it's not because I need more rules or some grand gesture to get back on track. I just need to be more present with the daily work of those relationships. With Jane, I need to look her in the eye and play with her, engage with her, snuggle her, show her that I enjoy her company. With Nate, I need to ask better questions, listen better, show love more intentionally. With God, I need to be mentally all-in when I try to commune through prayer. With friends, I just need to plan the time to be together, even if it's over video chat or text. None of these actions are difficult or expensive or demand elaborate checklists. They just require remembering my priorities and paying attention.

And that's what I try to do as we return home to celebrate a quiet Christmas. We listen to Nate's meticulously curated playlist of Christmas music, and I bask in his excellent taste and in the memories attached to so many of the songs. We visit a live nativity at a church downtown and I focus on Jane's and Nate's faces—her rapturous reaction to petting a real camel, his delight in being with his daughter. How lucky we are to watch our baby play with goats and a camel on the same day.

Later, Nate has to go to wait tables, and I send him off with affection instead of sadness or resentment. I put Jane to bed, and I try to enjoy her playfulness and her complete trust when she inevitably shouts me back into her room.

I'm alone in our still, cozy apartment. Our Christmas tree this year is eighteen inches tall, twinkling with something like five colorful lights. I probably wouldn't have thought of it as beautiful if Jane hadn't spent so much time staring at it all season. I pull out the gifts our parents sent and set them up—in a pile taller than the tree—to surprise Jane in the morning.

ART MODERNE

FIELD OF PUBLIC SERVICE, CELL 712: Tell the history of each historical spot in your own locality.

"OKAY, SO HERE'S WHAT WE NEED to know about Henry Ford. He didn't invent the automobile and he didn't invent the assembly line, but he did bring the two together to make a car that average Americans could afford. He took the assembly time of a Model T from twelve and a half hours to one and a half hours . . . so by 1920, half of all cars in the U.S. were Model T's."

Nate interrupts my reading to clarify. "Wait, but we're not going to Henry's estate, are we?"

"No. It's closed all year for renovations. We're going to Edsel's estate." Most of the historical spots in our locality are on the campus of the University of Michigan. We've seen all of that. My visit to the county historical society museum was exceptionally boring, but at least they could recommend a cool place for me to visit.

"Henry's son?"

"Yes. His only child."

"Got it. And did Edsel do anything important?"

". . . No? Let me see . . . he was known for preferring flashier cars than the Model T and for being less pacifist than Henry. He provided a *lot* of tanks, engines, Jeeps, and parts for World War II. Possibly for both sides."

"What a legacy. I didn't know Henry Ford was a pacifist."

"Yeah, unfortunately it looks like he was a pacifist *because* of his intense antisemitism, so not actually better than being a war profiteer."

"Ew."

"Yep. But apparently Edsel's other thing was collecting art. That big famous Diego Rivera fresco at the Detroit Institute of Art? He commissioned it."

"Oh, cool. I'm excited to go there with you—the pictures look amazing. This neighborhood is cute, by the way."

I turn my attention from my phone to the view from our car. Detroit is about a forty-minute drive from Ann Arbor, so the drive always reminds me of visiting Salt Lake City as a BYU student. Detroit has such a bad reputation these days that it's interesting to be in the city and see these darling old neighborhoods, cheerfully packed with unique homes and enough space for gardens. "Well, let's move here!" I joke, as always. Nate and I don't know where we'll live after Ann Arbor, so we're always subtly on the lookout for Jane's eventual hometown.

Within a minute, though, the houses start to get much fancier. "Oops, we've gone too far." We're passing a neighborhood of mansions with ever-expanding lawns and then, suddenly, we're passing Lake St. Clair itself.

The lake is gorgeous. I can see why, if you were very wealthy and you had to go to work in the center of Detroit, you'd build your castle right here. "There's the house!" Nate points out.

"I'm surprised we can see it from the road . . ." I remark. It's a grand building, though, stone covered with ivy.

Nate follows the driveway and we realize our mistake at the same time. What we saw from the road is only the gatehouse. And once we're inside, we still can't see the main house. Instead, there's just acre upon acre of naturalistic lawn with enormous old trees. It is incredibly peaceful and, in its own way, simple. We have incredible parks in Ann Arbor, but this one feels softer, more idyllic, and more private.

We unload our sweaty toddler and put her in the stroller. We find the non-original structure where weddings are held and tour tickets sold. The ticket clerk directs us toward the house and we have a few minutes before the start time of our tour to meander in that direction, admiring the harbor and the lagoon the Fords built (well, not personally) for their boats, along with the Powerhouse, which is an entire building full of boilers and fuse boxes. It is so hot and muggy today, but the shade of the enormous trees and the breeze coming off the lake makes it feel like we *might* survive the weather.

Eventually, we find the main house. It looks much older than a century—medieval, even, and very European. It is large—potentially the largest home I've ever entered—but I still remark to Nate that "it doesn't seem *that* big . . ."

"Maybe it's because we're from Utah," he replies. He has a point. I grew up in a neighborhood where extremely large houses were the norm. My parents would take us on Sunday drives to see the massive estates of Alpine. I've been desensitized.

We meet our tour guide, Nickie, and wait for the rest of our tour group to assemble. "It looks like you're all alone for the 12 o'clock tour," she confirms after a few minutes. "That never happens!"

Nate and I are soon very grateful to have no tour buddies for this. We should *not* have brought Jane. While the house was built in 1927, it was constructed from bits and pieces of old English castles and churches—every door, wall, window, or fireplace is from the sixteenth, fifteenthth, or fourteenth centuries. We are separated from centuries-old furniture and original Degas paintings by velvet ropes. Jane doesn't speak the language of velvet ropes and she's very fast. Nate has to pick her up to keep her off the artifacts, which doesn't help her mood. She wants to explore. She wants to put a fourteenth-century couch cushion into her mouth. It is so hot in here. We're all dripping, and the small stress of holding onto Jane feels bigger.

I can't believe that four children were raised in this house. Were they allowed to sit on these chairs?

I can't believe that the farmhouse we visited way back in Logan was built within a decade of this place. This mansion has a central vacuum system in the walls! There are walls of refrigerated cabinets in the kitchen, and then a separate room with refrigeration for all the fresh flowers. There was a butler and a large staff: they used a light-up board to manage calls to various rooms in the large house.

In the dining room, Nickie tells us, "This is the only room in the house without electric lighting. The Fords had black-tie dinners every night and they ate them by sunlight, firelight, or candlelight. Exclusively." I can't believe they were so set in this decision that they didn't even put in light fixtures. I assume their four children ate dinner somewhere else? How does a toddler wear black tie? How did this family even work?

Upstairs, in the children's rooms, we finally see more modern styles—I refer to the look as Art Deco, and Nickie corrects me: "This style is actually Art Moderne, which wasn't really available to the general public until the forties." The Fords were so wealthy that they could bring together styles they liked from five centuries ago and styles from the literal future. Their master bathroom could be transplanted into any modern house and still look fashion-forward.

The master suite includes a dressing room for Edsel's wife, Eleanor (where every panel in the wall hides another closet for her gowns), and another room just for sitting and writing letters to people. Would I answer my emails more promptly if I had a whole room dedicated to email-answering? Eleanor's full-time responsibilities were managing the household and entertaining important guests in high style.

"What did the kids do all day?" Nate asks Nickie. I think it's a solid question, but Nickie seems confused by it: "They went to school . . ." Right, I guess that's what we did all day as kids ourselves. It contrasts so sharply, though, with what we heard at the historic farmhouse in Logan—all the labor divvied up according to age and gender. It wasn't really time that separated the two families—it was wealth.

After our formal tour, we get to see Eleanor's wedding dress, which is pretty on the mannequin and completely magical in the softly-lit black-and-white photograph of the bride displayed next to it. The dress's style is strongly Russian, Imperial Russian, with a beaded, almost triangular crown supporting the veil. A Ford wedding was a big deal, but newspapers at the time noted its simplicity; there were only a hundred guests, close friends and family in the bride's department-store-magnate uncle's library, and there was "No pomp, no magnificent ceremony: merely the old, old simple ritual of marriage." A wall placard in the exhibit claims that "The nuptials were such as are within reach of any middle class American bride." Nate and I share a look.

"Um . . . how many middle class Americans do they think can fit a hundred people into their household library . . . ?" Nate says.

"Yeah, that's not normal. And look at this. Eleanor told a reporter, 'We are going to live very simply after we are married.' What changed?"

"Maybe Edsel didn't share the same priorities? Maybe they changed their minds? Or maybe . . . this is what they thought of as living simply?"

I picture them in their custom-designed forest, filling refrigerated rooms with flowers during the Great Depression. It's kind of . . . gross.

When we're out on the grounds, it becomes a little clearer what the kids were doing all day. There are boats. There's a swimming pool, designed to look like a natural pond in the woods, and a tightly controlled French-style rose garden. Edsel's and Eleanor's daughter, Josephine, was given a *house* for her seventh birthday: a playhouse that is a two-thirds scale working model, with electricity, running water, and miniature furniture. (Josephine didn't even really like it, but her eventual children did.) There is a tennis court. There are lawn games. There is a recreation room for hanging out and for playing squash year-round. The children went to school and then they played.

🦋 ⚘ 🦋

The lives of the Ford children are a great illustration of the appearance of adolescence in its current form. When I first began studying the Young Women program, I wondered whether Latter-day Saints were unique in creating organizations for their young people. Other churches had existed much longer, but I couldn't picture many youth pastors working in colonial America or during the Inquisition or anything . . . I had to look this up.

The short answer to my question is no, the Latter-day Saints weren't the first to think about their youth. But they were following mid-1800s trends that were completely shifting the way young people were thought about at church, and that all began with the Industrial Revolution. In the cities, young factory workers would spend their day off—the Sabbath—galavanting around and wasting time in a way that was seen as egregious by many older adults. Well-meaning people began offering Sunday Bible study and other literacy-oriented classes. Churches saw the value of the idea and began reaching out to young people with free education programs of their own, largely to convert the youth and retain their loyalty for life. One author, Joseph Kett, describes this widespread rush to provide youth ministry as "the final act of a melodrama which . . . had exhibited sundry attempts . . . to 'save' youth from cities, gambling dens, grog shops, and bawdy houses."

Why a melodrama? I read more and more, trying to figure out how this youth ministry movement was different from whatever came before. Surely adolescents have always needed education?

Well, in a way, adolescence (and adolescents) didn't exist until youth ministry existed. There were teenagers, of course, and they still had to undergo puberty, but they were not separated from adults to live a completely different lifestyle as they are now. Teenagers were truly considered young men and young women, who worked alongside adults (their parents, relatives, or masters of apprentices) and gradually took on adult responsibilities, including contributing to the financial support of their parents and siblings.

I know when I was a teenager, my main "job" was to do well in school so I could scholarship my way through college. I was employed, a little, but that money was considered *mine*, to spend on myself even if that meant saving it for the future, and my parents would never have claimed ownership in it (especially since they benefitted far more from claiming me as a dependent on their tax return). It

seemed normal and right to everyone that I should continue going to school with my peers and that the police
could get involved if I didn't show up. Before I turned 16, I
couldn't legally get a job beyond teaching piano lessons and
babysitting, anyway. But compulsory high school and child
labor laws, along with a juvenile justice system that separated teenage offenders from adults, are all developments of
the last 150 years. Whether or not they are good, these ideas
I took for granted are very new in human history.

Another author, David Alan Black, also decries the new
adolescence as a period of "psychological moratorium,"
and "extended childhood," where "permissiveness and
playfulness are encouraged." Again, I'm not convinced that
keeping still-growing teenagers out of back-breaking labor
or discouraging fourteen-year-old girls from marrying
is a misguided goal, but I'm intrigued by this comment:
"There even developed organizations to turn youth from
adults into children. With the invention of the Boy Scouts,
the Girl Scouts, and boys' and girls' agricultural clubs,
adults officially began calling people in their teens 'boys'
and 'girls.'" I suppose that indictment includes Beehive
Girls as well. Several authors I read are appalled that young
people are considered dependent children for a decade or
more after reaching sexual maturity.

But there is at least one biology-related reason to stop
using puberty as the beginning of adulthood. Puberty has
been inching earlier and earlier for the last century and a
half, so that it starts (on average) six years earlier now than
it did then. Some see this as a positive thing—a result of
improved nutrition due to increased societal wealth—and
others as a very negative thing—the result of absurd levels
of chemical exposure. Either way, this is a massive deal.
So much happens internally for a kid between twelve and
eighteen. It feels very different to decide that an eighteen-

year-old with armpit hair is an adult than to decide that a twelve-year-old with armpit hair is an adult.

Meanwhile, many modern cultures have come to value individual choice to the point that young people are expected to select their *own* occupations and their *own* spouses. Before the modern age, normal parental responsibility included setting up sons with some kind of livelihood (a farm, say, or an apprenticeship) and finding daughters a suitable husband to support them. Again, I'm not convinced that getting to choose your life's work and your life's partner is a change for the worse, but it does dramatically complicate the decisions that young people have to make.

High school is supposed to prepare kids to make those decisions, but "in segregating adolescents into groupings by grade, the secondary school promotes the development of age-specific adolescent peer groups that carry distinctive subcultures," distinguished by "styles in dress, music, clothing, language, and recreational activities." Teenagers generally spend their resources—time, energy, and money—on thriving in their own subcultures. While these pursuits may seem petty or pointless to the parental generation, they are at least goals and associations chosen by the young people themselves, not "busywork" invented by adult leaders to spend the awkward in-between time of adolescence well. Deprived of adult roles, teenagers (and advertisers!) find ways to fill the void. I find it fascinating that early Latter-day Saint teenagers and twenty-somethings organized *themselves* in Nauvoo for gospel lectures and discussions, but were organized by older leaders after crossing the plains.

Discussing biblical teachings about growing up, writer Mardi Keyes relates an anecdote about a high schooler raising his hand at the end of a "teen issues" class to say, "This was meant to be a class in 'teen issues,' but all we talked about was sex! I am struggling with a lot of other issues—intellectual, political, economic, religious, vocational—that I'm going to have to make decisions about in the next few years. Aren't they teen issues? I was hoping to get some help with those!" I really appreciate Mardi's points about how adolescence is stressful because of the "shifting balance of dependency and independence," and that our culture does kids a disservice when it "virtually defines adolescence in terms of sexual maturation and the social life that flows from it."

> The teenage years are unique in that kids are old enough to be thinking seriously about many adult issues, but without the weight of adult responsibility that will come soon enough. Yet so often this special time is squandered, which prolongs and exacerbates the process of growing up.

Squandered? I think about my own adolescence, searching for squandering. . . . I mostly did schoolwork, often at truly absurd hours of the night, and hung out with my friends. I worked in a library, taught piano lessons, and babysat a *lot*, saving money for my mission. I don't think I thought seriously about any adult issues at all, though. Life after college was a black box. I guess at church we were always trying to prepare for marriage and motherhood, but never in a "serious adult issue" kind of way. More of a "here's how to behave on a first date" way, or a "here's how to bake cinnamon rolls" way.

I'm a millennial, part of the generation constantly criticized for its failure to grow up in a timely manner. Millennials laughingly compare stories about "adulting," our attempts to navigate various adult responsibilities for the first time: investing, paying our taxes, renting and buying homes, keeping a clean living space complete with food and clean clothes, moving, working with doctors and in-surance, paying bills on time, applying for "real" jobs, et cetera. I haven't seen anyone talk about family planning and parenting as part of "adulting," but that's important stuff too! We were such well-cared-for children, but some-times it feels like we have walked into adulthood with mostly Google to guide us.

Meanwhile, the Laurels I teach spend seemingly all of their Mutual nights decorating t-shirts and playing Capture the Flag with the boys. Are we thwarting them? What else could we even do? It feels complicated. Practicing making phone calls to strangers would be a seriously strange Mu-tual activity. What about laundry? Tax returns? Taking the city bus? Is it even the church's job to teach random life skills? What could we do to prepare youth for their adult roles at church?

Other churches with youth ministries are concerned about many of the same issues. Research has shown that 70% of Protestant young people will drop out of church in the years after high school and only 35% of those will return to regular attendance eventually. "It seems the teen years are like a free trial on a product. By eighteen, when it's their choice whether to buy into church life, many don't feel engaged and welcome," Scott McConnell said in response to his team's findings.

One blogger/youth ministry coordinator, Dave Wright, has identified several main issues that have made youth ministry ineffective long-term, and I can certainly see a re-flection of our own church programs in the problems he's describing. "First, we segregated youth from the rest of the congregation." Youth don't feel part of the "adult church," miss out on relationships with older people, and feel out of place after graduation from high school. "We incorpo-rated an attractional model that morphed into entertainment-driven ministry." The youth come only to have fun and once things become less fun they have no reason to stay. Then, "we created a consumer mentality amongst a generation that did not expect to be challenged at church in ways similar to what they face at school or on sports teams. In the midst of all this, church leaders and parents came to expect that successful youth ministry is primarily about having fun and attracting large crowds."

As I work on this project, people often ask me about my agenda—do I think that Personal Progress should be more like Beehive Girls? My answer is a definitive no. Sure, the assumption that Beehive Girls was a cooler program is what motivated me to try it out, but I've come to appreciate that Personal Progress is designed to focus more on gospel skills and to invite more honest goal-setting on the part of individual Young Women. That idea has merit. However, studying the invention of adolescence sparks questions for me as a Laurels leader and as a mom. How do I stop forcing my own perspective and schedule onto their curriculum? How can I facilitate real gospel learning and gradual growth into adult roles? What real responsibilities could I hand over to them? And how? And when?

THAT IS ALL
VERY WELL,
AS FAR AS IT GOES:
THE STORY OF
EMMELINE B. WELLS

FIELD OF RELIGION, CELL 9: Give brief account of the life and labors of four other local women who have done much good in Church service.

AGES AGO, when Jane was a newborn, I attempted to take a daytime Institute class on that Relief Society book *Daughters in My Kingdom*. It was a brief attempt. But there's a striking quote in there (page 64) about living peaceably in times of war. The quote is by Emmeline B. Wells and, when I check the index, she actually comes up many times. I don't know her. It's time to change that.

Emmeline Blanche Woodward was born in 1828, definitely *before* the invention of adolescence. At fourteen, she was baptized into the Church of Jesus Christ of Latter-day Saints along with her mother and a few of her siblings. She finished her schooling and specialized training and started working as a teacher. She married upstanding Latter-day Saint boy James Harvey Harris when they were both fifteen, gave birth to their son Eugene, and left her job behind to move to Nauvoo with the Saints. Before she turned sixteen, baby Eugene had died, James had left Nauvoo to find work, and Joseph and Hyrum Smith had been shot in Carthage Jail.

James never returned and Emmeline, still a young teenager, resumed teaching school to support herself.

After a few more years in Nauvoo, Emmeline became the plural wife of Newel K. Whitney. She crossed the plains to Utah with his family in 1848 and they had two daughters in Salt Lake City. Two years later, Newel died. Emmeline lost "as good a man as ever lived": her supporter, the father of her children, but also her own father figure and point of calm and security. She later wrote, "I looked to him almost as if he had been a God; my youth, my inexperience of life and its realities caused me to trust most implicitly in one who had power and integrity always at his command."

Emmeline returned to teaching, a single parent of two young girls. Two years later, though, plural marriage was finally acknowledged publicly and she decided to propose to Newel's close friend Daniel H. Wells. She wrote a letter asking him to consider her "lonely state" and take her on as a plural wife. Daniel was prospering in Salt Lake and remembered Newel with love—he married Emmeline six months after her letter. While his first five wives shared the "big house" on South Temple Street, Emmeline and her (eventual) five daughters lived in a separate home nearby.

The living arrangements and size of Daniel's family often left Emmeline excruciatingly lonely. She wrote "O how enthusiastically I love him; truly and devotedly if he could only feel towards me in any degree as I do towards him how happy it would make me." I can't imagine the pain of caring deeply for someone who lives a few blocks away with his five other wives and married you to do you a favor. Yikes.

Eventually Daniel's investments began to fail and financial stability, too, was missing from their marriage. Emmeline fell back on her teaching career to support herself and her daughters, whom she resolved to "train . . . in habits of independence so that they never need to trust blindly but understand for themselves and have sufficient energy of purpose to carry out plans for their own welfare and happiness." I wonder if Emmeline had expected, as a fifteen-year-old first-time bride, that her needs would be provided for for life. Obviously, she was already setting an example of "sufficient energy of purpose" for her daughters, but I wonder how she meant to train them in "habits of independence."

Everything I've mentioned so far is only the prologue to Emmeline's major work and service. Her early life built her, yes, but raising a family in no way led into a quiet life of old age and retirement for Emmeline Wells.

The Latter-day Saint women's periodical *Women's Exponent* was established when Emmeline was forty-four (in 1872). While she was not involved in its founding, we know from her diary that she began submitting writing to the paper almost immediately under the *nom de plume* Blanche Beechwood. She was concerned about the way Latter-day Saint women, especially those living as plural wives, were represented in the political conversations of the federal government. Emmeline wrote for national publications, countering images of Latter-day Saint women as chattel by pointing out that they were voting, attending college, practicing medicine and law, and heading organizations when most other American women could not. She explained that they practiced polygamy out of sincere faith, not because they were oppressed, weak, or uneducated.

(White) Utah women were indeed granted the right to vote in 1870 (fifty years before the nineteenth amendment!), but United States leaders assumed that they would use their votes to rid the Territory of Utah of polygamy. When white Utah women voted for seventeen years without doing any such thing, a federal act punished them with disenfranchisement. I've heard about (some) women in Utah voting early, but I didn't realize that they lost their right to vote so soon after.

Emmeline and others appeared before various congressional committees to defend their religion. Emmeline was the first Latter-day Saint woman to visit a president to plead on behalf of her fellow Latter-day Saints—she ended up doing so five times. When that didn't work, she focused on embedding (white) female voting in the Utah Constitution as the territory suspended polygamy and prepared for statehood.

In 1877, Emmeline was appointed editor of the *Exponent*. As editor, she continued writing about women's rights and politics under her own name. Emmeline had built a close friendship with Eliza R. Snow and, with her newspaper, was able to give Eliza's Relief Society an unofficial voice.

Emmeline also wrote on more conventional women's magazine topics: reflections on childhood, friendship, motherhood, and romantic love. In one sassy article, she mused, "Is there then nothing worth living for, but to be petted, humored and caressed, by a man? That is all very well as far as it goes, but that man is the only thing in existence worth living for I fail to see." Her diary, though, shows that she was a romantic at heart and still ever so lonely. "O if my husband could only love me even a little and not seem so perfectly indifferent to any sensation of that kind, he cannot know the craving of my nature, he is surrounded with love on every side, and I am cast out." She maintained her strong public facade and dedication to causes she believed in, even when devastated by the deaths of two of her daughters as adults.

The work and writings of Latter-day Saint women caught the attention of national suffragist leaders, who invited Emmeline Wells and Zina Young Williams to the 1879 meeting of the National Woman Suffrage Association in Washington, D.C. There, Emmeline began a thirty-year friendship with Susan B. Anthony and won over other women's leaders, in spite of their deep, unresolved ideological divide on polygamy. Bridge-building was one of her most important talents as she proved herself a true friend to people of all sides. She was on the National Council of Women (a reporter called her one of its most interesting members), presided over a plenary session at the 1893 World's Columbian Exposition in Chicago, and spoke at a meeting of the International Council of Women.

For Emmeline, feminist endeavors were rooted in her faith, not contrary to it: all of God's children were trying to progress toward perfection and prepare for eternal rewards. The restoration of all things meant the end of man's wrongful dominion over women. To her, it was intensely significant that the Seneca Falls Convention took place six years after the organization of Latter-day Saint women into the Relief Society, when Joseph Smith "turned the key in favor of women." Though she did not reach the City Beautiful in time to participate, she had felt connected to the Nauvoo Relief Society from youth via the recollections of her first sister-wife, Elizabeth Ann Whitney—one of the counselors to President Emma Smith. Emmeline saw the newly re-booted Relief Society as a wonderful vehicle for breaking the bonds of oppression for women:

> It has given to woman, in its rise and progress, influence on almost all subjects that pertain to her welfare and happiness, and opportunities for expressing her own thoughts, views and opinions; all of which has had a tendency to make her intelligent in regard to matters which before were considered incompatible with "woman's sphere" and unintelligible to her "weaker" mind.

I think of Relief Society as the center of compassionate service and excellent crafting in a ward, so I'm intrigued by Emmeline's take. The Relief Society was powerful? It gave women a voice? It was involved in issues not normally seen as women's issues?

As I've mentioned, Emmeline's brand of feminism was not universal in her time and place, but it wasn't edgy either. Brigham Young had called upon Latter-day Saint women to obtain the highest education possible—in fields as untraditional as accounting, telegraphy, typesetting (Go Mattie!), and medicine—and I found this quote from future-President Joseph F. Smith that completely shocked me:

> Why shall one [sex] be admitted to all the avenues of mental and physical progress and prosperity and the other be prohibited, and prescribed within certain narrow limits? . . . It is all right for them to be qualified for any and all positions, and possess the right or privilege to fill them, but that they *must* do so does not follow.

Smith goes on to say some less than generous things about women who prefer the status quo. You don't need to see that. The point is that this is the most meaningful acknowledgement I've ever seen from an apostle that women were oppressed at all. I've never seen such straightforward support for *any* women's movement from Church leadership.

As the president of the Utah Woman's Suffrage Association, Emmeline traveled to suffrage conferences in the East ("with the blessing and financial assistance of the Church") and urged her *Exponent* readers to be politically active and ready to participate when they gained citizenship. In 1896, Utah was granted statehood and suffrage for white women was written into the state constitution, largely thanks to Emmeline's advocacy.

Though Emmeline was aging, life still had a few great joys and a few great disappointments in store for her. This is where we get back to the cute romances. At age 62, Emmeline was surprised to find that she and her husband Daniel were falling in love. He would write to her and visit her frequently, and she wrote that "We are more like lovers than husband and wife for we are so far removed from each other . . . there is always the embarrassment of lovers and yet we have been married more than thirty-seven years—how odd it seems[.] I do not feel old, neither does he." Finally, *finally*, Emmeline got the kind of partnership she'd wanted all her life. I'm so sad that it only lasted a year before Daniel passed away, leaving Emmeline all alone again.

When Emmeline was nearly eighty-three, she was surprised with a calling to be the General Relief Society President. She'd recommended her own daughter, Annie Wells Cannon, for the position, and considered herself too old. Again, there was no rest for Emmeline.

Long before, in 1876, Brigham Young had assigned Emmeline to head up a program to store grain for times of famine. Her early efforts had become a massive, signature Relief Society project in the early 1900s. After four decades of building up the grain-storage program, Emmeline's 200,000 bushels of grain were instrumental in feeding soldiers during WWI. However, the sale to the United States was made by the first presidency without consulting (or even informing) Emmeline. The money from the sale was never turned over to the Relief Society. What?! While I don't think she had a problem with helping the war effort, she was dismayed and frustrated at the complete takeover of what she considered a major part of her life's work. The demise of the grain storage program is just one example of the long process of "Correlation," or centralization of authority in the Church of Jesus Christ of Latter-day Saints, but it is one that mattered deeply to Emmeline.

She was also disappointed that the Relief Society general board chose not to take on the *Woman's Exponent* as its official publication. She had been its editor for thirty-seven years when lack of financial support forced the paper to shut down. The Relief Society began a new periodical, *The Relief Society Magazine,* with Susa Young Gates as editor. In her final editorial, Emmeline wrote that the *Exponent* "has surely performed a mission in the midst of Zion for the women of Zion, holding as it does within its leaves the history of their work." That record ended up continuing its mission in the seventies, when a group of Latter-day Saint women in Boston found it, read it, and were inspired to found their own magazine, named in direct homage: *Exponent II.*

When Emmeline passed away at age ninety-three, her friend Susa Young Gates wrote in tribute, "She is sensitive without smallness, she is wise without narrowness, and religious without bigotry. She is a tender, loving link between the women of the Church and those without, both of whom reverence and love her for the good she has done. She is sarcastic at times . . . but her repentance follows swift on the heels of her offense." Wow, I want to live up to every part of that description. And have you ever heard of a pioneer described as sarcastic? What a wonderfully intimate observation! Susa goes deeper, though, pinpointing

Emmeline's sense of humor as key to her character, the thing that has "prolonged her life and preserved her reason in the midst of crushing trials." Emmeline was funny, and that kept her going.

Emmeline is apparently one of the best-known of early Latter-day Saint women, but she's a new character to every friend I mention her to. I can't stop bringing her up. Relief Society birthday party? I'll talk about Emmeline. Visiting teaching? Every topic relates to Emmeline. Dinner party with people who aren't even Latter-day Saints? Emmeline. I'm grateful to get to read both her bold, public words *and* her vulnerable inner thoughts. I'm grateful for the community work that happened under her leadership as well as the Latter-day Saint women's literary tradition she fortified. I'm also grateful for her example of living a life that just gets more interesting with age.

WITH THE STARS
SHINING UPON
OUR BEDS

OUT DOOR FIELD, CELL 535: Select a location and
erect a tent (May have the help of one girl).

THE LOCATION I HAVE SELECTED IS . . . my living
room. I've borrowed a tent from my neighbor because we
are nomadic students who own zero camping equipment.
It looks like it's going to rain, and I'd rather not get the tent
all muddy for no reason.

This is a five-man tent and it's going to take up the
whole room. Jane helps me move the furniture out of the
way as only an eighteen-month-old can. She helps me pull
out the tent's components and dumps out all the pegs—we
technically won't need them on the hardwood, but they're
just the right size to be toddler toys. "Okay, here are the
instructions, Janie," I narrate. "Let's see how this works."

It's a fancy tent, advertised for its miraculous one-minute set-up. The directions are given entirely in pictures. I
carry them as I pace around the flat tent, trying to figure
out what on earth I'm supposed to be doing. One min-

ute? The circling and nudging and head scratching have already taken much longer than the average tent-raising.

I go to YouTube and find someone demonstrating the remarkable mechanism of the fancy tent. It gives me the courage I need to do more than nudge. I start putting things together. Once I've seen the video, it only takes three more minutes for me to put up the one-minute tent.

Jane ambles in and out, stuffing the pockets with whatever strikes her fancy. But without the thrill of breathing mountain air and without relying on the tent for shelter, the exercise feels meaningless. I don't feel any more accomplished than I did before.

When Jane loses interest, I pack up the tent. By the time Nate gets home from school, the only evidence of our adventure is the photo.

It feels relevant to watch "Once I Was a Beehive" in the midst of this project. If you haven't seen the movie, it's the story of a teenage girl (Lane) who ends up attending a Latter-day Saint girls camp without really knowing what she's getting into. In portraying a culture of odd camp songs, inept camping, themed *everything,* and weepy testimony meetings, it would have been easy for the movie-makers to turn this into a showcase of the most bizarre elements of Latter-day Saint girlhood. Instead, though, they focus on the sincerity and unity of a successful girls camp. Lane comes to love the girls and their leaders and to feel like she has been welcomed into something beautiful. I've heard negative reviews but I freely admit that I like the movie, in spite of (or maybe because of) the fact that I have a terrible fever when Nate and I watch it.

From the preppy girl with full make-up to the girl living in pajama pants, the costume designers nailed girls camp. There were completely accurate prayers on screen, containing all the deeply-felt details that we love to pray about. The overblown admiration for any teenage boy within a few miles was also spot-on. I'm not sure where the characters got the ingredients for apparently spontaneous meals and the crafts seemed a little more impressive than ours ever were, but overall the movie was so true to life that it provoked serious reflection on my own days at camp.

At the tender age of twelve, I was beyond eager for my first week of wilderness survival. The young women prepared by making matching jungle-themed pajama pants (for the first-years, the fabric was orange and covered with swinging monkeys) and by going through the motions of "certification," where we were instructed in first aid, fire-building, etc. Our poor leaders, unprepared by any pertinent experience, read and regurgitated the manuals for us. I'm grateful for them, but believe me when I say that none of us deserved any certificates.

We whiled away our days at camp making jewelry and fluffy flip-flops (the ugliest, but most unifying craft in the world). But there *was* a stunning five-mile hike—I remember taking pictures of the view and all the wildflowers with my disposable camera—and we *did* get to sleep in tents (which the men in the ward pitched for us before we arrived).

My first night at camp, the older girls took us hunting for some small creature they called a "snipe." I was pretty sure they were just messing with us, because why wouldn't I have heard of a local mammal with glowing eyes and fangs? I went along anyway, an eye-rolling twelve-year-old, impossible to trick . . . until someone ahead started screaming that she saw a bear. As my fellow first-years and our teenage mentors turned and ran past me, I backed away slowly. I remembered from certification that we were supposed to back away slowly, making as much noise as possible, and I was stressed out that none of my friends were following best practice.

That bear was not real.

That same night one of our leaders heard a bear in the woods. Was this bear real? No one would ever be quite sure, but it didn't matter: we had to sleep in our equipment trailers for the rest of our time in the mountains.

The other thing I remember about that first year is that the fifth Harry Potter book had just come out and the girl who'd brought it with her was dyslexic. I gained access to the coveted copy by reading it aloud for her. And then somebody gave away the ending and we were all livid.

There were always toilets at girls camp, and usually showers and cabins. We always ate legitimate meals, planned and mostly prepared by the best cook in the ward. (We "helped.") We tied no knots and built no shelters. We tried to accumulate charms for our charm bracelets. It never felt like real camping and that always bothered me. I assumed that early girls camps were more like the High Adventure trips that the teenage boys always took for Scouts.

But now, when I look it up, I learn that "real camping" was never the goal of girls camp. In 1913, the presidency of the YLMIA in the Liberty Stake (in Salt Lake City), reported in the Young Woman's Journal the success of the first Latter-day Saint girls camp, put together to meet the needs of their young working women, who were increasingly "engaged in offices, department stores, and factories, and others . . . in school." The women tended to continue working year-round without pause for rejuvenation. The M.I.A. leaders sought to provide "a place where the girls could enjoy nature's luxuries to the fullest extent and at the minimum cost." The stake YLMIA president, Emily H. Higgs, believed that "joy, rest, recreation, and companionship under beautiful conditions is the rightful heritage of every girl whether rich or poor."

This meant a quiet, forested plot on a farm, complete with a screened-in sleeping house, cots, electric lights, farm-fresh produce, and (for safety) chaperones and telephone access. Other than some cooking duties, the girls were free to spend their time however they wished. The camp housed twenty girls a week for six weeks that first summer, with every week ending in a large "Mother's Day" celebration with hundreds of visitors, including many of the girls' parents. There were "bonfires, candy-pulls, concerts, and open air dances." Each week was carefully planned so that it would cost the girls no more than $3.00 to take a vacation. There was no certification.

That first camp at Liberty Glen expanded and the concept spread readily, with many stakes setting apart wilderness property for vacation homes for girls. Claire N. Hulme, writing as the chairperson of the Summer Home Committee in the Cache and Logan Stakes, discussed the expansive vision of sending girls into nature:

> The consciousness of God is a gradual growth with most of us, and we understand best the power and goodness of the Creator of all by acquaintance with and appreciation of His works. Through sleeping among the tree-tops, as we do in our camp, with the stars shining upon our beds, there are moments when the most thoughtless girl realizes, if but dimly, the wonder and glory of it all.

It's interesting to see that this thought—that we connect to God when we're out in nature—is really what ties modern girls camps to the originals, not a desire to teach wilderness skills. When I went to camp as a kid, we were given plenty of time to ponder, pray, write in our journals, and enjoy nature. I did my best to find God in nature because I knew I was supposed to. But usually . . . there were bugs. And it was hot. And I was sitting on a rock trying to write in a journal. It struck me as a little hokey and then I'd feel guilty about not feeling the Spirit when given the best possible opportunity.

It took growing up and hiking with my own family to really understand the spiritual side of being in the mountains. When Jane was eight months old, Nate and I took her to one of our favorite trails in Payson Canyon. It was a perfect spring day. "Bees were humming, sweet birds singing" and all that. Jane fell asleep in her backpack, so her dad and I were quiet. As we walked, I was filled with joy to be with them in a place we had visited over and over and to which we would always return. It was like a ritual.

As I walked, I thought of other hikes: the foothill behind Nate's house in high school, when I was twitterpated that he held my hand even though I *knew* it was purely to help me down a steep spot. Taking pictures for him from the top of Timpanogos while he was a missionary missing his mountains. Our giddy first road trip to Southern Utah when we were planning to get married and no one else knew yet. Scrubby little hills on our honeymoon. Through snow and mist right after we found out I was pregnant with Jane. On that sunny hike with my spouse and our baby, I thought about the miracles that brought us here, God's love for us, and our place in the whole Plan of Salvation. I knew experientially that a mountain could be a temple.

Today, I'm driving a carload of girls to camp and I've put together a special playlist. The music is going to have to stand in for a personality today—my migraine has been really intense lately and I'm menstruating heavily. These aren't my Laurels and they don't know me, but I don't have the energy to engage with them today. I can't believe that I'm the grownup here, the one who has a car and knows how to drive it, the one who has a credit card and can be looked to in emergencies. We'd better not have any emergencies.

I drive westward on the highway to Jackson, Michigan, and then through the forests and farms. It's a hot day, with such a bright blue sky and such big, billowy clouds that it feels like a big road trip (through Montana, maybe?) as soon as we're out of the city. I never really think of Ann Arbor as "urban"—it's not known for skyscrapers—but the sky is much bigger out here. Every other driver is trying to go 20 miles per hour over the speed limit, which stresses me out. The girls chat happily in the back of the car and, to my relief, no one complains about the music. I wonder if I'll ever stop stressing about whether the teenage girls think I'm cool. Of *course* they don't think I'm cool. Pull it together, Kayla.

They don't even notice I'm here, which I'm not really used to. At home, unless I am completely alone, someone is always touching me, always talking to me, always trying to get my attention. Nate and Jane do not know how to be in a room with me without some kind of affectionate contact. And at work, well, I'm the teacher. People definitely notice whether I exist. Maybe it's nice to be a little incognito.

On the flip side, driving with a migraine this bad is severely unpleasant. If Nate were here, he'd tell me to pull over: he'd give me a hug and switch places with me. If Jane saw me like this, she'd stand on a chair to get my "cold hat" out of the freezer, then quietly hold my hand (for at least four seconds). Shelby would hand me a banana. My mother-in-law would pull painkillers out of her purse. Even my students would ask if I was okay. I would lie to my students, but I'd be grateful all the same. With these Beehives and MiaMaids, I can't even bring myself to ask them to laugh less raucously.

I mentally calculate how much longer I'll be behind the wheel today—only 90 minutes with the girls, but I'll have to turn right around and go back to Ann Arbor this afternoon for a doctor's appointment. Then back to camp. Phew. I'm praying it'll be worth it. I hope my doctor will be able to prescribe a new medication or recommend a new treatment or *something* to make life a little easier.

We pull into the camp minutes after the other car from our ward, driven by my friend Brooke, who directs us to the schedules, t-shirts, totes, and other camp paraphernalia. Everything has coordinating branding. Brooke sees my elevated eyebrows as I look around—she laughs with me, "Yeah . . . this is a *production*."

Brooke and I attend the first couple of activities with open hearts, but we have no responsibilities here and it's weird. "Should we go set up the tents?" she suggests. I hesitate. I still resent that I didn't ever get to set up the tents for girls camp as a kid, so I thought that I was adamantly against denying the girls the opportunity here . . . .but we've seen their schedule. "They have back-to-back activities all the way through campfire songs," Brooke points out.

"Yeah, you're right," I concede. "I don't want to teach them how to pitch tents in the dark. Let's go." We hike back to our ward's camp site and unpack the equipment. These aren't fancy, one-minute tents, but Brooke and I are pretty smart and we get them up anyway. I really do know how.

It's good to be with Brooke. She's excellent with the Young Women, fun and young, an art teacher and newly-wed and returned missionary. "I'm not sure I'm going to be able to deal with the cafeteria," she tells me now. I wait for her to announce . . . and she does: "I'm like eight weeks pregnant and this is *rough*. I might disappear a lot to take naps."

"Congratulations!" I tell her. "And you are doing such a great job staying cheerful for the girls. Holy cow. I wouldn't have guessed." I mean, I definitely guessed, but only because I'm really good at guessing.

She laughs. "Thanks. We'll see how long I can keep it up."

Did my Young Women leaders ever have migraines? How many of them came to camp pregnant? I never considered what they were leaving behind or fighting through to be there with us.

Anyway, no one gets to nap right now. I get back in the car and start the long drive to my doctor's appointment.

Then there's traffic. Standstill traffic at two in the afternoon. My migraine and I have already waited so long and done so much driving today—I am stressed out and powerless to hurry. My doctor has a 15-minute grace period, which I blow right through.

I walk into the office, just in case.

The receptionist tells me that I'm late and my doctor can't see me today.

From there, I have a few seconds to move out of her sight and grab a drink of water before I start sobbing. I didn't expect all of my emotions to come out like this—in public, in front of someone who did nothing wrong. I'm so bitterly disappointed and so tired of being in pain.

The kind receptionist comes over to check on me, trying to conceal her alarm. She schedules a new appointment for me, but it isn't today.

And then I'm back on the road, not to my Nate and Jane, but to a gaggle of teenage girls who are looking to me for leadership through a fun and spiritual camp.

🌼 🦋 🌸

The stake camp leaders worked so hard to make this camp happen that all I have to do is show up. I don't have to cook or teach any classes—I am just here to supervise and deal with nighttime. I set up my hammock so I have somewhere to read and write in snatches of time—as the mom of a toddler, any moment alone feels luxurious. I pick a big handful of wild blackberries on my way through the forest to breakfast. The heat and humidity drive me back inside to do crafts and listen to classes wherever there is air conditioning (yes, there's air conditioning at this "camp," and some poor kid still ends up with heat exhaustion).

The girls are a little overscheduled and we get more and more behind as every event on the docket goes overtime, but the second afternoon they get an hour or so to play in the lake. They ask me to join them. I have no desire to do so.

But maybe this is a sign that they think I'm cool? They want me to come with them, to play with them, like I'm their mom or their cool aunt. I'm going for it, grabbing this moment of acceptance.

I spent my teenage years very self-conscious about things like wearing a swimsuit, menstruating, and growing hair on my body. Today, I'll be doing all three simultaneously. I commit internally to making zero disparaging remarks about my body. I will show my girls that it's feasible to frolic in a lake while being an adult woman! Sure, they won't notice or care, but I want to set the uninhibited example I wish I'd seen from more women as I was turning into one.

I have to hike back to our campsite and get my suit (and another Excedrin), then change in a restroom so I can deal with the period situation. It's awkward to carry a wad of clothes and smelly camping garments through the forest. I think briefly of the ticks that are probably leaping from the trees onto my exposed shoulders. The activation energy for this activity I don't want to do feels extremely high.

But finally, I'm walking across the beach and into the water. In all this preparation, I forgot about something big: it feels *good* to swim in a lake on a hot day. It feels so good. Getting ready feels like an annoyance until you're in cool water, with buoyant limbs and sun on your face, surrounded by happy kids having playfully aggressive races and splash battles. Moms are missing out when we stay out of the water.

🌸 🐝 🌼

Of course, there are over a hundred girls at this camp and maybe eight showers, so it takes a hubbub to get ready for dinner after our swim. We start dinner when we're supposed to be on a treasure hunt, start the treasure hunt when we're supposed to be having a fireside, and then start the fireside when we're supposed to be doing a campfire. The fireside itself is . . . well, it's two hours long. A fireside for kids shouldn't be two hours long. It's not my responsibility, though, and this gives me so much time to just sit in a cooling breeze, with a great view of the sunset. The trees sway in the wind, becoming shadowy as the light fades. I'm not a kid, so no one is trying to make me feel the Spirit out in nature. It just happens.

The landscape here is different, but just breathing forest air is "lace" for me.

The campfire is canceled for the night. The girls invite me and Brooke into their tent to play games before lights-out. After tonight, I'll be back in the thick of being a parent and partner, but tonight I'm going to stay up laughing with teenagers until the schedule says it's time to tuck myself into my hammock under the stars and get some sleep.

OH, BUT I HAVE DONE A TERRIFIC JOB: THE STORY OF MINERVA TEICHERT

FIELD OF RELIGION, CELL 9: Give brief account of the life and labors of four other local women who have done much good in Church service.

WHEN IT ISN'T SUMMER—when I'm teaching seven classes, jumping between two institutions and still working together with Nate to take care of Jane without paying anybody to help—I stay connected to my Beehive Girls project by making slow progress on the Local Women sketches. My mom has told me a few times over the years about a really cool Minerva Teichert exhibit she saw at the Museum of Art at BYU. She always says her favorite part was learning about the artist's life, but that's all she says. Beehive Girls finally gives me an excuse to go look it up. What's Minerva's story?

Minerva Kohlhepp was born in 1888 to a Latter-day Saint family and spent her childhood in Idaho and northern Utah. (Oh, my mom's from Idaho. No wonder she liked this story.)

When she was four, her mother gave her a set of water-color paints and from then on little Minerva thought of herself as an artist, carrying a sketchpad and charcoal at all times. When she was fourteen she worked as a nanny for a wealthy family as they traveled to San Francisco and Los Angeles. In California Minerva went to an art museum for the first time and also attended her first art classes at the Mark Hopkins Art School. She taught younger grades while she was in high school, to help support her family during her father's mission to Switzerland and Germany. As the end of high school approached, Minerva was advised to attend the Art Institute of Chicago, but for an unaccompanied young lady who was also very poor, Chicago was a big dream.

Minerva taught school for a couple of years, saving up money and giving her parents time to accept the idea of her going East for school. Eventually, her father arranged for her to go as the first woman "art missionary": she was set apart for service and sent to live at the mission home in Chicago while she attended art school.

The first five art missionaries were sent to Paris for training in 1890. Their work was considered "missionary" not because they were meant to focus on preaching the gospel while they were away but rather because they left the Saints on assignment: the Church gave them financial assistance in exchange for the promise that the artists would later paint temple murals and church portraits. Their training with the great Impressionists helped the young artists overcome their lack of sophistication and their limited technique. Their work also helped cultivate interest in art in the territory. Their students became the next wave of art missionaries to Paris. Other Latter-day Saint painters, including women, made the pilgrimage to Paris to study without any kind of "mission" arrangements; I don't know why Minerva went to school as a missionary, but I suspect that her poor, rural background may have been relevant. She needed support from the Church. And how cool is it that her parents helped her find a way?!

School and city life were still so expensive that she had to bounce back and forth between home and the city several times, taking semesters off to work as an elementary school teacher, but she was buoyed up by the confidence she was gaining in her own work. In Chicago she once confronted her mentor, John Vanderpoel, because he criticized her work so much more harshly than classmates whose work she felt was poorer. She later wrote, "I shall never forget the disappointment on the dear little man's face when he answered in a choked voice, 'Miss Idaho, can it be possible you do not understand? They're not worth it, they will drop out, but you—ah, there is no end.'"

Minerva finished her course of study and returned to Idaho to claim a homestead by "building a dwelling, establishing residence, and making improvements." She slept alone at the isolated new cabin with a gun under her pillow. She taught more school and saved money she earned painting china sets and working for a newspaper. She courted a wealthy young man and called off the wedding when she learned that he didn't want to be married in the Church. She didn't know any young men who *were* Latter-day Saints. She enjoyed the company of "gentle cowboy" Herman Teichert, but told him to marry someone else when she moved to New York City to study at the Art Students' League.

In New York, Minerva plunged into an exciting world of

music and theater as well as art: her school refused money from patrons, so wealthy people would instead donate tickets for students to see the latest important plays, operas, and symphonies. The city was full of museums and many of Europe's great artists had fled their home countries due to World War I, so mentors abounded. To pay for her education, Minerva sketched cadavers for medical schools, painted portraits, illustrated children's books, gave dramatic readings, and performed rope tricks and "Indian dances" in vaudeville shows. (Minerva wore a distinctive headband for the rest of her life, and this may be where it began.) As Nate and I are in the middle of paying for (basically) art school ourselves, I appreciate Minerva's resourcefulness. How do I land a paid gig doing dramatic readings? I'm already hanging out with cadavers for money.

She thrived in school, working under Robert Henri, an important figure in American art history. Trained in realism and then French impressionism, Henri combined ideals of both to create a style all his own, one he hoped would be less academic. He painted in large, quick brushstrokes, with many details left out. After his death, one journalist wrote that, "Robert Henri might have developed into America's greatest painter had he not chosen to become America's greatest art teacher."

Minerva was critically acclaimed for her paintings of animals and had a scholarship to continue her studies in London. She was poised to become a major American artist, but she always prioritized her family: she wrote them frequent, thoughtful, and entertaining letters and turned down the London scholarship. She continued attending church, where another woman's testimony of the joys of marriage and motherhood reminded Minerva of Herman. "Back on the Idaho desert, herding his cattle and branding his calves was a man more nearly meant for me than anyone else in the world." I love that she describes him not as her soulmate, but more nearly her soulmate than anyone else. I don't technically believe in soulmates, but sometimes Nate makes me forget.

Minerva decided to go home and marry him, knowing full well that she was committing to a life of raising children and managing a ranch. Her living room was the center of her home and—in the moments of down-time during meal preparation and after their (eventual) five children were sleeping—her art studio as well. For forty-three years, she painted in the cramped space regardless of its shifting light and the children and grandchildren playing around her. Many of her works were too large to work on in that space, so she'd fold her canvas to work one section at a time, looking the wrong way through a pair of binoculars to see what it would be like from a distance. What must it have been like for Herman, a rancher who had never been to Chicago or New York, to have this remarkable artist and all her stories in the house? What was it like for Minerva to choose a quiet life at home after so many adventures?

Before she left New York, her teacher Robert Henri had commissioned Minerva to "tell the great Mormon story." This concept framed Minerva's artistic life. Painting in such isolation from the rest of the art world helped Minerva develop a style all her own. Henri had taught her that "When the story is told, the picture is finished," so she often left unimportant elements in her paintings vague and sketchy. She saw landscape as background and focused on people, animals, and narrative. Thus, she *could* be described as an illustrator . . . but "illustrator" doesn't convey the artistic sophistication of what she was doing, nor its physical size. Minerva liked to paint on a large scale. She painted more than forty scenes from the Book of Mormon on three foot by four foot canvases. She traveled to Mexico to gather ideas for ancient patterns, headdresses, etc., but she wasn't attached to historical accuracy. She loved confident lines and splashes of rich color. She loved dramatic moments. She loved the Latter-day Saint pioneers. She also cared deeply about depicting women: many of her paintings draw on stories of women that are not usually featured, like the wedding celebration uniting Lehi's and Ishmael's families or the dancing daughters of the Lamanites.

Her isolation had its downsides too, of course. More than anything, Minerva dreamed of sharing "the great Mormon story" with her fellow Latter-day Saints, but they hadn't heard of her. The church declined to publish her Book of Mormon paintings and they rejected her applications to paint murals for the Idaho Falls Temple, the Bern, Switzerland Temple, and the Los Angeles Temple.

Still, Minerva always found other ways to serve. When relatives were in need, they found a home with the Teicherts. When young men needed work, she hired them and paid them well. She prayed over injured neighbors. She used her art talents for service as well, teaching lessons to children, planning creative activities for her young women, and selling paintings to BYU to defray tuition costs for her children, grandchildren, and anyone else who asked. After years of paying tithing and supporting Minerva's Church service, Herman joined the church when the youngest of their five children was six.

Finally, when she was fifty-nine, Minerva was selected to paint the world room of the Manti temple. She recorded that the room was "21 ft. high, 60 ft. long, abt 24 wide." While most world rooms are decorated with landscapes, Minerva envisioned large figures portraying "poverty, pride, oppression, and hatred." She stayed true to her own artistic style, sometimes leaving out facial features that weren't important to the story. She and her assistant

Frank had to recruit their spouses for the mad rush to their (self-imposed) deadline, but Minerva found the whole thing exhilarating. She wrote,

> "Oh but I have done a terrific job. It's wonderful that my health held up, and I was able to go through with it. The authorities could hardly realize that it was ended. They had heard that I was working very fast, and I sure did. No mural decorator in America ever beat that — nearly 4,000 sq. ft. in 23 days. They must approve before I am paid."

I haven't fact-checked her claim, but I love this diary entry so much. I love her excitement at a job well done, especially a job that she'd waited for all her life. I'm grateful that the work was approved. I've been in the room she painted, before Beehive Girls, before I knew her, and it was the first time I was ever challenged by art that I saw in a church setting. I felt the gravity of what I was seeing, but I didn't understand all of it. Her World Room isn't just a dark and dreary landscape: there are 120 people in it! The figure at the head of the room especially confused me: he looked like an Indian chief, but he had his arms out and palms open—was he supposed to be a symbol of Christ? Some kind of idol? Just a stereotyped symbol of the American West? I genuinely didn't know what he was doing there and I sat there puzzling during the ordinance. Whatever Minerva's real intent was, she made me think.

By the time a hip fracture ended her painting career at the age of eighty-two, Minerva had created something like a thousand works of art. She wrote, "I want . . . to be able to paint after I leave here. Even though I should come back nine times I still would not have exhausted my supply of subjects and one lifetime is far too short but may be a schooling for the next."

The more of Minerva's letters and stories I read, the more I admire her. She was a ranch wife *and* a real artist, determined to finish her mural in a fraction of the time anyone expected so that she could be home to help with calves and lambs. She taught her painting assistant human anatomy lessons and simultaneously taught him not to bother painting noses because noses aren't expressive. She had to prove that some of her scenes existed in the scriptures, since she was drawn to stories that no one else noticed. She was completely confident in her unique set of paradoxes. I want to be like her: building the family I want with the person that I love *while* continually making progress toward unrelated goals and passions, finding ways to be entirely myself.

UNNECESSARY READING

IN JUNE, WE TRAVEL HOME, knowing that our fortnight in Utah is going to be busy. My brother is getting married. Nate is putting on a concert of the music of Spanish Latter-day Saint composer Francisco Estévez. We need to spend time with each of our siblings and parents. We want to visit all our friends. We're walking in the Pride parade with Mormons Building Bridges. I'm going to visit the Mormon History Association conference. My birthday is happening. We would love to catch a couple of outdoor Shakespeare productions. And somewhere in there, we hope to hike in the mountains and go on a romantic getaway.

But on this, our first day, I'm off to the Church History Library in Salt Lake City. Technically, this visit doesn't fulfill any Beehive Girls cells, but there are some mysteries I want to look into. Everything I've found about Beehive Girls so far has been about the YLMIA board's vision for the program in 1915 and their glowing reports of how it was going by 1955. I haven't seen what any actual Beehive Girls thought about it. I haven't seen what any swarms chose to do with their time. I don't know how big the program got or how long it lasted. I don't know whether WOMAN-HO caught on. For all I know, I'm the only person ever to choose a personal symbol. I hope to find some clues in the archives.

I park in my secret free parking place and take the train to the Temple Square stop. The place is populated by young missionaries, old missionaries, church employees who dress like missionaries, and tourists in shorts and tees: business casual feels snappy almost anywhere, but my slacks are out of place here. I enter the library and am immediately greeted by a senior missionary, who shows me how to get to the reading room.

I'm over-prepared for this visit: I've pre-registered, watched all the orientation videos, and have an online bookshelf with all the documents I want to request. My driver's license is already in my pocket so I don't have to rummage. I already know that the librarians can check manila folders out to me one at a time. I wipe my hands down with the provided towlettes while they weigh my item, "Gay A. Mitchell's Beehive scrapbook from 1950," then I take it to a quiet desk.

I smile involuntarily as I open the folder to find nothing but a blue felt bandelo. It's like a homemade version of what the Boy Scouts use to store their merit badges, covered with little felt insignia, and after a year of working on this project it is the first evidence of actual Beehive Girls that I have held in my hands. The felt medallions are stamped with all kinds of symbols: a beehive, flowers, a bee, colorful honeycomb cells, colorful bars, a house, trees, a bird, stars, a young woman's face captioned "Honor Bee," a pair of "M"s, and a smiling sunshine. The badges seem homemade, but perhaps a centralized entity produced the stamps. The most complex badge is large and round with a scalloped edge and a layered mountain pieced together from four colors of felt—it doesn't have the commercialized crispness of Scouting as I know it, but surely this one was mass-produced. The pieces are all carefully stitched on and there's one food stain, as though the bandelo was actually worn. The food stain makes it real.

And I love this object . . . but that's all there is to say about it. I return it to the desk (where it is re-weighed, just in case I stole a merit badge or something), and pick up the other part of the file: the scrapbook itself. It is breathtaking. Or rather, it's breathtaking to me, a person obsessed with Beehive Girls. The scrapbook is bound in a wooden cover with a leather cord serving as a hinge. It is painted with a snowy purple mountain, the same as the big badge from the bandelo. It belongs in a museum, not in a never-used folder in a vault. I am so excited to open this thing.

It's all here. I can't believe it.

Gay has copied in "Spirit of the Hive," the Womanho song, the purpose of Beehive Girls, all of it. She records that her stake symbol is the sun, her class symbol is a rose, and that her personal symbol is a mountain. In tight lines of junior high cursive, she explains why she chose her symbol:

> All of us have to climb mountains and if we choose the highest mountain with peaks nearer to the sky we have all the more need for help to ascend. Whatever our ambition and goal in life may be so we choose our mountain to climb. If we wish to attain eternal glory and be nearer to the Lord we have chosen the highest mountain with many obstacles to block the way. When we choose this mountain it means work and struggle all of our earthly lives but is our earthly existence for any other purpose than to gain eternal glory? If we pray to God and always have faith in Him and strive hard to reach our goal, the obstacles and the steep path will be passed as easily as possible and we will reach the highest peak among the clouds.

Okay, that's lovely. Did she really write that herself? Gay strikes me as extremely enthusiastic, but maybe she was just well guided. Or maybe I've been underestimating tweens. She made the fancy wooden scrapbook at a Mutual activity; same goes for the fancy mountain badge (it was not mass-produced!). She lists each cell she filled in her book: playing the violin at Mutual, babysitting for free, covering for her mom so her mom could leave for a couple of days, taking care of someone sick, roller skating, posture training, building a first aid kit. There are real pressed wildflowers and leaves.

Mostly she just writes down the requirements and that she fulfilled them, but I love finding any glimpses of her own personality. She read for three hours from the book "The Presidents of the Church" and reported that she enjoyed it very much, as she was concurrently trying to improve herself by cutting down on "unnecessary reading" (Ouch. Who told her to read less?). She made a map showing the locations of all ten temples and visited the Manti Temple in October 1949 (when Minerva Teichert's murals there were new, though Gay wasn't endowed and wouldn't have seen them) to do work for the dead for twelve hours. She watched cheese being made (by mid-century, it was certainly not part of the regular household work); she made five interesting flower arrangements; she earned a dollar and sent it to a missionary. She babysat for fifteen hours to earn $3.00 and recorded, "I like this work quite well. I tend kids often and have learned to be more patient and kinder with small children."

When I finish reading everything Gay has to tell me, I take a lunch break. When I return, there's a different librarian on duty to check out my materials. She asks if I'm working on the Young Women Project and I say that I am. Then I really understand what she's asking. "Wait, I'm working on a project *about* the Young Women, but I didn't know there was an official project. What is that? What's happening?"

The librarian offers to introduce me to one of the Church historians working on the real Young Women Project.

And that's how I get to meet Brittany Chapman, co-author of the *Women of Faith in the Latter Days* series and *Fearless in the Cause: Remarkable Stories from Women in Church History*. She seems young, a little too close to my age to have accomplished as much as she has, and I secretly hope that she just ages well. She's friendly, helpful, and not condescending in a situation where it would be easy to look down on me: I'm no historian.

I ask her the question that has been on my mind all along. Where are the first-person stories from the Beehive Girls? I have only found Gay's scrapbook. The last history of the YLMIA was written in 1955, and the program seems to have been strong and successful at that point—why did it end? The minutes of the Young Women General Board who must have made the switch to Personal Progress are in this very library, but they are closed to research. My grandmas and Nate's, who all should have been Beehive Girls, insist that they've never heard of such a thing.

Brittany's answer is, in a way, comforting: the black hole that I've encountered between 1955 and now is real, and there basically aren't any reports of what Beehive Girls was like. "If we can't get records from the girls, the next best thing would be reminiscences from years later, of course. We don't even have those."

She points me toward some recommended reading. It's fun to chuckle with a real historian about good old Susa and the drama of her every sentence.

Back in the reading room, the rest of my items are on microfiche, so I get to learn how that works. They turn out to be a disappointment. Though labeled "Beehive Scrapbooks," they are resources compiled by adult leaders—

games and recipes, but no stories or comments from the Beehive Girls themselves.

I do at least find a reminiscence by a woman named Mary Teerlink about her summer (in approximately 1936) at one of the earliest girls camps—Brighton Camp, which is still operating today. I don't *endorse* Mary's fake connection to indigenous culture, but it does sound like a pretty classic camp experience with a bunch of white, teenage, Latter-day Saint girls from Utah.

> Lake Martha was my favorite, for I was a nineteen-year-old romantic. There was a lovely little island in the mountain lake, with evergreens, low vegetation, and two close-standing pine trees, apart from the rest. And so I made up a romantic Indian story about the two evergreens and the island, with a sad ending which the girls listened to as we sat on the edge of the lake. As the sad fate of the Indian lovers was told, the teen age girls, listed with tear-filled eyes, a sob in their throats, and we ended with singing the Indian song I added to this *tour de force*. It was the only Indian song I knew, which may have told how the Indians grew corn, but it sounded wonderfully sad and impressive in a slow and minor key.
>
> It was always surprising to me, however, how close we all got during the week. When a girl's week was over and her parents came for her, we all circled round her and sang our goodbye songs and everyone cried that this special week was over.

I notice that Mary doesn't bring up her memories of testimony-strengthening experiences, nor does she mention any wilderness skills she picked up at camp. It was all about the company. I think the wisest YLMIA leaders have always understood: you can plan the most incredible orienteering course or deliver the most poignant devotional, but what the girls are really going to take away are memories of being together and feeling close.

But that's camp. It was barely associated with Beehive Girls. In the whole Church History Library, are these really the only records we have?

LET THE REST GO:
THE STORY OF
CHIEKO OKAZAKI

FIELD OF RELIGION, CELL 9: Give brief account of the life and labors of four other local women who have done much good in Church service.

WHEN I WAS A KID, the ultimate praise for us kids to get from Mom was that we'd been "kidkidsuko," which she told us was a Japanese word that meant doing what needed to be done without waiting to be asked. I was always exceptionally bad at being kidkidsuko, but not for lack of excellent parenting.

Now, as an adult, the vaguely-Japanese-ish word has started to sound suspicious, especially with such a *convenient* definition. So one day, I ask her where she got her information.

"I'm not quite saying it right," she acknowledges, "and I don't know how to spell it . . . but it's a Japanese word that Chieko Okazaki used in a General Conference talk a long time ago."

That's plenty of information to look it up, even without knowing the correct spelling of the word. It turns out to be kigatsuku. I'm actually blown away that Mom was that close, since Sister Okazaki gave that talk when I was an infant. ("Spit and Mud and Kigatsuku," from April 1992.)

Reading through it, though, I can see why the message has stuck with my mom for so many years. It's excellent. Also, I've heard "Aloha!" over the pulpit plenty of times, but Sister Okazaki used it over the *tabernacle* pulpit. Who was this lady? I'm about to find out.

❀ ❦ ❁

Chieko Nishimura was born in Hawaii in 1926. Her parents were Japanese Buddhists, plantation workers who were determined to give her a life beyond farm labor. Chieko studied hard at her local schools—one in Japanese and one in English.

Chieko met missionaries from the Church of Jesus Christ of Latter-day Saints when she was eleven years old. For four years she enjoyed being a Latter-day Saint *and* a Buddhist, but at fifteen she was officially baptized into the church. It was that same year that the Japanese military bombed Pearl Harbor. Japanese Americans made up a third of the population of Hawaii at that point and, for the most part, avoided being forced into concentration camps with their mainland counterparts from 1942 to 1946. Chieko's uncle was among the unlucky ones.

After the war, Chieko went to college. She didn't know how her parents managed to pay her tuition to the University of Hawaii until decades later, when her mother told her that she and Chieko's father and brothers used to weave leaves into sandals to sell for fifty cents a pair. Their love and sacrifice paved the way for her to become a teacher.

In college she met and dated a fellow student named

Edward Okazaki. She recognized him as "a good man and a strong Christian," even though he was not LDS. They married in 1949 and he was baptized ten months later. They moved to Salt Lake City, Utah for Ed's graduate schooling and Chieko began teaching at Uintah Elementary.

In Utah, where so many Japanese Americans had been incarcerated, the Okazakis faced deep suspicion for their Japanese heritage (even though Ed served in the United States military during World War II). Three mothers had their children removed from Chieko's class before the year began and other parents were not subtle about their close scrutiny. Her students came to love her in no time, though, and the parents adjusted.

Chieko and Ed were surprised at how often they encountered racial hostility in "Zion," but they remained committed to the principles of the gospel and found ways to show love and patience in spite of it all. Chieko's mother's counsel helped sustain her: "Know that you know the truth and others haven't learned it yet. So just hold fast and let the rest go."

A great job offer for Ed took the couple and their two sons to Colorado, where they found a dramatically more open environment. Chieko and Ed finally felt free to associate with their neighbors and ward members. They could discuss their difficult questions about the gospel aloud and challenge racist thinking without being shunned. Chieko earned a master's degree in education and then a degree in educational administration. She eventually became an elementary school principal.

Chieko was called to serve on the Young Women general board in 1961 by President Florence Jacobsen. Elder Ezra Taft Benson interviewed her and told her, "Chieko, I want you to know that you are a pioneer." She was momentarily confused, recalling, "It had certainly been impressed upon us that we *weren't* pioneers like those who had crossed the plains." Then she realized that she was the first non-Caucasian to serve "on any of the general boards or any part of the Church hierarchy."

In 1968, Chieko lived in Japan for the first time when Ed was called to serve as the president of the brand-new Okinawa mission. She credits the church's missionary program as a key to gradually moving away from a culture of racism and exclusion: "When the missionaries were sent out into the different parts of the world, they began loving the people they worked with. This broadened their scope of understanding about what all human beings have in common. They began to understand the concept of 'Other sheep I have which are not of this fold.'"

Chieko had served on the boards of all three women's auxiliaries by the time president Elaine L. Jack of the General Relief Society called her to be her first counselor in 1990. Chieko began to have speaking assignments at Relief Society Conference, General Conference, and elsewhere—she would arrive in bright colors, often wearing a Hawaiian lei, and greet her enormous audience with an enthusiastic "Aloha!" Because of modern technology, I can pull up videos online and see her speak. While everyone I've written about for Beehive Girls has left behind diaries, articles, or other words, she's the first whose face, voice, and presence I get to experience.

Her speeches were masterpieces that she worked over for weeks and practiced delivering aloud. But the addresses were important for far more than their beauty: Chieko was one of the first to use a church setting to discuss abuse, the balance between work and family, homosexuality, blended families, and coping with racism. As her friend Kathleen Flake described it, "She took real and pressing problems and not only comforted, but led women in how

to constructively engage those problems using the resources of the gospel."

It wasn't Chieko's intention to cover the most difficult
topics. It began when she was assigned to speak at a stake
Relief Society conference in Oregon. As always, she con-
sulted the stake Relief Society president about the needs of
women in the area, but was surprised to hear what she was
asked to speak on: sexual abuse. "I was thinking, 'You must
be kidding,'" Chieko recalled in an interview, "but I said I
would and then I prayed and prayed." Her talk represented
a major breakthrough in church discourse and people never stopped thanking her for that speech and others like it.

Chieko's patriarchal blessing promised, "Thou shalt be
an influence and power for good. . . . Thou shalt not lack
for friends and associates, especially among those of thy
sex, for they shall come unto thee seeking counsel and advice." It was in her highly visible role in the Relief Society
general presidency that Chieko felt that this blessing was
fulfilled. She was prepared and fearless. When President
Gordon B. Hinckley set her apart, he twice blessed her to
speak freely.

Chieko had a gift for observing and talking about problems in church culture and hierarchy without any bit-
terness or resentment. As the curriculum counselor in the
Relief Society, she once began writing a new manual with
lessons that focused on how to implement gospel principles in dealing with modern-day problems facing women
of the church. I love this idea. Sometimes at church, I long
for us to be able to apply the principles of the gospel to
relevant, real-world challenges people face. I want to talk
more about politics and conflict, not less.

The Relief Society presidency was excited about the
project, but the Curriculum Committee rejected their ideas
in favor of yearly manuals on the lives of the prophets, the

first of which had just been compiled by a group of five men. The women hadn't even been informed that it was in the works.

In this and other situations, Sister Okazaki did not throw a fit, but she did ask why. Why were the women not included in this decision? Why were the women not included in the writing process? In response to her advocacy, three women were called to the Curriculum Committee and included from then on. Though change was (and is) slow, she had the courage and optimism to push for positive developments.

After Ed died in 1997, Chieko traveled the globe, speaking to groups of all sizes and ministering to individual women who felt lost or alone. She survived multiple bouts of breast cancer before she passed away in 2011, at the age of eighty-four.

❁ ☙ ❀

Chieko was alive until the year I was married. It's remarkable to me that I didn't grow up knowing who she was, but (thanks to those manuals) I guess we mostly focused on the brethren in church, in seminary, and at BYU. Her books and talks survive, though, and I want to read them all. She understood and discussed aloud such a variety of life experiences that tend to remain unspoken at church. She was optimistic and patient without pretending everything was always okay.

UNTIL YOU
HAVE WON THEM

BRITTANY CHAPMAN, the Church historian, gave me an important lead. Without a pile of scrapbooks or interviews available, old Church periodicals are my best resource to find out more about life in a Beehive Girl swarm. All of the magazines—"Young Woman's Journal," "Juvenile Instructor," and "Improvement Era"—are freely available on archive.org. Thankfully, they're all searchable. I search for "Beehive" (spelled multiple ways) and spend weeks reading literally every reference in the periodicals between 1915 and the end of the program. There are hundreds, and they are an absolute treasure trove of information I've been hoping to find.

One account, of a large 1916 "Day of the Swarm" celebration in Preston, Idaho, describes a parade of 200 young women, dressed to match their swarm symbols, marching and sounding "Womanho." They were led by a Queen bee and her eight princesses. There was a program, an awards ceremony, lunch, and a dance. Two *bona fide* pioneers attended.

There's a list of names and symbols chosen/invented by real-life Beehive Girls. All of the girls chose flowers for symbols, and most chose real names, but to me the highlights are always the hideous and hilarious mash-ups of virtues: Lopurice (love, purity, patience), Loinco (love, industry, courage), Ugladin (youth, gladness, industry), and Trovesty (truth, love, and honesty). I hope this isn't the next baby-naming trend to take off in Utah.

One Young Woman's Journal article tells the story of the Edaha Swarm camping near Blackfoot, Idaho when two of their members became very sick. Their adult leader (their Beekeeper) had forgotten her consecrated oil, but the swarm prayed together, united in their faith, and the sick girls recovered. The Beekeeper carried consecrated oil to use herself? And it was normal enough to mention in the *Journal*?

I love a letter from Kansas that was included in the Young Woman's Journal. While the local leaders did not expect the Beehive Girls program to work well with such a small Latter-day Saint population, "the girls each brought their friends, and they in turn brought their friends," so that the program was 22 girls strong even though only four Latter-day Saint girls participated. "All worked energetically during the entire summer. The parents were interested; it was a new thing to have their girls take their mending and patching to 'club' or spend the afternoon having a cooking lesson, or literary meeting. We had also two 'hikes,' a fishing trip and a picnic at Mulberry grove."

After two years of Beehive work, the YLMIA general board reported on the scope of the program.

"While it was originally intended especially for the Junior girls, we are pleased to know that it has been adopted also by many of the Senior members, and has been appreciated by the parents, particularly the mothers, who, in many instances have seen much in it that would be helpful to them as wives, mothers, and homemakers, and have joined the work in organized adult classes." This last quote vindicates everything I've been doing for the last two years! I'm not the first adult to be interested in being a Beehive Girl.

I also find extensive advice on making a scrapbook.

> A Beehive scrapbook may become one of the most cherished possessions of the girl who makes it, for into it goes information which she values for itself and also for the memories and interesting associations connected with it. [. . .] Anyone can make a scrapbook which is of general interest. Only you, yourself, can make your scrapbook which on every page will mirror you in some mood or trend of thought. [. . .] To know what kind of poetry interests a person is to know the person better; to read little random thoughts which he has jotted down is to understand better his mental processes, his ideals, and his dreams.

I mean, this is exactly what I want from the Beehive Girls. I wish I had a few dozen more scrapbooks like Gay's to read through. Where are they, if not in the Church History Library? Local historical libraries? Attics? Landfills?

The Beehive Girls seemed to perform for audiences much more frequently than I ever did in Young Women. The magazines include reports of musical numbers for church, sure, but also pantomimes, playlets, pageants, plays, operettas, and operas! Frequently, girls performed material they had written themselves. Have we lost anything in the change? When I did perform as a teenager—piano solos, piano duets, orchestra concerts—my goal was to make the highest-quality imitation possible of what already existed. I didn't try my hand at creativity that expressed anything personal or new.

Wait! There was one time. I wrote a cello duet for the worldwide art competition that was part of Joseph Smith's 200th birthday celebration. It was a cello duet so that I could perform it with my cute and talented crush, Nate. I was a strategic fourteen-year-old. And it's not like my one and only composition was *good*, but I remember rehearsing with Nate and collaborating on little flourishes to add in. I remember the rap the young men performed for the contest (specifically my dad's beatboxing performance). I remember Nate's parents coming to watch us play. That was truly a community event. Surely one way of making a program more youth-directed is to make the youth literal directors (and writers and choreographers and composers) instead of handing them a script and telling them to stick to it.

Actually, contests like that one seem to have been a staple: every year, wards participated in some combination of contests for sports, drama, speech, storytelling, scrapbooks, sewing, singing, debating, painting, drawing, folk dance, cakes, stunts (skits or games), and swarm songs. Until 1930, the ward winners progressed to the stake level and the stake winners from the entire church competed at June Conference. It was a really big deal.

One of the first things that stands out to me is the way the Beehive Girls and Boy Scouts are so often mentioned in the same breath: a choir made up of Beehive Girls and Boy Scouts, Beehive Girls and Boy Scouts marching in a parade, flag demonstrations by the Beehive Girls and Boy Scouts, etc. Especially in the early years, these were made up of kids the same ages and had most of the same functions.

Many Beehive Girls activities were comparable to Scouting. The girls hiked, cooked beans over an open fire, cleaned up their communities, and practiced first aid. They helped sick and lonely people, swam, played baseball, and made all kinds of tchotchkes. Some activities, though, feel more gendered: the girls planned and hosted a *lot* of events. They decorated everything in sight. They sewed linens for their summer camps. They learned the details of making beds and bathing babies. They were recruited as servers for weddings, dances, and—sometimes—Scouting events. I doubt it went the other way.

Beehive Girls were encouraged to report their activities to local newspapers, with one of the girls assigned to be the official reporter. Some wards also tracked their comings and goings with their own publications.

While personal symbols are only mentioned once in the original Beehive Girls handbook, they come up again and again in the periodicals. The girls wore their chosen symbols on their uniforms. They stenciled symbols on lampshades. They embroidered symbols on aprons. They watercolored symbols on their Beehive Girls record sheets. They stamped symbols on Christmas frames for their mothers. They shaped symbols out of metal to make cookie-cutters. They wrote symbols into Beehive Girls songs and poetry, including this one, from thirteen-year-old June Wheeler in 1936.

CAN I?
When life like a river
is solemn and sad,
Can I, like a river,
Make it cheerful and glad?
When hardships, like stones,
Stand thwarting my way,
Can I, like a river,
Be sparkling and gay?
Can I visit the homeless,
the sad and the lorn,
Like a river goes wending
through thicket and thorn?
Can I teach little children
to dance and to play,
Like a river waves reeds
That grow by the way?

I'm including the entire poem because it is excruciat-ingly rare for actual young women to say anything in the Young Woman's Journal.

The General Board emphasized frequently that every Beehive Girl should be prepared at any time to explain what her symbol was and what it meant to her. The idea was to let each girl choose her own ideal to aspire to . . . and then put it all over everything she owned. Honestly, I would have *loved* this as a junior high kid. I already wanted to spray-paint silver stars onto all of my t-shirts as though a five-point star was my own logo, invented by me. (The very fact that I haven't switched over to wearing lace cloth-ing every day since choosing lace as my symbol is evidence that I *have* grown up, a little.)

By going through every issue of every periodical, I do gain some clarity on the ages that participated in Beehive Girls. The Beehive Girls program was originally for any girl or woman fourteen years old or older. The Junior and Se-nior classes of YLMIA—with the coursework in physiology and world literature—were conducted during the school year and Beehive Girls was for summer fun. Over time, though, the vision shifted. The YLMIA classes began run-ning year-round and the Beehive Girls became the young-est class: the fourteen- and fifteen-year-olds. The older Beehive Girls, though, seemed bored with the program while the oldest Primary girls were clamoring to become Beehive Girls.

Soon twelve- and thirteen-year-olds could choose whether to affiliate with the Primary or the Beehive Girls. This led to disarray: some girls were already on their sec-ond rank at thirteen while others wouldn't begin for an-other year. To simplify things, the twelve-year-olds be-came automatic Beehive Girls and the fifteen-year-olds were bumped up into Juniors. Instead of earning each rank to begin the next, the girls were simply promoted a rank with each year in Beehive Girls. By the 1950s, the girls were re-sorted into Beehives, Mia Maids, and Laurels.

Reading through the Beehive Girls section of every magazine does get boring after a while. It feels like hundreds of minute descriptions of essentially the same, unremarkable church party (no offense to church parties). Full menus are included. Full scripts for programs are included. Costuming details are included. Numbers of people present are included. There isn't space for the general board to include the party planning for the Swarm Day of every single ward—complete with every single "Spirit of the Hive"-themed script—but one gets the sense that they would have done so if at all possible. I can't fathom who would be interested in this information.

But that's because I grew up with the Internet. Imagine that your bishop calls you into his office and asks you to plan a Yabodkin Commemoration. You'd probably say yes and then go straight to Google. Is this a happy event or a sad one? What do we eat? Who is supposed to be there? What do we wear? What time of day? Should there be musical numbers? Games . . . ? I end up scouring the Internet for ideas every time I need to plan so much as a bridal shower for someone, and I've been to way too many bridal showers. Pinterest exists for a reason.

But (as you may have already discovered) nothing comes up online when you search for Yabodkin. I made it up to make a point: the first Beekeepers were planning events with no precedent. The guidance they got from the periodicals was *all* they got because the whole program had just

been invented by the general board. The Beekeepers brave-
ly took this task on, co-creating the traditions of the Beehive Girls by experimenting with their own ideas in their
own swarms. The general board clearly welcomed this bot-
tom-up leadership, reporting their favorite ideas "from the
field" and encouraging YLMIA leaders to send more.

I understand the microfiche scrapbooks now, the adult-
centered books I scanned through with so much disappointment. They were the Pinterest of the early twentieth
century. The Beekeepers cut out ideas from periodicals and
kept them at the ready. These scrapbooks weren't meant to
show off their unique thoughts or their taste in poetry, the
way the girls' scrapbooks were. They were resources, re-
positories of Beehive Girls knowledge so that a Beekeeper
didn't have to reinvent every single wheel. I wonder whether individual Beekeepers passed them around to each other or kept them after being released, knowing they could
not easily re-create their work. (It probably depended a lot
on individual circumstances, as some Beekeepers scrap-
booked creatively enough to participate in annual contests
at June Conference.)

Reading so much Beehive Girls advice in the periodicals makes something else very clear: they were written for
the Keepers, not the girls. This, for example: "Appreciation
night affords opportunity for the girls to express themselves for the blessings they are enjoying in life. The object
of this evening is really to have a testimony meeting. We
think, however, that calling it 'appreciation night' will be
more appealing to the girls." Oh, man. How many of us
have been pressured into bearing a testimony because of
all the tearful soul-baring happening around us?

Another major topic of discussion in the Beehive Girls
department of the Improvement Era is fundraising. Before correlation, the Beehive Girls received no money

from the ward, whose "budget covers the expenses of such activities only as are open to the entire membership of the ward." Hence, each swarm had to figure out how to pay for every picnic, campout, temple trip, and sewing project. The dime fund mentioned in the handbook was a single dime per year contributed by each girl; this amount did inflate over the decades, but was never enough to pay for everything. Many of the Beehive Girls contests and performances were put on for the express purpose of raising money: their wards supported them through buying tickets to their shows. The girls made and sold products such as candy, children's toys, aprons, underwear, cakes, flower arrangements, donuts, quilts, and various handicrafts, sometimes at their own Beehive Bazaars. They also grew and sold produce, did housework, and babysat.

🐝 🐝 🐝

I've given a lot of credit so far to the general board (for inventing a cool program) and the girls (for doing cool things). Realistically, though, behind every camping trip, literature lesson, service project, award ceremony, and opera there was a Beekeeper. Looking through Beehive Girls columns in periodicals, I can see that Beekeepers were supposed to give the weekly lessons all winter and plan the weekly activities all summer, but there was so much more.

The ideal Beekeeper would be working with a swarm of other Beekeepers from the stake, filling her own cells and attaching them to her own uniform. She was to read all the reading course books and use them to teach. She had to pass a test to make sure she knew enough about the program. She was encouraged to "stay alert for supplementary material concerning the adolescent girl," to understand

234 de MIKAYLA ORTON THATCHER

her girls better. As many priesthood leaders were unfamiliar with the Beehive Girls program (throughout the *five decades* of its existence), the Beekeeper needed to fight for ward attention to the program and for suitable space in the church building. For the Beehive Girls Silver Jubilee year (their 25th), the Beekeepers were supposed to throw a special event every month and they were supposed to enjoy it. And while I respect the ingenuity of teenagers, I'm sure the girls did not coordinate all their fundraising plans on their own. (Some casualties of correlation make me sad, but I'm delighted that we don't have to fundraise for the young women.)

For all this, after three consecutive years in the calling, a Beekeeper was rewarded with a three-year Service Pin and a check for a million dollars. Oh wait, no, just the pin. All I do for my young women is teach a lesson or two every month, and I'm already burned out.

A great deal of the calling's intensity, though, was not in the busyness, but in the weighty philosophical underpinnings. "Beekeepers," pleads one column, "can't you feel as if you were serving in a missionary capacity as worthwhile as a foreign mission? Who are more precious than the Daughters of Zion? No others, go where you will, I am sure." The point of all this recreation was to help kids explore their interests, practice making and reaching goals, and "to find joyous uses for their abundant energies" through the difficult transitions of the teenage years. And "B work is more than anything else dependent upon the interest and will to do of the Beekeepers."

Beekeepers, though, were well aware that their most important objective went beyond preparing the girls for a happy life. "You shall account for every boy and every girl in your ward of Mutual age," explained the Improvement Era, "that you shall list them, that you shall keep a record of them and work on that record until you have won them by some of these means and facilities that have been given to us. Until you have done this, your task is not fully performed." I know that that's an underlying hope for youth leaders today, but I can't really imagine anyone saying that out loud. The Beekeepers were called to be unrelenting missionaries of the Church, proficient in the missionary tools of recreation and fun.

So how did the Beekeepers learn to do all of this? The YLMIA leaders acknowledged that "the one cry which comes to the general board from the stakes is more training in this work." June Conference in Salt Lake City was the major annual event for Beekeeper training and idea-swapping. Latter-day Saint Institutes of Religion at all the colleges in Utah held seminars so that Beekeepers could learn first aid and handicrafts from real experts. Those outside Utah had to cobble together information from their Beekeeper handbooks, church periodicals, other periodicals, and experts local to them. Individual Beekeepers also corresponded with the general board about their questions. At one point, a specific general board member was even designated the "craft expert" and all Beekeepers were welcomed to write her letters. As "motion pictures" came into existence, the general board dreamed of one day showing June Conference trainings and contests to worldwide Beekeepers via film, but that was not yet an option.

For one particularly technical Beehive Girls lesson, the board made this recommendation: "You may prefer to have this lesson given by a professional nurse, an MD or a physiology teacher. If not, prepare yourself carefully and you will be all right. Read a physiology text if possible. Read Beekeeper Book page 123 to 127 for a simple treatise." It turns out that my particular skill set would have been more useful to the girls in my ward seventy years ago than it is now. Now we only need to know Church stuff. Yet again, Correlation has made the program *way* more do-able worldwide, even though we may have lost something cool in the process.

I wonder how Beekeepers felt about all this. Was Beekeeper a dreaded assignment? While I would never, ever, ever, ever want to do this calling (except for the physiology lesson), I can see how other personality types in other eras could have found it fulfilling. Beekeepers might have relished the many, many creative processes involved in running the program. They might have liked the company of the girls and serving as a leader and mentor. They might have enjoyed the variety and playfulness of so many Beehive Girls activities. They might have appreciated the excuse to learn so many things and practice so many skills. They might have wanted a way to serve in the ward or to have busier weeknights. They might even have just loved the checklists, rules, salutes, uniforms, symbols, and being part of a tightly-organized group.

The United States entered World War I in 1917, when the Beehive Girls program was only two years old. The war became, temporarily, the entire focus of Beehive Girls. A new handbook was written specifically for wartime, simplifying the broad program down to mostly food conservation and Red Cross work. "The two cells that must be filled in each field, to attain rank," leaders explained in the Young Woman's Journal, "are only sufficient in the opinion of the General Board, to keep a balance and prevent the tragedy of war from taking too terrible a hold upon us." Instead of competing to bake the best cakes, the girls competed to grow the most potatoes on a given plot of land. Instead of cash prizes, there were war bonds. Instead of sewing dresses, they made bandages. There was a new motivator available, too: a special Beehive Girls War Emergency Pin, frequently advertised as an analog to the medals the young men would bring home from battle. In this time period, messages to the Beehive Girls were unapologetically U.S.-centric, with no acknowledgement of Latter-day Saints in "enemy" countries.

Swarm leaders were asked to record the girls' efforts and send the numbers (bandages made, vegetables canned, fruit dried, hours volunteered to the Red Cross, etc.) in to the Journal. One swarm reported the following:

> March: Made fifteen convalescent gowns for the Red Cross and collected $175.00 for the Y.W.C.A.
>
> April: Gave a Charity Ball, proceeds of which $290.00 were turned over to the Red Cross, made and donated 200 towels to the Red Cross.
>
> May: Made 1800 bandages for the Red Cross.
>
> June: Made 35 pairs canvass [sic] gloves, knit twenty-seven sweaters, 12 pairs of socks, and studied the food value of Rhubarb, canning hundreds of quarts of the same to supply our diet with the necessary mineral salts so that we can release the usual supply of tomatoes for use by the Government.
>
> We have $2950.00 in Liberty Loans.
>
> We have $566.00 in War Savings Stamps.

Those are some serious contributions to the war effort! I've seen Young Women spend a morning laying down fresh wood chips at a campsite or tying knots to finish fleece blankets, but this kind of sustained teamwork among the youth sounds incredible (in spite of the devastation of war itself). I wish I knew what the girls thought of it. Was that the worst summer ever? Or was it the most united and efficacious they'd ever felt?

The program resumed its more regular pace after the war (and after an interruption during the deadly 1918 influenza pandemic). The Great Depression's main impact on Beehive Girls seems to have been a heightened concern for giving the youth something positive to do with their time, surrounded by so much joblessness and hardship. The Improvement Era nudged, "This year of all years is the time to go to camp, when everybody is affected by the financial slump and many cherished vacation plans will be abandoned because the money cannot be had to realize them." A few days at a stake camp were dramatically cheaper than other vacations.

The Beehive Girls' response to the second world war was dramatically different from its response to the first. I suspect that it's because the organization was truly international by that point. The Improvement Era had dedicated a lot of space to praising German Boy Scouts and Beehive Girls and describing the events of their MIA conferences: there was no way to demonize those same kids now that they were compulsory members of Hitler Youth. Within a year after the attack on Pearl Harbor, the Beehive Girls message included reports and photos from a swarm in Hawaii and a swarm in Japan on the same two-page spread. Was it intentional? There's no acknowledgement of the juxtaposition in the text, but I think it was definitely on purpose—someone's powerful, silent statement about shared humanity and sisterhood. While girls in the United States were encouraged to write to soldiers, and while some swarms *did* focus on earning War Emergency Pins (an award created in response to popular request), the mission of the Beehive Girls program did not change for the war.

Instead, the wartime changes were logistical. As gas was rationed, stake and general MIA leaders replaced visits with phone calls. The Beehive Girls office announced shortages of some of its pamphlets and pins, then that none remained "for the duration." Uniform requirements were relaxed: under the circumstances, girls were welcome to just participate in whatever activities were happening. If meeting at night was no longer practical, daytime meetings were encouraged. A highly-anticipated Beehive Girls column in the Deseret News was canceled after only eight weeks to conserve space. Youth were encouraged to make their homes the centers of recreation for their families, since there wasn't food or money to spare for frivolities.

In the Church periodicals, I don't find many Beehive Girl voices. What I do find is a clearer picture of a program that changed constantly, adapting to serve Japanese Saints, Utah Saints, and non-LDS kids in Kansas. It served twelve-year-old girls and grown-up women. It gave them work to do during war and during peace. It changed whenever the girls got bored. It changed whenever girls were getting left behind. When I first read the program's requirements, I laughed at its localness, its specificity, but it certainly grew out of that over the years. I don't know how you measure "effectiveness" of a youth program, but this was definitely a program that did its best.

SOMETHING OPENED:
THE STORY OF
JULIA MAVIMBELA

FIELD OF RELIGION, CELL 9: Give brief account of the life and labors of four other local women who have done much good in Church service.

I KNOW, I KNOW: I've already given brief accounts of four Local Women. This is my favorite part of my project, though. I don't want to stop. Besides, I'm well aware that every woman I've mentioned has been American. This is a world-wide church! I know I can't tour the globe in one little book, but surely I can find a story or two.

I start looking. I assume that the Ensign and New Era would be full of them, perhaps in their stories about the Church in other countries. It turns out, though, that those columns usually just refer to a mission president and "his wife" without sharing any quotes or details. I scour online lists of "famous Mormons," but they're all from the U.S. and/or men. Maybe there are more stories about women in the various language editions of the Liahona?

Most of what I can find is in upcoming books about Mormon women's history. I'm sure they're going to be cool, but I can't use them for this project. Not even with the power of interlibrary loan.

I find Julia Mavimbela on the Church website. I read various versions of her story—articles and videos produced in the nineties—and, you know, it's a nice Ensign story. Very spiritual. A whole life summarized in 600 words. Apparently, she was honored at BYU? But I don't know a ton about South African history and I'm missing some context. Maybe I'll move on to someone else . . . not that I have a lot of other options.

I start reading about South African history. I read sources that aren't focused on Julia's Church membership. As my brain integrates these different angles on her life and work, my heart opens up. I love Julia. I want to emulate Julia however I can. And I definitely want to share her story.

❁ ⚘ ❁

Julia Nompi Nqubeni was born in 1917 in South Africa. Her father died when she was four, leaving her mother to raise her and her four older siblings. They spoke Zulu in their home, but the children were legally required to study English and Afrikaans—the languages of their oppressors—under Apartheid. Julia was eventually fluent in seven languages.

Julia received a formal education in psychology with financial help from her sister. She became a school teacher and was one of the first Black women in South Africa to serve as a school principal. Without permission from her higher-ups, she taught an additional class of 40 students who couldn't afford to attend regular school. During the Great Depression, when there were no paychecks for the teachers under her care, Principal Julia fundraised for them.

In 1946 she met and married John Mavimbela, whom she called "a very special man, one out of one hundred." John and Julia ran a little butcher and grocery shop together. He was a sweet husband who did dishes while she had friends over, helped wash their babies' diapers, and made sure she always had her own money. Julia was happy. She built positive relationships with John's former wife and their two children. While raising all of their children and running the store with John, Julia formed and led community groups to learn thrift and homemaking skills in the wake of World War II. She taught bored little boys various sports—they started competing and winning prizes. She organized groups to increase literacy in her area, especially among mothers. No, I have no idea how she made time for all of this, but she amazes me.

She was 38 and pregnant with their fifth child when John died in a car accident in 1955.

As if the grief and stress of losing her husband and the father of her children were not enough, Julia was also burdened by rage. Another driver had swerved into John's lane, killing him. The courts blamed the accident on John, citing racist stereotypes as their evidence. The police who dealt with the scene stole a large sum of money that John had been carrying when he died. Anger and resentment haunted Julia for two decades, as she raised five children without John.

Her personal tragedy and its aftermath were, of course, part of a much larger pattern of abuse and injustice that would soon come to a head. Starting in 1975, the South African government required Black children to be taught half their school subjects in Afrikaans, instead of studying Afrikaans as a separate subject. Controlling the languages in schools served to separate children from their native culture. It wasn't the only injustice the students had endured, but it was the final straw.

In June of 1976, children in the town of Soweto, where Julia lived, went on strike from school and organized a mass demonstration in the streets, involving between 10,000 and 20,000 kids. They were met with extreme police brutality: law enforcement shot directly into the crowd, wounding over a thousand people and killing 176 people (though the official government count is 23 and some estimates are as high as 700). Fifteen hundred police officers were deployed to Soweto by the next morning, along with their automatic rifles, armored vehicles, and helicopters. Over the following months, many public buildings—especially schools and libraries—were burned.

The town was devastated by the intense violence and the loss of so many children. The schools remained closed for the next two years and many adults were out of work. Black teenagers, especially, were constantly harassed and detained by law enforcement.

Two entire years with no schooling available for anyone. I can't imagine the grief and hopelessness the people must have experienced.

Julia's own children were grown by now, but she had an idea that only a mother/teacher/psychologist/grocer such as herself could have come up with: she began to teach neighborhood children to garden. She established a community garden and helped families get permission from landowners to clean out and cultivate vacant lots. She used seed packets and old workbooks to teach kids to read, channeling their desire to learn when no one else could.

She taught nutrition classes in her home. The people of Soweto had fresh vegetables and blooming flowers. They gradually cleaned up the rubble and destruction left in the wake of the state violence. She recalled, "As others watched us struggle with the overgrowth of stubborn weeds, they too became involved, and I moved from corner to corner of Soweto replacing the useless and the ugly with the beneficial and beautiful."

She used the work to teach the children about forgiveness and healing and felt her own burden begin to dissipate.

> "I would say, 'Now look, boys and girls. . . . Let us dig the soil of bitterness, throw in a seed, show love, and see what fruits it can give. Love will not come without forgiving others. Where there has been a blood stain, a beautiful flower must grow."

As the schools reopened and as her heart continued to heal, Julia began working with various women's groups. She co-founded Women for Peace, a group that tackled a variety of issues: literacy, infant care education, fair pay for teachers of all races, legal protections within common-law marriages, the Matrimonial Property Act (allowing a widow, rather than the eldest son, to inherit her husband's property), integrated playgrounds, prison reform, and reform for criminal justice for young people. Women for Peace was eventually fifteen thousand strong, with women from all races illegally mixing into a single group. Julia was its co-president. While she'd never heard of the Relief Society at this point, Julia's work reminds me of Emmeline's—varied, energetic, and not limited by narrow views of what constitutes "women's issues."

In 1981, when she was 64, Julia was asked to head up a rebuilding project at a boys club. She visited the site to see what she could do and saw two young white men working alongside the townspeople to clear the rubble. This was unexpected. She talked with them. Of course, they were missionaries from the Church of Jesus Christ of Latter-day Saints. They asked to visit and she told them to give her three days to clean her house first. While I, too, require three days of cleaning before I let a stranger into my house, Julia was really asking for time to think, since letting white people into her house could be seen as traitorous in her community.

After three days, the missionaries really did show up (Julia was surprised) and she was brave enough to let them in. Their first visit did not impress Julia. They brought a companionship of sisters on the second visit and Julia still felt nothing. Finally, on the third visit, they asked about Julia's and John's wedding photo, which led to a discussion of temple ordinances. (As a side note, this extremely busy woman was so kind that she let these kids come back after *two* lackluster visits.)

Julia was shocked at the idea of vicarious baptism and later said, "Something opened in my mind." In her church, it was considered heretical to speak of the dead at all, let alone to talk about reuniting with them in the future. "Their words had touched a very delicate place in my heart," she later recalled. I can only imagine how she must have felt, after so many years of avoiding speaking of the losses she and her community had experienced. She, her mother, her siblings, her children, and her neighbors had all mourned in silence. She invited the missionaries back.

Julia was baptized less than two months later and was endowed in 1985, just eight years after the priesthood and temple ban was finally lifted. She was one of the first temple workers in the Johannesburg South Africa Temple. She was sealed to her parents and to John. (Thank you, Jane Manning James, for paving the way.)

From then on, she served as a sort of unofficial companion to any LDS missionaries she met, introducing them to people and getting them inside people's homes. As a 71-year-old woman, she quit her teaching job to be a self-appointed full-time missionary. Of course, she remained a community leader and organizer until she passed away in 2000. In 1989 she told her story at BYU Women's Conference and closed with this, "We are not where we can say all is well. But we say all can be done and we feel it will be done." I love her statement of optimistic faith, especially because she knew from experience the work that change would require. She'd already gardened a burned city, changed laws to protect women and children, organized thousands of women, and taught decades of elementary school. Her hopes weren't based on wishful thinking. They were based on her dedication to leadership and tireless work.

PURSUING RELIGION
AS AN OCCUPATION

FIELD OF PUBLIC SERVICE, CELL 710: During three
months, assist the Relief Society in their work of caring
for the poor and sick.

I'VE BEEN IN THE RELIEF SOCIETY since I was seventeen. I've been a good visiting teacher for practically all of
that time, so technically I *do* aid in the work of the Relief
Society. I take on this Beehive Girls requirement, though,
to force me to do something I've never been brave enough
to do before: I ask the Relief Society president what I can
do to help.

I don't know the Relief Society president. I'm not sure I
want to know the answer to my question. I'll be committed
to doing who-knows-what and I'm already close to being
overwhelmed at home and at work. There's a part of me
that genuinely wants to serve, though, and I really do love
the Relief Society . . . hopefully it's okay that it's a writing
project that is pushing me into being brave.

In response to my email, the Relief Society president
has a woman named Alex call me. Alex is a visiting teacher
to Sue, who has terrible arthritis. Sue doesn't get to leave
her house often and she lives alone, so housecleaning is vi-

tal support for her. Alex visits and cleans diligently, but it's a lot for one person. Alex is pleased to hear I have a physiology background: she figures that I've seen and smelled enough difficult things to be ready to visit Sue with a smile. Alex joins me the first time I go, since Sue wouldn't take kindly to a stranger showing up with cleaning rags. I don't know what to expect. I pick a time when Jane can stay home with Nate.

I spend that first visit in the kitchen doing dishes. For two hours. At home, I have a policy of limiting dish-washing sessions to ten minutes because it hurts my back, but here I just muscle through. I have a lot of time to think, to form long-term plans about how to keep helping. Sue lives near Shelby and her family, so maybe I could leave Jane there when I come here to clean? I guess Jane could come with me if I trapped her in a pack-n-play . . . ? The place is dirty enough that she probably shouldn't be running free, plus Sue says her dog is bad with kids.

Sue says a lot of things, to tell you the truth. Some of it is about the new housemate she has moving in—a young man, the son of her former neighbors—and how clean things will be once he's around to help. She talks about drama with her own adult children and her worries that they'll leave the church. She talks about ghosts she's seen and how important it is that a painting of Jesus is hanging over her bed in the living room. My back hurts more and more every minute, and the buzzing in my temple is spreading into my left ear and eye, but I'm happy to listen. I'm happy to be here for someone who really needs it. I'm happy to be serving in a way that makes me uncomfortable. It feels like a legitimate effort to follow Christ.

The next day, our car breaks down across town from where we live. (Yes, I get stranded more than once in this book.) The repair process is beyond convoluted. We are without a car for weeks and weeks in the middle of winter. Our friends shuttle us around with endless patience.

I haven't visited Sue and I haven't spoken to Alex. Alex will think that I didn't want to help. The logical thing to do is to get an update from Alex, but I've let it go too long and I'm embarrassed. I can't call her. I just can't.

I never find out what ended up happening with Sue and her new roommate. Does he help out around the house? Are things still rough? Does she still feel haunted? Every passing week makes it more impossible for me to ask.

And that's the end of this attempt to assist in the work of the Relief Society.

Emmeline's words about the Relief Society giving women a voice have been bouncing around my head ever since I read them. I start reading about the Relief Society in between Nauvoo and now.

The women of Nauvoo organized themselves as a charitable group, meeting at Sarah M. Kimball's invitation in her home. They asked Eliza R. Snow to draw up a constitution and bylaws for them before Joseph Smith co-opted their meetings, widened their aims, and promised them spiritual blessings. Emma Smith was unanimously elected the President of the society. The Female Relief Society of Nauvoo focused on clothing the workers constructing the Nauvoo temple and on caring for the sick and needy of the city. I did know all of this from Relief Society lessons and that "Daughters in My Kingdom" book that was handed out at church.

In 1843, President Emma Smith delegated some of her oversight to a "Necessity Committee," who visited families "to discover all instances of sickness and distress and report these findings to the president." These original visits have been pinpointed as the origin of the visiting teaching program. Cool! I never realized that visiting teaching came before home teaching.

Polygamy tore the Relief Society apart in 1844, which is something I do *not* remember discussing at church. Plural marriage was not yet taught openly, or even admitted to, but Relief Society devolved into Emma Smith defending Joseph's honor in the face of all kinds of accusations. Joseph was killed two months after the Society's last meeting. Brigham Young, then president of the Quorum of Twelve Apostles, laid the blame for Joseph and Hyrum's deaths on Emma's resistance to polygamy, and in the process blamed the Relief Society itself. To me, that doesn't seem particularly fair. He told the men of the church, "When I want Sisters . . . to get up Relief Society I will summon them to my aid but until that time let them stay at home." (This was followed by some stronger language that doesn't belong here.)

So for twenty-three years there was no official women's organization. I've never really recognized that before. Some of the Saints' most difficult trials—losing the prophet Joseph, leaving Nauvoo, crossing the plains, sending off the Mormon Battalion, and trying to establish a new home in Utah, and the Utah war—were during that gap! Sisterhood still grew, of course, out of proximity, necessity, and the gradual acknowledgement of plural marriage. Sister-wives could identify themselves and find kinship in their shared trial of faith. "Older wives mentored younger ones, delivered their babies, coached them in their exercise of 'the gifts,' while younger ones performed tasks for their older sister wives, visited with them, honored them with the title 'Mother.'" I know there were bad things about polygamy, but this concept of families with many mothers is beautiful to me.

In Utah, women banded together into all kinds of charitable groups, but nothing church-wide or church-endorsed.

A core group of sisters experienced the Nauvoo Relief Society, Winter Quarters, *and* plural marriages to prophets and apostles. Most of them ended up living in downtown Salt Lake City, where they became the social, political, and ecclesiastical elite. Eliza R. Snow was the queen bee for decades, as I've already mentioned. She gained status being a plural wife of Joseph Smith and, later, Brigham Young. She officiated as a matron in the Endowment House, served as secretary in the original Nauvoo Relief Society, and was called in 1867 to reorganize the Relief Society in Utah. While she had no official title in her early Relief Society work, the women knew her as a prophetess and hailed her with such epithets as "Presidentess of the female portion of the human race." Other prominent women included Zina D. H. Young, Presendia L. Kimball, Elizabeth Ann Whitney, Sarah M. Kimball, Bathsheba W. Smith, Mary Isabella Horne, and Phoebe Woodruff. At this point, I recognize a lot of these names, but it's interesting to finally name and consider the shared experiences that made them leaders.

It took two attempts to re-initiate Relief Society in the Salt Lake Valley, but by 1869 every ward had an independent organization quietly working to meet local needs, stockpile grain, and make silk. (Yes, this is the part that overlaps with Emmeline B. Wells' story.) In 1887, white Utah women were disenfranchised in a government attempt to force the end of polygamy. The aims of Relief Society expanded to public advocacy for polygamy and brought them into contact with women's rights activists across the nation.

When Latter-day Saints gave up polygamy in exchange for Utah's statehood, the Relief Society began fighting for white women's suffrage in the new state constitution. "Relief Society meetings, their spiritual and charitable business completed, would dismiss into suffrage meetings in which the women addressed their political concerns and planned their campaigns." Wow, so pro-suffrage views were even more mainstream among LDS women than I realized when I read about Emmeline. Is that because of *Exponent* or was *Exponent* so pro-suffrage because women were? I don't have any way to isolate variables and show causation, but it's still important context. The women were, after so much charitable organizing, prepared for this political action. They saw pro-suffrage work as perfectly aligned with their faith: they believed it was the secular application of the Savior's statement that "all are alike unto me."

By 1895 the Utah constitution—complete with votes for white women—was in place and the Relief Society moved on to goals that largely mirrored those of the Progressive Movement throughout the United States. To make medical care more accessible and affordable, especially in rural areas, the Relief Society offered nursing classes: nurses were trained for free as long as they committed to do a certain amount of nursing work at little or no charge. The Relief Society opened a maternity hospital, staffed with volunteer nurses (and with general board members to do laundry for the first few weeks). The Relief Society sewed linens for LDS Hospital and for displaced children in Europe. The Relief Society sent delegates to conferences on world peace, and it lobbied for laws guaranteeing equal guardianship for mothers and fathers, pensions for widowed mothers, and a minimum wage for women.

To me, this feels like an entirely different approach to relief than that of the modern church. I've made blankets and various "kits" to give to people, but back then the Relief Society worked to restructure society as a whole and break down oppressive systems instead of just giving people a little extra help surviving in those systems.

Individual chapter by individual chapter, it cooperated with community agencies working for public help and community betterment. Meanwhile, the Relief Society Social Service Department took advantage of the latest professional research to organize relief, train workers, connect workers to potential employers, and facilitate adoptions. (To be clear, not all of these endeavors had positive results. Many "adoptions" took Native American children away from their families and communities, a practice that was extremely destructive and based on entirely racist ideas.)

Something that strikes me as I get to know Latter-day Saint women's history is the amount of time, energy, and money that everyone seemed to give to the Relief Society. This isn't an exclusively Latter-day Saint phenomenon, though: American women of the nineteenth century have been described as "pursuing religion as an occupation" because it was in their churches that they found engaging outlets for their talents in moral, missionary, educational, and charitable endeavors. While men organized in government and commerce as well as at church, the religious voluntary associations were where "women wrote and debated and amended constitutions, elected officers, raised and allotted funds, voted on issues, solicited and organized new members." I've never thought about church as the place women could practice the skills of leadership when they were barred from actually governing.

The nature of their Church work—unpaid and focused on care-giving—allowed women to see it as a natural extension of their domestic roles rather than a trespass into the world of men. In 1910, suffragist Jane Addams wrote, "As society grows more complicated, it is necessary that woman shall extend her sense of responsibility to many things outside of her own home if she would continue to preserve the home in its entirety." By the early twentieth century, volunteerism had brought Latter-day Saint women into every element of public life.

Personal acquaintance with the Prophet Joseph Smith and clear memory of the hardships of crossing the plains were not the only vital memories shared by the leading sisters. These women had strong spiritual gifts and taught their daughters and granddaughters about accessing the powers of heaven. In blessing meetings as early as Kirtland, women prophesied, spoke in tongues, and gave blessings of healing. In current Church teaching this would be considered improper, but Joseph Smith's response to questions at the time was unconcerned: "If the sisters should have faith to heal the sick," he said, "let all hold their tongues." Fair enough, Brother Joseph!

The rules about exercising spiritual gifts got more complicated under Brigham Young, with a variety of conflicting messages from the brethren, but the sisters continued their blessing meetings through the difficult days of crossing the plains, the early Relief Society in Utah, and well into the twentieth century. Parents often gave joint blessings to their children. Sisters came up with rituals of washing and anointing each other during sickness, before surgery, and in preparation for childbirth. Oh my goodness, of *course* there should be a blessing for childbirth. That is so beautiful. And this wasn't something sneaky that people did in the privacy of their own homes—blessing rituals were propagated through the Relief Society itself, with some sisters even called and set apart to perform them.

I find one surviving record of a blessing before childbirth. There's no way to tell whether it's someone's transcript of one blessing or a script used to give many blessings, but it is so full of empathetic specificity from one mother to another. The pregnant mother is blessed that her hips "might relax and give way for the birth . . . that the child shall present right and . . . the afterbirth shall come at its proper time." Her breasts are blessed that her "milk may come freely and [she] need not be afflicted with sore nipples as many are, [her] heart that it might be comforted." The night before Jane was born, I asked Nate to give me a blessing. I treasure that memory. But it's not like he thought to mention the afterbirth or the difficulty of breastfeeding.

"What do all of you think," the bishop asks the assembled ward council, "about making our Giving Tree this year a project for Syrian refugees?" I've never been part of the ward council, but I'm invited today because if they decide to do this, it's my job to make it happen.

People have questions and ideas. "Is there a lot of need in the ward?"

"Not really," the bishop responds. "There's one family who has asked for a couple of things, but that's it." That's good to hear. There are so many student families in the ward who are living on student loans, but we're all privileged enough to be going to school and to have what we need (even if we get it from among the cast-offs next to the neighborhood dumpster).

"Oh, we have that really generous donation we didn't end up using last year! We could use that to get started."

"Christmas is really soon . . . how are we going to find families to help?"

"We've gone through a refugee organization before—Sister Thatcher can talk to them again."

"Is it weird to bring Christmas presents to Muslims?"

I can answer this one. "I mean, let's not bring them Christmas trees. But I don't think any of them will mind receiving food and clothes and toys."

"I have a lot of old stuff I can donate and I bet I'm not the only one . . ."

"Well . . ." I've been learning a lot from a friend about this one and I have to pass along what I've learned. "We could maybe pass along really gently-used coats, but basically everything else should just be new. We want to make sure we're not passing along our trash. We want to offer the best we can."

"How will we communicate with the families? None of us speak Arabic."

"Great point. We'll figure it out."

The questions and input subside. I look around the room at all the decision-makers. I think everyone is happy to take the Giving Tree in a different direction this year. "Okay," I say, "how many families do you want me to commit to? Two? Three?"

After a brief pause to consider, the bishop says, "How about ten?"

I'm floored. "*Ten*?!"

"You'll be amazed," he reassures me, "at how generous this ward is."

It's already near the end of November and I'm not going to be in town for Christmas. I have my work cut out for me.

I mean, technically a Christmas deadline shouldn't matter at all because we're bringing presents to people who don't celebrate Christmas . . . but this project is only *mostly* to benefit them. If we only cared about helping, we would pull out our checkbooks and give directly to the Syrian American Rescue Network (SARN). But we want something our kids can participate in, with individual gifts for individual people. We want something that feels like Christmas. And we definitely want to see strangers look happy and surprised when we show up at their homes on Christmas Eve.

I've been in this calling for a few months now, the "I am a Stranger" . . . Liaison? So far, all I've done is go to information sessions and talk with my friend Jess, who works on refugee resettlement professionally. I care so much about this work, but the need is so overwhelming that I haven't been able to figure out how our ward can contribute. Our new neighbors need jobs. They need help navigating WIC and Medicaid in a foreign language. They need cars. They need affordable housing near friends in their own community. The best thing we could do would be to donate a lot of money.

But, since I don't have a lot of money and I *do* have a ward full of people ready to donate Christmas presents, we'll do it that way. I call my contact at SARN and ask her to make me a list of ten families that could use our help the most. I ask for their addresses, ages, their genders, their clothing sizes, and some items they want right now. My contact assures me that SARN has "mentors" with Arabic skills who have a relationship with each family, so it will be no problem to get good lists and get some help coordinating delivery so that no household will be completely surprised. They're excited that we want to get involved. Well, great. Then I can just make tags and put them on the tree and it will all be smooth sailing from there.

I hear nothing for more than a week, even though I ping my contact more than once. Nothing is smooth sailing in a non-profit—I think that literally everybody I've spoken to has been a volunteer. I'm trying to get information out of volunteers during the holiday season. Finally,

I get a list. Well, I get a photograph of a handwritten list, with many things crossed out and not nearly all the information I hoped for. I have no way to contact any of the mentors. I know so little about the families, but there are a couple of heartbreaking footnotes about which people have survived torture, which have been diagnosed with PTSD, which parents have no jobs because of complex disabilities. It's so much. There are a couple of scrawled notes about what the kids need for their school uniforms and it looks like basically everybody needs winter gear. Oh no. It's already December and they're living in Michigan without winter clothing?

It's my job to turn all this need and all my questions into cheery gift tags that ward members can take from the tree and guide them on a merry shopping spree. It's a strange juxtaposition. I'm the only person who is going to see this list.

Okay, so the kids need school clothes. But the list only has ages, not the sizes that I asked for. An eight-year-old can be *so many sizes*. I make tags requesting gift cards for clothing for all the kids. I have sizes for the adults' coats, and I know that the women want long ones, so I can make tags requesting coats. I definitely need to stop and think about logistics before this gets confusing. Time to make a spreadsheet.

Most of the tags for the tree end up being gift cards so that everyone can choose clothing that works for them— their size, their taste, their own modesty tradition. No one asked for toys, but I want refugee kids to have toys, so I make tags for toys. I do a lot of reading about Islam and children's toys—there's a wide range of scriptural interpretations out there—and finally just cross my fingers that we will choose things that are appropriate. And if we get the toys wrong, the grocery gift cards should make up for it.

I stay up very late preparing tags for the tree. It's the second Saturday in December and I've got to get the tree up before church.

My ward members descend upon the Giving Tree like a miraculous flock of seagulls on a swarm of crickets. No one in the ward complains about buying boring gift cards, which is a big relief to me. They see a tag that says "woman's coat, size medium" and understand that there is a medium-sized woman out there with no coat. While they haven't seen my list, I think they see what is needed and why.

While the ward is gathering gift cards and toys, I am researching Syrian cooking. I want to bring groceries, but I want them to be groceries that taste like home: the right spice mixtures, the right legumes, the right grape leaves. I've invited people who don't have money to spare to volunteer instead—to pick up groceries, to sort the gifts, to deliver everything. Coordinating the volunteers is a lot for someone who is low-key afraid of phone calls, but it works out. When I leave town, I have a right-hand woman to leave with my house key so everyone can drop things off and pick things up, move them around, and deliver them.

I'm not there when the gifts and groceries are delivered. I don't know how awkward it is or any of the aftermath— do our neighbors get what they need? Do their coats fit? Do they have to throw away the toys? I hear good things from my ward members who got to deliver, but I have no sense of the whole thing from the other point of view.

I hope it was good. I'm glad we did *something*.

The work of the Relief Society has never been perfect. We're not professionals and we never operate without rookie mistakes. Is our work pointless because it's a little problematic? I hope not. I know that my ward members were happy to participate in welcoming refugee families to Michigan and I hope that the recipients felt loved and welcomed, even if the groceries weren't exactly right. We couldn't give them everything they needed, but we showed up in the way we could. Maybe that imperfection is "lace" in and of itself—connecting us to every Relief Society there has ever been.

🐝   🐝   🐝

BUILDER IN THE HIVE FOUNDATION CELL 9: Every day for one month do at least one good turn, quietly and without boasting. It may be done at home, to a member of the family, as well as elsewhere.

I'm still sore from my failure to help Sue. I'm too embarrassed to go back and fix it. Maybe "do a good turn daily" will be more accessible?

I pick a good day to start, nail the second day, miss the third and fourth day, and then give up. Then I do it again. *In my defense*, I've made the rules much stricter than they would have been for a Beehive Girl: nothing in my own household counts. If I could count "cleaned the bathroom without being asked" or "made lunch for the whole family" as good turns, this wouldn't be a goal at all. I want to use this requirement to practice looking outside myself.

My downfall, on my first two attempts, is that I can't think of things to do for people. Everyone is shut up in their own little households. I know there is more to do in the world than bring people cookies . . . but how do you get close enough to people for them to tell you what it is they need? How do you create that kind of intimacy and trust?

For my third attempt, I give myself a back-up plan. I'll do whatever service comes up, but if I get to the end of a day without having found something to do, I'll reach out to someone. I'll make a phone call, send an email, write a letter, anything to help a friend or family member feel loved and thought-of.

Between my back-up plan and a new record-keeping system (I'm always finding new apps to obsess over), I'm ready for another attempt.

The first day, I volunteer for a babysitting job that intim-idates me. Four hours with my friend's two kids plus my own doesn't sound like an ideal Saturday to me (I'm not awesome with kids), but I can do it. I send my aunt a pic-ture of Jane, finally wearing a dress my aunt made for her as a baby gift. I don't normally reach out to my extended family, so it feels good to make a connection and show her that I remember her generosity.

The second day, nothing comes up organically. I mes-sage two friends I haven't talked to in a while and ask how they are. One never answers, which is fine, but the other chats with me and I get to follow up on her new life in a new place. I haven't forgotten our friendship.

On the third day, Nate is taking Shelby and her family to the airport and I relieve him of his duty so that he can work or rest or whatever he needs. Before I drop them off, I ask the Barneys if they'd also like me to come back and pick them up a week from now and I'm delighted when they agree—that's a day's good turn already planned! Nailed it! Normally I guard my time carefully, but I find myself *looking* for ways to give it away. I'm tossing it out like parade candy.

I follow through on my babysitting commitment and, oddly enough, enjoy it a lot. Later, I do a wardrobe switch from Jane's winter to summer clothes and realize she has twice as much as she can use. I reach out to Autumn, my friend who "lives in my ward," and share the bounty of hand-me-downs for her daughter.

The next day, Sunday, Nate and I try to invite Catherine and Jesse over for dinner, even though our house is, once again, way too hot and my migraine is, once again, the worst. They're booked all week. Shucky darn. (I'm relieved.) But I get to talk with Catherine and she geeks out with me about a professional success I've had recently and my day is 1000% better because I called her. I text my little brother to see how his latest date went. He's so good to call me frequently, and I want him to know that he's on my mind, too.

On Monday, my other visiting teachee needs help dropping her car off for repairs. I've never hung out with her outside of structured visits and I enjoy laughing with her about how poorly-acquainted we still are with downtown Ann Arbor and how badly I drive as soon as someone is with me. Again, I get to *offer* to bring her back to get her car the next day, instead of silently hoping she'll ask someone else.

One day, I show up for my neighbor's party. This doesn't sound like service, I know. But I don't watch soccer and I don't drink and this is a party that's completely about soccer and alcohol. Plus, I'm in the middle of devouring a really great book. For me, this is a way to be less selfish about my time and my preferences and celebrate my neighbor and the things she loves. It's a good turn.

Another day, I meet up with a couple of ward members for some Frankenstein fitness event called "Bollyfit." It is not at all inside my comfort zone, but I would like to be friends with these women and I will go try the thing they want to try. Due to a clock malfunction at my house (really!) I show up an hour late and miss it. But my leap of faith in showing up is rewarded: I still get to hang out with new friends.

One night, when I haven't done anything for anyone outside my own house, I get Natalie to video chat with me from Utah. I get updates on her family, her work, her health, her feelings and thoughts and dreams. I learn about what she's reading—"The Miracle of Mindfulness"—and about the harp string shortage caused by a shift in meat regulations in England—a big deal for a professional harpist. Fifteen hundred miles apart, we spend an hour and a half together, much of it laughing. It makes me so happy.

I hate to admit this, but it is honestly easier for me to have a long conversation because I am checking off my good turn for the day. What does it mean about me that I have trouble making time for my best friend unless it's *mandatory*? What has happened that has turned my life into a quest for productivity?

One Sunday, I volunteer to substitute in nursery! Have I mentioned that I'm not great with kids?

I get ridiculously excited when one of my Laurels asks me for a ride. I have been her adviser since moving here and have never stopped feeling uncertain and awkward (generally uncool), so it's a big deal to me that she finally trusts me enough to ask for something.

Someone invites me to a last-minute game night and I come with a pan of lemon bars. Games are not my thing. I do not tell them.

One night, I'm falling asleep when I realize that I haven't done a good turn for the day. I grab my phone to jot a Facebook message to literally whomever, and then I stop. I still want this moment to be thoughtful, not random or self-serving. My record of days isn't as important to this

266   MIKAYLA ORTON THATCHER

goal as doing good turns that are actually good. I spend thirty seconds thinking and praying about who might need a note and what it should say.

My college roommate Christie pops into my head. She gave birth to her first child a week ago. I send her a message asking how things are going, including the question "What is The Worst part right now?" Then I go to bed. I hope my message leaves some space for her to talk to me openly, not just tell me that the baby is "so perfect" and they feel "so blessed."

In the morning, I have messages from Christie. The week has been harder than she expected, by a lot. She isn't getting any sleep. She feels infinitely worse than she did late in her pregnancy. "Can you tell me that things will get better?"

I absolutely can. I have a two-year-old who sleeps for twelve straight hours at night and another hour or so during the day. She's funny and sweet. She can feed herself. She can tell me why she's crying. Yes, things are going to get better. Christie and I haven't been close in the last few years, but maybe her new baby is our opportunity to start talking again.

During my thirty days, a new family moves into the apartment directly across from ours. They turn out to be in our ward (for real)! They seem wonderful right off the bat and they have three little boys, one of whom is Jane's age.

I know exactly what my good turn should be. I should invite the new neighbors to have dinner with us. It's their move-in day—they're tired and their dishes are probably packed up. It would be a good way to launch a friendship. But . . . they have three *entire* children. I've never cooked for eight people before in my life. And I don't know what they like to eat—kids are fickle. Do I even have enough dishes for that many people?

Okay, Kayla, time to stop making excuses. I invite them and they accept. There's a picnic table in the courtyard between our homes: we can all fit there. I make a big batch of sweet potato black bean tacos—it's the same meal that another ward member fed us right after we moved in two years ago. That feels kind of like "lace" to me. We have four dinner plates and four dessert plates, which is precisely enough. We share a simple dinner with our new friends on a beautiful June evening. I have no regrets.

I wish I were just naturally unselfish, but my daily good turns make excellent training wheels. I am being mindful of others. I am finding ways to fit other people's needs into my own busy life. I'm setting the kind of example for Jane that I want to set. My friendships are getting stronger.

Some of my good turns wouldn't count as service to someone more outgoing than me, or better with children than me, or wealthier than me. My efforts to show love are unique because my strengths and weaknesses are unique. I attend events I don't technically want to attend. I pop in for visits when I know scheduling won't work, even though I usually make a point of never knocking without texting first. I volunteer for things immediately instead of waiting a few hours or days. It's as small as that.

Of all the things I've done for Beehive Girls, this is the one I truly recommend.

FOR DREAMS AND INSPIRATION, FOR RECORDS OF OUR DEAD

FIELD OF RELIGION, CELL 23: Memorize five hymns from the L.D.S. Hymn Book, selecting those which you like best.

I REMEMBER FULFILLING this exact requirement for Personal Progress as a kid! This time, I'm going to use the cell as an excuse to jump into old hymn books. All I really know about where our hymns came from is that Emma Smith was called to compile them and that I'm descended from the poet who wrote "High on a Mountain Top" (it's a major point of family pride).

I look up old church hymnals and the first thing I learn is that there were quite a few, used for various purposes and spans of time. The first several were pocket-sized, with no musical settings included. Choristers' jobs got much easier in 1889, when every hymn in the latest "Psalmody" was matched to a tune. Early in the twentieth century, various auxiliaries created their own hymn collections. One of these, "Deseret Sunday School Songs," became tremendously popular and was embraced churchwide until 1948, when the General Music Committee put out a new hymnbook that took over as standard.

Interestingly, Emma's original book is less of a predecessor of our modern one than I thought it was. Before her second edition came out, several members of the Quorum of the Twelve on missions in England, including Brigham Young, published their own "Manchester Hymnal." The project was unauthorized and Joseph chastised the apostles at first, but he soon came to appreciate their finished product. The Manchester Hymnal leaned more toward "bold, millennialistic, group-oriented hymns," while Emma's focused more on "personal solace and the intimate, graceful Savior." Since Brigham Young traveled west to Utah after Joseph's death, his favored hymns and hymn style remained important as the Church of Jesus Christ of Latter-day Saints developed. Back in Illinois, Emma continued collecting hymns all her life. Her work is foundational to the hymnody of the Community of Christ.

Since I'm here to learn about Latter-day Saint women, and since there were apparently plenty of hymnal options to choose from in the early twentieth century, I pick up the Relief Society Songbook from 1919. Many of the songs are familiar (Battle Hymn of the Republic, Did You Think to Pray?, Our Mountain Home So Dear—okay, maybe that one doesn't count as familiar). The first few new-to-me hymns I see have that same grandiloquent aesthetic that makes the Young Woman's Journal somewhat difficult to enjoy. Nothing catches my attention.

Well, except the names. Since most of the texts and tunes are by men, it's special every time I find one by a woman—especially by a Latter-day Saint woman, written specifically for Latter-day Saints to sing. In total, thirty-one of the 157 hymns have female poets and twelve have female composers (there may be a few more of each who went only by their initials). Our old friends Emmeline, Susa, and Eliza contributed a lot, but I don't recognize the other names. In all, there are five hymns that are collaborations between Latter-day Saint women composers and lyricists. I'm including my two favorites below. They're actually both by the same two women and the lyricist was the first editor of the *Exponent*!

67. My Friend
Words: Lula Greene Richards
Music: Lucy May Green

My Friend, I look to Thee most kind and true,
To shield and comfort me life's journey through
Darkness and death extend with wild increase
And still with Thee, my Friend, is perfect peace,
Is perfect peace.

I have no pow'r to fill life's great design,
Save as I learn Thy will and make it mine,
Help me to understand Thy faintest call;
Let me but touch Thy hand, I shall not fall,
I shall not fall.

Sure is Thy promise true to all who hear,
And Thou wilt guide my feet I have no fear
So all life's journey through until the end,
I'll trust Thy love most true, my perfect Friend,
My perfect Friend.

Wow, why don't we have any remaining hymns with God described as a personal friend? I love that this one is full of faith and a very specific plea: that the speaker will be able to understand the divine plan and follow it. And the poetry is so dang good! That is honestly a special thing in hymns.

80. We Thank Thee, Heavenly Father
Words: Lula Greene Richards
Music: Lucy May Green

We thank Thee, Heavenly Father, for sacred, holy ground,
Where blessings of the Gospel and precious gifts abound;
For true and loyal people whom Thou hast planted here,
from continents and islands, all nations far and near.

We thank thee for the temples wherein Thy people throng,
For friendship, love, and union, which make us glad and strong;
For dreams and inspiration, for records of our dead,
and faith to help redeem them as by the spirit led.

We thank Thee for the spreading of gospel truths abroad,
The light of which shall vanquish all ignorance and fraud,
that all who will may gather, rejoicing in Thy grace,
And stand in holy places, prepared to see Thy face.

This one reminds me of "We Thank Thee, O God, for a Prophet," because it's just a list of things that we are communally grateful for. It has the added benefit, though, of not being so familiar to us that we accidentally mishear it as being about the prophet throughout. I love the Latter-day Saint specificity of lines about redeeming the dead, spiritual gifts, missionary work, and being brought deliberately to the promised land.

FIELD OF PUBLIC SERVICE, CELL 736: Write a story, a poem, or words or music for a song which is either accepted for publication or adopted for use in some organization.

You've seen Nate mainly as my helpmeet in this story, so you may not remember, but I'm married to a composer. Nate's life playlist includes music from every time period and culture, and he learns something from every composer he listens to. He is immersed in his field for his academic, professional, social, and recreational life in a way that most people could not stand to be immersed in theirs—sometimes I resent when people ask him to sing or play random things at the last minute and he simply smiles and reminds me, "I *like* music."

Nate sings in an early music choir, which performs mainly masses and other religious music, so he is exposed to a huge variety of church music. Like many trained Latter-day Saint musicians, he is often frustrated by the limited musical language that is culturally acceptable in the church. Of course, that means he wants to contribute, so setting whatever text I write appeals to him . . . even when I tell him I want it to sound relatively normal for a Latter-day Saint hymn. He treats it as a good, healthy challenge.

Of course, I start by doing a little research. Even though we call our green book "the hymn book," I learn that a narrower definition of a hymn only includes the kind that is formatted like a prayer—directly addressing God. So it's "How Great Thou Art" instead of "How Great He Ist." Does that sound like every church song to you? It's actually just under a quarter of them (I counted. For research.). We also have songs of admonition ("Count Your Many Blessings," "Keep the Commandments"), songs of camaraderie ("We Are All Enlisted," "Who's on the Lord's Side?"), songs of testimony ("I Stand All Amazed," "I am a Child of God"), and a variety of other song types, including the just plain weird ("In Our Lovely Deseret"). No, these are not academic categories. I made them up.

Of course, none of these formats is inherently less valuable than the true hymn, but for this project I want to write a prayer. I want it to be tied very tightly to the scriptures, I want it to be about Jesus Christ, and I want it to be distinctly Mormon without being tacky.

I brainstorm, thinking about Christ's many roles and the roles that matter the most to me. I make a list of stories of Christ from the scriptures, concrete references I could make in a hymn. I list scriptural phrases I love. I commit to using only straightforward language and phrasing. I've watched enough primary choristers try to teach children the line "'To fulfill the law,' said Jesus when the Baptist questioned why" that I know the kids have no idea what they're repeating. I have excessively lofty ideals for my first round of hymn-writing.

As for meter, I decide to just write words that fit an existing hymn and then pass the words to Nate without telling him what I used as a template. This will allow me to lay things out in an organized, proven way, but it will still let Nate come up with his own melody and rhythm without being influenced by the template hymn. I choose "We Love Thy House, O God" because it keeps popping into my head. With all of this spelled out, it's time to start writing.

My first big surprise is that hymns are *short*. I've mapped out a nice four-verse progression of ideas about Jesus, but trying to capture what I meant to say in each verse with just four phrases makes me sound like a child. Fancy turns of phrase aren't possible when each line is seven syllables long. Further complicating my syllable usage, I want to use the traditional and respectful thee/thou that I was taught to use in prayer. Thee and thou don't take extra space, of course, but sometimes the verbs surrounding them get . . . complicated.

In spite of my difficulties, I love the writing as an exercise. I love finding elements to use in the scriptures. I love choosing something to say and organizing the scriptural elements to support my "thesis." I love the problem-solving of fitting the words into the rhythm of the template hymn. When I finish, it still feels embarrassingly simplistic, but I hope adding music will fix that. I can sing it with friends in sacrament meeting and it will be great.

Thou hast shown us once again
thy power to still the storm.
Thou hast filled us with Thy peace;
with Thy love we are transformed.

With loaves and fishes, Lord,
thou blesses us with daily bread,
And with Thee to feed and guard
the future holds no dread.

We have come before thee, Lord,
to give away all our sin.
O, root out this evil spirit
that Thine may enter in.

We know by whom we're led.
We praise Thee for Thy sight.
We have seen Thy hand and learned
what Thou touchest fills with light.

Nate sets my lyrics. Or rather, he tries to set my lyrics. It becomes painfully apparent that rather than counting syllables, I was mentally stretching words to fit "We Love Thy House, O God." It works great in my head. The first line of my first and second verses have completely different syllables and accent patterns (skansions). Nate tweaks it as much as he can, but in the end it will only be good for a ward choir that has a little time to put in. A congregation won't be able to figure out what to do with the words. Shoot.

And that could be the end of my hymn-writing story, just another of the mild disappointments that inevitably happen when you try out a lot of new things in rapid succession, if it weren't for the Center for Latter-day Saint Arts Festival. Nate's publisher, Glen Nelson, invites him to present at the festival—not on his own music, but on his book about Spanish composer Francisco Estévez (nicknamed Paco). Glenn is flying Paco in for the festival and it's a big, happy deal for everybody. There's going to be a sing-in at the festival, a big crowd of people sight-reading hymns written in the last fifty years, and Nate wants to submit something. This time, with one collaborative attempt under our belts, he writes the music first. Then he drafts some lyrics and asks for my help.

The rough draft isn't a good poem, but it's an excellent place to start because it captures the message that he wants to write about: this is going to be a hymn about trusting in God when our faith is challenged and we don't feel connected to heaven. I help him focus in on exactly what he wants to say. I structure the flow of ideas. I choose the best imagery and get rid of phrases that are pretty, but off-topic. I offer phrases that we can use.

It takes several evenings of happy, intellectual arguing, but we finally step back and realize that we've made a hymn we love. I laugh as Nate adds my name to the top of the music as a co-lyricist: I was vital to the writing of the poem, but I'm not sure that any of the lines were technically *written* by me.

> From our God is all we own—
> Every breath and beat we've known.
> Beating halts too soon,

Breath wanes like the moon.
Our days pass like smoke before us.
Fear and trembling fill our bones.

All we have must pass away.
We meet silence when we pray.
When light seems to leave,
Can we yet believe?
Stripped meaning seems all suff'ring.
How canst Thou still hide Thy face?

In the world we are dismayed,
But Thou hast endured our pain.
As Beloved Son
Thou hast overcome.
Thou hast promised joy for ashes,
Joined us in our home of clay.

Though we have not understood,
We have trust that Thou art good.
We have seen Thy hand—
Not the promised land.
May we, as Thy wand'ring children,
Comprehend Thy Parenthood.

Our hymn is chosen for the festival sing-in.

It's the summer that Jane is two-and-a-half. Nate's aunt, Elizabeth, cares for her in New Jersey for the first two days of the festival, so we can fully participate in listening to presentations (The whole thing is on YouTube, if you're interested!), hosting Paco and his daughter, and making new friends. On the last day, though, I bring my daughter into the city—walk, bus, subway, walk—to hear the music. She gets to meet Paco. She gets to explore the pop-up art exhibit (her favorite piece by far is an animation by Annie Poon, but that may be because it involves a TV). She runs around with poet Rachel Hunt Steenblik's four-year-old daughter for at least an hour, giggling more loudly than is appropriate.

There are so many people that I never get a binder with copies of the music. I'm getting nervous about the audience. Our hymn is . . . a little raw. It is technically about trust and gratitude, but it acknowledges some more difficult emotions. Our hymn is one of the few with the composer present, so Nate will be conducting the crowd and everyone will know who he is. What if they are disgusted? I suddenly wish we'd submitted our first hymn, the lower quality one, just because it is more happy-go-lucky.

But it's too late. The crowd is singing our hymn. A nice woman, whose toddler is taking turns with mine using the Annie Poon headphones, is trying to converse with me and I rudely cut her off to listen. The makeshift choir grows more confident verse by verse, as they figure out the melody. When it's over, Craig Jessup (the former MoTab director running this event) congratulates Nate and Nate points me out in the crowd, telling everyone that I wrote the words.

It's an overstatement, because he's generous, but it ends up mattering beyond just getting credit. Because he pointed me out, people come up to me for the rest of the day to thank me for the hymn. I get hugs from strangers. I cry with strangers. They tell me stories about faith crises and cancer and miscarriage. Maybe some people *were* perturbed by our hymn, but they'll recover. This is more important. I feel so blessed to get to meet people who connect with what we wrote. We don't need to feel alone when we encounter doubt or fear. We don't need to feel like an aberration when we can't hear the answers to our prayers.

🌸 🐝 🐝

When the Church calls for original hymns and hymn suggestions, I fix the scansion in my first hymn so it will actually
work. Then I write one more new text and Nate sets it. Nate
and I submit all three that we wrote together. Then I recommend the two Lula Greene Richards/Lucy May Green collaborations from the old Relief Society hymnbook. There's
a slight chance that my work for Beehive Girls will influence
the future of Church music.

ALL THE STEPS BEFORE

FIELD OF DOMESTIC ARTS, CELL 126: Pluck, dress, and cook a fowl.

WHEN I CALL THE CHICKEN FARMER, Daniel, about plucking my own chicken, he laughs. "You know that you'll need to do all the steps before that too, right?"

"Yes! I'm planning on it. I just felt weird about asking a stranger aloud to help me butcher a chicken. It sounds so . . . violent."

"Then yes, I can help you. And don't worry—it really won't be violent. It's not weird to know where your food comes from."

I guess he's right. I keep running into that ethic here in Ann Arbor—there's so much organic, local, and free-range food here. The farmer's market runs year-round; the local community college hands out heirloom seeds every spring for people to use in their gardens. It feels like half the populace is vegetarian.

I'm not used to thinking about any of this. My family growing up was so large that my mom prioritized nutrition, cost, and taste. No one had time to think about carbon footprint or animal cruelty.

Nate and I have been slowly changing our own cooking as we look around and learn. We certainly don't have money to eat high-quality meat regularly, so our repertoire of vegetarian recipes just keeps growing. Thank goodness for beans! Because of the many Indian and Arab immigrants in this part of Michigan, we have access to a huge variety of legumes and delicious spices, which makes learning to cook vegetarian food way more fun. It turns out that I *love* cooking without needing to touch meat, thaw meat, or hope I've properly cooked meat.

So as I plan a time to visit Daniel's farm, the chicken-butchering cell feels even more dramatic than it would anyway. A live chicken seems a very long way from dry beans.

Daniel has kids and welcomes kids on the farm . . . so it's yet another summer outing with the whole family, on our way to yet another farm. Beehive Girls has taken us to the countryside so many times in the last two years! I didn't realize when I began that farms would be such a strong thread through this project. I'm grateful, though. It would be so easy to settle down in the city and let Jane assume that food comes from the grocery store.

"I can't believe how many big trees there are out in these fields," I remark. "I haven't seen anything like this in Utah or Idaho."

"Yeah," Nate acknowledges, "but all of this used to be forest, so if you think about it that way . . ."

"Wow, good point. This is clear-cutting in Michigan. I can't even imagine how many trees there must have been."

The roads turn and keep the same name, or else continue straight and change names. The GPS is a necessity. The ground is pretty much flat here, so we don't see anything "across the valley" the way we would at home.

"I love these roads where the trees arch over. We're practically driving through a tunnel."

"It's so magical. It reminds me of those houses in London that used to jut out on the second floors so that they almost touched over the streets."

". . . Is that a thing?" This comparison doesn't ring any bells for Nate.

"Um. I think so? I think it's something I learned in *The Prince and the Pauper* as a kid? I guess I have no idea."

Daniel meets us at his home and introduces his wife Leanne and their two little kids. We hand over the homemade cookies we've brought. I'll pay actual money for the chicken, of course, but I want Daniel to know that we appreciate the tour and the tutelage.

"We have ten and a half acres here," Daniel begins, "and it's split up into fourteen little paddocks so the cows can rotate through and have a fresh place to graze every day. The grass and weeds in a paddock have two weeks to bounce back before the cows take it down to stubble again." He points out the chicken coop, which is on wheels. "The coop is portable, so the laying hens can follow the cows around, but three days behind."

"Three days behind? Why?" I guess the insect population needs time to bounce back as well . . . but three days seems very specific. I'm missing something.

"Well, the cows produce manure and flies lay eggs in the cow pies. By the third day, the eggs have hatched into maggots, which are like a protein-packed superfood for the chickens. Plus, the chickens end up scratching the dry cow pies apart, so I don't have to think about waste removal. Nothing builds up."

Oh my goodness, that is ingenious. He's taking good

care of the land, the cattle, and the chickens all at the same time! "How did you learn to do this?" I ask, prepared to hear that he learned from his father, who learned from his father, who learned from his father.

"I read a lot of books and taught myself!" he answers instead. He tells me about his career as a scientist, a pharmaceutical researcher interested in psoriasis and lupus. He and Leanne bought their acreage five years ago. "My in-laws were inside, carefully inspecting the house, and I didn't care whether it was a shack," he told me with a smile. "I knew immediately that I wanted this land." At this point the farm barely pays for itself, but he doesn't seem to mind. "I still have my job, so there's income. I love getting to experiment and learn from my mistakes every season. And I get to feed my family such good food!"

"Speaking of which, here are the meat chickens," Daniel changes the subject as we arrive at the front yard. "These guys grow really fast—they get to full size when they're eight weeks old." Yeah, these chickens are huge. They were clearly bred for a different purpose than the laying hens. "I keep them in these smaller coops that I can slide to a new spot on the lawn twice a day because they get really anxious about grazing if they have too much space."

This might be the end of the tour. It might be time for me to begin my real business here. We stand silently for a moment, looking at the chickens, before Daniel gives me the verbal nudge I'm waiting for: "Okay, get in there and choose one."

I, like the chickens, feel a little panicky in the face of too many options. It doesn't really matter, though, because I can't actually "choose" a specific chicken and catch it. I don't have the skills. I get into the pen, grab, miss, and just keep grabbing until I finally fill my arms with a large, light-brown chicken.

My left hand supports her breast, above the reach of her clawed feet, but the other hand is trickier. "Wait, how do I hold it? Is my hand supposed to be under her wings or on top?"

"Whatever you want!" Daniel reassures me without actually helping. "She's fine." Hand under wings feels more stable, but allows her to flap her wings in my face when she feels like it.

She's settling in, though, calm and finished with her flapping.

The only other non-bugs I've killed have been lab mice (for diabetes research) and they never stop trying to bite. To pick up a lab mouse and give it an injection, you have to pinch the scruff of its neck between your index finger knuckle and your thumb, simultaneously restraining its legs with your pinky. It is frustrating, stressful, and often painful. You respect the mouse's will to live and understand that it is frightened, but you're still kind of . . . relieved . . . when it's dead. You'd never touch one without gloves on. By the end of grad school, I had been bitten enough times that I wouldn't handle a mouse without two *pairs* of gloves on.

The hen is different (and not only because she smells so much better than a mouse). I'm cradling her, in no rush. I can feel her warmth in my hands, feel her soft feathers, feel her heart beat and her wings beat and really take in that she is alive.

Then Daniel takes her from my arms and puts her upside down into the "death cone" and hands me a pocket knife. A pocket knife?! I was not expecting a pocket knife. Jane wanders by and I'm not sure whether to have Nate take her away or not.

With mice, I always felt a step removed from the sacrifice, since giving a lethal injection was exactly like giving a routine insulin injection. The mice were dead before I ever cut into them and harvested their organs.

Slitting a throat, though, is a very intimate way to kill a creature. The chicken is alive and I make eye contact with her. I basically have to grab her face to do my work. The cartilage of her trachea (anatomy factoids help) is difficult to cut through with a pocket knife—shoot, shoot, shoot— what a time to fumble. Crap. This poor hen. Her blood is all over my hands, warm and red and sticky as mine, painless as one of my spontaneous nosebleeds. I'm acquainted with this creature in a way that I couldn't be if I'd shot her from a hundred yards away.

When I've made it through the trachea and esophagus, Daniel has me step away so I don't have to see the chicken thrash around in the first minutes of death. I wash my hands. The historic rituals of slaughter and sacrifice make a lot of sense to me right now. I wish so badly that I had a good prayer to say, of thanks or repentance or whatever is most appropriate.

Repentance doesn't seem necessary, though. I'm okay. This is new, but it feels normal. Confrontation leaves me shaking with adrenaline, while killing a chicken with my bare hands doesn't. Even Jane lost interest and walked away of her own accord. Daniel is heating water now for the next step, one I didn't know about before this very moment: scalding the chicken in slightly soapy water, to break down the waterproof oil layer and loosen the feathers.

"So how do you usually process chickens?" I ask Daniel. "Like, if they're going to the grocery store then they have to be FDA compliant, right?" I don't know much about the law, but I doubt that pocket knives are the standard in commercial meat production.

"Well," he answers, "I drop them off somewhere, alive, and then I come back and they're all wrapped in plastic and frozen."

"Oh. Yeah, that makes sense."

"I butcher them myself for my family, but yeah, there's a whole factory apparatus that makes everything quick and simple and up to code."

I tell him about my conversation with the re-enacting carpenters back in Utah—that if people back then had had the technology that we have now, they would have been only too thrilled to use it. "I totally agree," he says. "It seems fun at first to do every single thing the old-fashioned way, but isn't sustainable. Farmers have always been under so much stress just trying to survive and keep their farms. They can't control the weather year to year, so they focus on making their other tasks a little faster and easier."

The soapy water is hot enough to scald and the chicken is still. Daniel shows me how to hold the carcass by the feet—weirdly convenient—and dip it into the water. It takes around a dozen short dips. I keep getting tired and switching arms.

Then it's time to finish cutting off the head and clean out the body cavities. I hesitate a little. I want to see the chicken's organs because I am exactly that kind of nerd, but I'm not sure I want to do this with my bare hands. (Why didn't I think of this before the pocket knife moment? I don't know.) Leanne appears next to me with latex gloves. She has been hanging out with Nate and the kids, but she has apparently been paying attention. I'm immensely grateful. I put on the gloves and feel the emotional focus and clarity that comes with being prepared in such a familiar way.

I cut off the head, the feet, the little nub of a tail, and open up a cavity to scoop out the kidneys, gizzard, lungs, etc. It isn't gross or difficult. This really isn't a chicken anymore.

Daniel points out an organ I've never studied before, "There's the gizzard. Go ahead, open it up!" It's about the size and shape of a hacky-sack—a thick, muscular bag enclosing chicken feed and the pebbles the chicken has swallowed to help digest its food. It's amazing. I love seeing the intestines as still-living tissue, a healthy beige, hung carefully in their curving mesentery.

I expect some instructions on how to pluck the bird, but there aren't any. You just pluck it. It's time-consuming, but there's nothing to it. Daniel does not help—his only direct involvement has been to stuff the chicken into the death cone—but he sits with me as I work. We chat about death.

"It's weird to me that I've eaten meat my whole life without ever plucking a chicken . . . or even *seeing* anyone pluck a chicken. I got to eat a whole, fried fish on the beach once, and I hated that it still had eyes and scales and fins. That has to be a new thing for humans, right? To be so guarded from the transition from animals to meat that it grosses us out to see any evidence?"

"Oh, absolutely. And not just guarded from meat processing, but from death in general. Two hundred years ago, almost everyone farmed, so people would have been used to seeing dead animals—for meat, but also from sickness and accidents and foxes getting into the coop, you know?"

"Right, and human death would have been more present too! Most children didn't survive to adulthood and mothers died in childbirth and there wasn't much medicine to keep people from dying of little infections . . ."

"Well, and not only were people dying, they were dying at home, in the care of their families. They didn't die in the hospital and then get whisked away to the morgue. So everyone had seen dead bodies."

"Wow, yeah. I teach with cadavers all the time, but I would be completely taken by surprise to see a dead body in any other context. Like, if I *found* a body? I wouldn't know what I was supposed to do next. I would probably look back at the experience as out-of-the-ordinary—quite a story to tell."

"Right! Even though people die all the time." I think of a friend our age who died of cancer four years ago. I was surprised to learn that he passed away in the evening and his family stayed with him at home until finally calling the mortuary in the morning. I didn't know that was a possibility, that there was no huge rush to hand him over to "proper authorities." That last night together sounded so sweet to me, so human. His parents and siblings weren't afraid to be with him just because he was a corpse.

Soon I deem the plucked chicken "good enough" and I buy it for just over thirty dollars—between the money and the labor, I've invested way more in this chicken than I've ever invested in a meal. Cooking it well feels very high stakes.

"How do I roast this thing?" I ask Daniel, but Leanne has already written down her recipe for me. She is an excellent chicken-butchering hostess. "You don't want to cook it tonight, though," she warns me. "Stick it in the fridge for the next twenty-four hours so it can finish going through rigor mortis. Then cook it tomorrow." I'm glad that she pointed this out! I totally assumed that fresh-as-possible was best.

We say goodbye to Daniel, Leanne, and their kids, then start winding our way through small agricultural towns to get home. Coming around a sharp curve, Nate has to slam his brakes to avoid hitting a turtle crossing the street. After a rushed conversation about whether it's a snapping turtle—he says it isn't, though I'm not sure how he knows—he pulls over to give me a chance to run into the middle of the road and save the turtle. I pick him up by his large shell, which is peeling oddly (has he been hit already?). The turtle is the second animal I've held in my hands today, and my purpose this time is directly opposite last time. This animal shows its fear by peeing on me. Like, a lot. More than I thought possible. My pants are soaked as I dodge another oncoming vehicle to re-join my family in the car.

I roast the chicken the next day, as instructed. The recipe basically says to salt the meat ("A *lot* of salt," Leanne told me, "An awkward amount of salt."), stuff it with onions, and let it sit on the counter for one hour before putting it in the oven, keeping the breast temperature at 165 degrees ("And not a degree over, or it will be dry!") for something like another hour. I have to borrow a meat thermometer from a neighbor.

Roasting the chicken takes forever and our home, as you know by now, lacks air conditioning. I think of the summer kitchen at the heritage farm back in Logan. I check the chicken again. Did I accidentally leave an organ in there? It looks weird. It's gotta be time to take the bird out of the oven. Am I just ready to take it out because I'm hot and frustrated? We're closing in on Jane's bedtime. I'll just take it out.

I carve the meat sloppily, burning my fingers and inwardly grumbling that this had better be the best chicken of my life.

Nate insists it's fantastic and Jane keeps shouting for "Ma ticken!" but I find it slightly dry and completely underwhelming. I should have stuck with beans. Or if I *really* needed to eat chicken, I should have bought us a grocery store rotisserie chicken. What a waste.

Fortunately, there are chicken leftovers in the fridge for lunch the next day and I get to taste it again. This time there's no heat to deal with, plus no worrying about doneness or finding a neglected organ or making a big, juicy mess.

The chicken is delicious. The chicken that I "chose" and killed and plucked and butchered and dressed and roasted *myself* is delicious. And I don't feel disgusted or guilty for having seen the process all the way through—I feel responsible and connected, as though I'm following some kind of natural law of the harvest more directly than I ever have before.

FRESH AIR
FOR MY SOUL:
THE STORY OF
GEORGINA BRINGAS

FIELD OF RELIGION, CELL 9: Give brief account of the life and labors of four other local women who have done much good in Church service.

FOR MY LAST LIFE SKETCH, I want to find a new story to tell and I want it to be about someone living right now. I don't know how to look for that person, though.

There's a cool new international Young Women general board—perfect for Beehive Girls! I read through their bios and reach out to one of them through a friend who knows her. She agrees to an interview, but she has to send my questions to Church Headquarters for input before she answers me. She never gets back to me. Did she forget? Were my questions inappropriate in some way that I didn't realize? I move on without knowing.

An LDS woman is dean of the business college here at the University of Michigan. She'd probably talk to me, and we could speak in person! I kinda hate business, though . . . and she's from the United States, anyway.

I reach out to strangers on Twitter who seem to be Latter-day Saints in other countries. I search endless local Latter-day Saint newsrooms and blogs, using Google to give me rough translations. I talk to a friend who works for the Church in linguistics. I talk with returned missionaries about cool women they met on their missions. No one points me to any specific stories. Maybe a life sketch doesn't make sense when a person isn't dead.

There's another major weakness in my search: if my mystery lady doesn't speak English, I pretty much can't interview her anyway. My ability to do this is so narrow. The Church, with all of its money, connections, and talented employees, could find and tell these stories much better than I can.

My breakthrough comes one day as I'm browsing the winners of the International Art Competition that the Church History Museum puts on every year. The theme for 2019 is "Meditations on Belief" and there are 151 pieces in the online exhibit, drawing from every artistic style and using a wide variety of media. Some feel bold and contemporary, and some are gorgeous illustrations of familiar images. One piece, though, looks like five white frames full of, well, dirt.

The artist, Georgina Bringas, gathered one kilogram (specifically) of soil fragments from various parts of Mexico City, where she lives. Within the frames, she arranged the soil to form a rolling horizon line. In her statement, she wrote, "As we remember the ancient wonders of God and speak of His deeds, we can look to the sometimes diffuse and distant horizon with hope and gratitude. Hope is transformative and helps us broaden our perspectives 'like the beam of sunlight rising up and above the horizon of our present circumstances.'" (That last phrase is a quote from Elder Uchtdorf.) She totally turned in boxes of dirt and won. They were thought-provoking boxes of dirt. They fit the theme.

I love contemporary art with all my heart, and I'm already a big fan of any artist who thought that far outside of the box for a Church-sponsored art competition. I find Georgina's website and start browsing her work. Her portfolio includes all of my favorite things—huge installations, found materials, meticulously-executed concepts, colorful thread, minimalism, and lots of math. Her website links to magazine articles about her artistic vision, which Nate can translate for me because he speaks Spanish, but none of the interviews make any mention of her faith.

I get to reach out to Georgina on Facebook. She's surprised by my excellent Spanish (it's Nate's excellent Spanish), friendly, and willing to answer my questions. It's interesting to feel trusted to tell someone's story when we haven't met and she doesn't know a *lot* about what I'm doing (I do explain, but she doesn't ask for any more details). I guess it's what I already did with the other five Local Women, but I didn't get to ask them for their input or consent.

Georgina and I correspond by email, in a process that is strikingly different from researching long-dead pioneer women. I don't get to read her diary, and I don't know her innermost thoughts . . . but I do get to ask for whatever I want to know.

🐝 🤝 🐝

Georgina Bringas was born in Mexico City in 1975. Her family was Catholic until one of her mother's coworkers introduced them to the Church of Jesus Christ of Latter-day Saints. Georgina's mother and all the kids were baptized when Georgina was almost ten years old, and her father joined them six months later.

Her father passed away only a few months after his baptism. She told me, "It was a time of many trials and challenges for my family. My mother was now alone with five children and we decided not to let go of the Lord's hand in order to be able to keep moving forward." Georgina was already drawing, but not because she felt like she had any talent. "There was something in the act of drawing that made me feel and think that I could see some reality more closely, more clearly." She found the same kind of happiness and belonging in drawing as she found in the gospel.

Georgina felt guided and helped as she took entrance exams and prepared to study art in college. She was admitted to "La Esmeralda," which is the most important school of fine art in Mexico. She was excited and confident in her path.

As she began her studies, though, she became deeply uncomfortable with some of the teaching and culture in her school community ("many philosophies of men, much banality and frivolity"). Georgina knew she needed to find her own way to make and experience art in harmony with her testimony and values. Halfway through her degree, she left to serve a mission in the Mexico Tuxtla Gutierrez Mission.

She calls her mission "a breath of fresh air for my soul." She witnessed God's love for God's children. She learned to work to the end of her strength and then give a little more. She learned how to offer her best to the Lord. She found great mentorship in her mission president, Benjamin de Hoyos, and his wife, Evelia Genesta de Hoyos, and she looks to them for guidance and friendship to this day.

Georgina returned to La Esmeralda and, though circumstances at school hadn't changed, she says, "I began again . . . with a renewed spirit and with a clearer vision of my work as an artist." A fellow student, Ricardo Rendón,

began trying to date her, but as a newly-returned missionary she wasn't looking for romance, let alone with someone
who wasn't a member of the Church. She told me, "I talked with him about what the church was for me, about my
standards and the covenants that I had made. I spoke with
him about my goals of getting married in the temple with
a certainty that he would lose interest and I would continue
on my way." Instead, he asked her to give him a chance.

A few months into their relationship, Ricardo's mother became gravely ill. He lived alone with her and had no
other support, so he and Georgina stayed with her in shifts,
trying to care for her while keeping up in their college
classes. She passed away the same year. This experience
united Ricardo and Georgina emotionally and spiritually.
Their work and their grief made them a family and prepared them for their eventual marriage.

Georgina and her husband are both professional artists, but they keep separate studios: their one professional
collaboration ended in "disaster" and Georgina quips, "We
decided that our only perfect collaborations would be our
two children." They stay connected to their community by
inviting people to visit their studio. Georgina says that they
"explain, especially to the children, the artistic process that
we have and help them see that art serves the social function of showing us new ways of seeing the world. . . . That
interests me: being able to help people see that art is part
of life and not some sort of secret code that can't be understood." For years, she has taught workshops on aesthetic
education and contemporary art.

Georgina and her husband have lived in the same ward
for the fourteen years they've been married. Of that ward,
she says, "It is a family for me. They saw me as a newly-
wed, pregnant with my kids, and through the years I have
learned a lot from them." The ward was there for her fam-

ily when Ricardo was baptized and when they and their children were sealed in 2017.

I asked Georgina about her dreams for the future, and she told me that her dreams have already come true. She has the gospel, she has work to do in her ward, and she is joyfully homeschooling her children. She's also making art. She says, "It is a small sphere but it can affect the whole universe. . . . I just try with my work to understand and perhaps help someone else feel more that a heavenly light exists in the small and simple things."

As the last of my Local Women, I can't help seeing patterns, finding connections between Georgina and everyone else. Like Emmeline and Chieko, Georgina found the gospel as a child. Like Julia, she lost her father when she was very young. Like Minerva and Chieko, she chose to marry a good man who was baptized later. Like Minerva, she is an artist. Like Chieko, she has exactly two children. Like Emmeline, Julia, and Chieko, she is a teacher. Like Minerva and Julia, she lives near where she was born, deeply connected to the place and the people. Like Jane (and probably all the others), she sees her life as guided by God's hand.

But Georgina is the first of my Local Women to serve a regular, full-time mission. She's the only one to keep her natal name. And all of the others lived into their eighties or beyond, while Georgina is only in her forties! I appreciate hearing from a Local Woman who is a little more ordinary, a little less famous, living in the middle of her story with no idea how it will end. The dead heroines I selected all seem so accomplished to me, their lives so full and their service so varied. They're amazing—maybe even a little too over-the-top to emulate. Georgina is a few years younger than my mom and, in many ways, much like her and the other humble and faithful Latter-day Saint women I've known my whole life. My aunts, my neighbors, my Young Women leaders, my professors. I needed to meet Jane, Emmeline, Minerva, Chieko, and Julia, but I think that interviewing Georgina is closer to what this Beehive Girls cell was encouraging me to do.

Georgina, like me, is so happy with her life right now, but I know from the other stories that there are so many more phases ahead of her. Ahead of us. Who will we be in forty years? I've changed so much in my first ten years of adulthood and the changes will probably just keep coming. If someone decides to write a short sketch of my entire life after I'm gone, I only know what the opening paragraph will say. Only the introduction. But I feel like my Local Women have shown me a wide variety of directions a life can take in the second and third acts, and Georgina has reminded me how simple a story can look when you're only part of the way through it.

BUILDER IN THE HIVE

AFTER YEARS OF WORKING toward earning my Builder in the Hive, I still haven't found a real Beehive Girl to talk to in person. The Beehive Girls program existed until 1970! The former Beehive Girls must be all around me! One Sunday, I finally stand up in Relief Society and explain my project. "Is there anyone here who was a Beehive Girl once who would be willing to answer questions about their experience?"

Everyone keeps their hands in their laps and it's quiet for a few seconds until someone asks, "Could you tell us how we might . . . know . . . that we were Beehive Girls?"

"Oh!" I pause, considering. "Well, you might have been a Beehive Girl if you had a bandelo or if you earned badges." I see a couple of nods. "You might have been a Beehive Girl if you had a blue and brown uniform and hiked a lot in Young Women. You might have been a Beehive Girl if you put on a bee-themed play or sang bee-themed songs." With each hint I give, I see more nods in the group. A couple of hands go up. (Perhaps your own hand just went up, too. I'd love to hear from you if it did.) I start making lists and planning interviews.

Now that I know which details ring bells for people, I go back to Nate's grandma and ask again if she was a Beehive Girl. She still has an alibi: she was the only teenage girl in her ward in Wisconsin and no one ran a Beehive Girl program just for her. We suspect that *her* mother was a Beehive Girl but we only have circumstantial evidence: her Provo upbringing at the right time, her strong group of female friends, and the program from a comedic opera she and her peers put on as missionaries. Missionaries staging an opera—can you imagine?

When I go back to my own grandmother and give her additional details, there's finally a spark of recognition. She sends me a picture of her with her swarm at a stake activity in 1955. "I was a Beehive! I hadn't heard of Beehive Girls. . . . I was probably too young to even know there was a name for it, but of *course* I had a bandelo and of *course* I earned things!" She doesn't remember what they did for activities or how she earned badges, but she remembers that she had good teachers and enjoyed her time.

That's the same message I get from interviews with the former Beehive Girls I've found in my ward. Their memories seamlessly integrate Primary with Beehives and, by the fifties, apparently, no one called them Beehive Girls. My friend Diana recalls, "One of my duties at Camp Lamondi was to pick ferns to put in a vase on the mantle of the fireplace—each of us had different duties to do. We worked on crafts and we made little necklaces with a little piece of wood that we cut and polished and strung on a string." Diana tells me that, sure, a fifteen-mile hike she went on as a MiaMaid wasn't something she would have done with her family, but only when I start asking very pointed questions ("Did you get to try anything *new* in Beehive Girls that you otherwise wouldn't have?").

It was just church stuff for them. They went to camp. They sang songs. They made crafts. They had fun. Sixty or seventy years later, not much stands out at all. Maybe things would be different if I talked to a Beehive Girl of the twenties or thirties . . . but maybe not.

So after extremely close inspection, I can say that the purposes of the 1915 YLMIA seem very similar to those of today's Young Women program. Leaders provided a gospel education and taught teenage girls to do wholesome things with their spare time. Fun activities brought girls closer together, including girls who weren't members of the Church of Jesus Christ of Latter-day Saints. As a group, teenagers could serve their wards and communities, finding adult ways to belong and contribute. The Beehive Girls program left space for girls to explore their individual interests and develop new talents. Leaders also facilitated travel to temples, mountains, and conferences, sacred spaces where girls were receptive to spiritual experiences. All of this is familiar.

Also familiar are the generational differences that encouraged the YLMIA general board to create Beehive Girls in the first place.To the mothers of these girls, the education their high school students were receiving must have seemed unrecognizable. Higher education and a job outside the home—maybe even a career!—became an acceptable stop along the way to motherhood. There were new standards for caring for children and homes, standards communicated by pamphlets, periodicals, and physicians instead of by word of mouth from experienced mothers. As with every generation, there were new fashions of dress, speech, and behavior that left older people aghast and concerned. Then, as now, the United States was wracked with war, pandemics, and economic turmoil.

Some things about early YLMIA, though, look very different from now. The information available through the YLMIA was somewhat comprehensive, covering everything that high school didn't: if the girls couldn't learn anatomy, wilderness skills, and sewing through church activities and periodicals, they might not have anywhere else to learn.

It was also a time when general women's auxiliary leaders were in constant, public communication with ward and stake leaders and with the girls themselves. They actively encouraged wards to submit ideas for activities and programs, which they then published or, occasionally, instituted churchwide. The annual June Conference brought together youth and leaders from faraway stakes, where they performed together, competed against one another, and heard from their general leaders. This collaborative, egalitarian model is worth emulating through all kinds of organizations.

I'm sad about how forgotten the Beekeepers are. Beekeepers gave so much of themselves and felt that they had an enduring impact on their adolescent charges, yet most Latter-day Saints don't even remember the program, not even those who were Beehive Girls themselves. How is that possible? What other dedicated work have we forgotten?

For a while, I thought that Priesthood Correlation ended the Beehive Girls program once and for all in 1970, but that is only true on a technicality. I no longer care about reading the restricted minutes from the meeting where the program ended. The Beehive Girls program began changing as soon as it was created. Its transition from a corollary to the Boy Scouts to a corollary to the Young Men happened gradually, over decades. Instead of being a distinct summer program, the Beehive Girls became year-round and somewhat interconnected with the weekly YLMIA lessons. For convenience, girls stopped advancing from rank to rank based on achievement and started advancing class to class based on age. As high school social life engaged the older girls, the Beehive Girls age group got younger and smaller. The Young Woman's Journal merged with the boys' Improvement Era, then the co-ed Improvement Era came under the direct authority of the Quorum of the Twelve Apostles and turned into the New Era. Funding and oversight for all the auxiliaries became centralized. The girls were left with Personal Progress, while the Scouting-style elements were replaced with . . . well, nothing. Camp Certification. From what I've read of the Beekeepers' herculean efforts to keep the girls interested in hiking and badges, this might have been the best choice available.

I thought I would come away from Beehive Girls telling everyone around me to try it out too. I was wrong. Beehive Girls is like every other program adults come up with to keep the kids off the streets and out of trouble. It's based on what the grown-ups want the kids to learn rather than what the kids are really interested in. It has a reward structure that grown-ups hope will motivate kids to stay involved. While this kind of loving manipulation is pretty recognizable to most teenagers, it's completely transparent to me as an adult. Beehive Girls isn't a moral or religious good. It's just activities. I have no desire to start a Beehive Girls movement.

In 2020, Personal Progress, Duty to God, and Church-sponsored Scouting all came to an end in favor of new programs. The new material is meant to be more adaptable to various cultures, circumstances, and individuals. My guess is that it will also be dramatically cheaper for the Church and for individual participants. Hopefully, it will nurture Young Men and Young Women in a more equitable way. The YLMIA general board were pioneers in creating a program to meet Mormons' unique needs, and now the tradition continues.

I hope that we will never become complacent about our programming for youth—that we'll never stop asking the big questions. What is important for a teenage girl to know as she begins her adult life? What is the proper place of a church program in preparing young women? What differences make sense between the girls' church education and the boys'? Are there any differences that should be done away with? What does the Young Women general board do and why don't we hear from them anymore? What if the young women *did* hear from them and knew who they were? How can we help our youth connect with their church heritage? What is a spiritual education without manipulation? And now that adolescence has been invented, what should we be doing with it?

🐝 &⸮ 🐝

I've finished my rank. (If you've been keeping track, I need to reassure you that I played the games, I wrote the menus, I've studied first aid, and I attended plenty of lectures. They weren't worth writing about.)

By all rights, there should be a ceremony where I receive my Builder in the Hive and maybe pantomime the work of gathering honey in costume, coordinated with my swarm. There's not going to be a ceremony, though, and not *just* because I don't have a swarm: Nate and Jane and I have transplanted ourselves once again, this time to St. Paul, Minnesota. We have some extended family here, but we left behind all of the people, places, traditions, and work that made Ann Arbor home. In the move from Utah to Michigan, my Beehive Girls project served as a tie to my homeland and culture. Now, I carry its lessons with me.

I think back to the empty new hive in The Life of the Bee: "Here, in the new abode, there is nothing; not a drop of honey, not a morsel of wax, neither guiding-mark nor point of support. . . . But useless regrets are unknown to the bee; or in any event it does not allow them to hinder its action." I've learned some skills. I know how to re-build.

As a Beehive Girl, I dipped my toe into a lot of things that I would not normally do, learning which I'd like to pursue and which I would not. I allowed myself to spend time on activities that I did not get paid for and that nobody required me to do. I did things I was bad at without an accompanying bad attitude. I looked outside myself. I stuck with a goal even when it felt overwhelming. I had failures and tried again. I looked for mentors and asked for help. I spent time with people more creatively than social norms encourage. I got to know my Latter-day Saint foremothers in all their day-to-day creativity, diligence, and love. I learned about a century of Church history that I'd somehow missed before. I learned values that will shape my decisions from here on out. I gained confidence in my ability to decide. I called multiple strangers on the phone.

If there were a Builder in the Hive ceremony for me, the list of invitees would spiral out of control. Cole would be there, Aunt Andrea, Patti, Amy, Catherine, and Shelby, for sure. They actually know about my project. Others—the goatkeeper, the chicken farmer, the Chief of Police and his wife, the reenactors, the lacemakers, the beekeepers, the tour guides, the librarians, my young women—have no idea how important and timely their influence was. And since getting all of these people to one place at one time is already a fantasy, my ceremony might as well defy the space-time continuum to include Susa, Mina, Adella, Mattie, Great-Grandma Erma, and all my Local Women:

Jane, Emmeline, Minerva, Julia, Chieko, Georgina. And my family, of course. Always my family.

What felt routine for all of these people did not feel routine to me. Their stories and generosity will always be part of me. And maybe in the end, my adult perspective just gives me a more mindful, grateful version of the regular Beehive Girls experience. The love, thought, and effort of countless leaders blended together to become, for generations of young Latter-day Saint women, the very air they breathed.

WOMANHO.

APPENDIX

AS A SCIENTIST, I can't shake the feeling that every sentence of this book is supposed to have a citation, but I've been informed that that is not how it works in creative nonfiction and memoir. Instead, I've included a short list of resources relevant to the history covered in *Beehive Girl* plus some of the modern-day organizations and locations I encountered along the way. I'm including the hymns I've written with Nate, in case your ward choir or barbershop quartet is interested in something new. Most exciting of all, I'm including the entire original Beehive Girls manual so you can get a swarm going in your own neighborhood.

Just kidding. Mostly.

RELEVANT WEBSITES

@evoluo.art
> My incredibly talented friend, Brenna Adams, did the embroidery for the cover of this book—check out her Instagram handle to see more of her work

http://www.georginabringas.com/
> This is the website for Georgina Bringas, the artist I wrote about for the last life sketch in the book.

https://whitelotusfarms.com/
This is the farm where I tried my hand at milking goats. If you're ever in the area, you should go on a Saturday and get a pizza!

https://www.fordhouse.org/
You too can visit the estate of Edsel and Eleanor Ford!

https://www.awhc.org/
The American West Heritage Center is the historic farm I visited in Cache Valley, Utah.

https://www.a2b2club.org/
I was never really a member of Ann Arbor Backyard Bee-keepers, but they were *so* welcoming and I'd recommend them to anyone local who wants to learn about bees.

http://www.keepapitchinin.org/
This is the most amazing "amateur" blog about Latter-day Saint history, run by Ardis Parshall. She doesn't know me, but I owe her a huge debt of gratitude for teaching me about our history and showing me that it's okay to be passionate about it even if you don't have all the right scholarly credentials.

https://history.churchofjesuschrist.org/landing/church-history-library
You too can visit the Church History Library! Photos, documents, old bandelos—they've got it all.

https://www.centerforlatterdaysaintarts.org/
This is the organization that hosted the festival where we sang my hymn. If you're interested in music, dance, theater, visual art, or literature by Latter-day Saint and adjacent artists, this is where you'll find your people.

https://archive.org/

This is where I found scans of all the Church magazines I read during the course of researching this book: The Young Woman's Journal, Woman's Exponent, Juvenile Instructor, Relief Society Magazine, etc. You can also find the entire Beehive Girl manual!

https://exponentii.org/

This magazine (and blog) are the spiritual successors of the original Woman's Exponent.

RECOMMENDED READING

Daughters in My Kingdom: The History and Work of Relief Society

Women of Covenant: The Story of the Relief Society, by Janeth Russell Cannon, Jill M. Derr, and Maureen Ursenbach Beecher

Keepers of the Flame, by Janet Peterson and LaRene Gaunt (This is the book about the presidents of the YLMIA.)

Women and Authority: Re-Emerging Mormon Feminism, edited by Maxine Hanks (This is the book where I got the accounts of women giving childbirth blessings.)

History of the Ladies' Mutual Improvement Association of the Church of Jesus Christ of L.D.S., from November 1869 to June 1910, by Susa Young Gates

Emmeline B. Wells: An Intimate History, by Carol Cornwall Madsen

WITH LOAVES AND FISHES

Mikayla Orton Thatcher

Nathan Thatcher

With loaves and fish - es, Lord, You give us dai - ly
You've shown us once a - gain Your pow'r to still the
We come be - fore You, Lord, to give a - way our
We know by whom we're led. We praise You for Your

bread. You feed and guard us well:
storm: You've filled us with Your peace; sir - it,
sin, To root out this e - vil Spi - rit,
sight. We've seen Your hand and learned

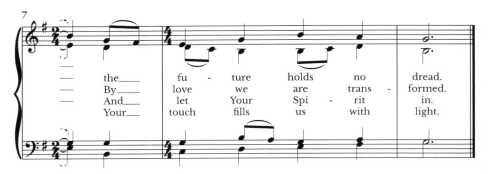

the fu - ture holds no dread.
By love we are trans - formed.
And let Your Spi - rit in.
Your touch fills us with light.

FROM OUR GOD IS ALL WE OWN

Mikayla Orton Thatcher

Nathan Thatcher

GOD OF OUR CHILDREN

Mikayla Orton Thatcher   Nathan Thatcher

God of our chil - dren, help us make a home for them—
God of the need - y, show us how to tru - ly give
God of the out - cast, par - don us where we have failed.

Ha - vens of safe - ty to learn and to grow.
Our hearts and sub - stance, so all may be filled.
Help us make space for all souls to be - long.

God of our el - ders, teach us how to love through
God of the help - less, we will, with Your aid, build
God of cre - a - tion, we strive to be one, by

GOD OF OUR CHILDREN

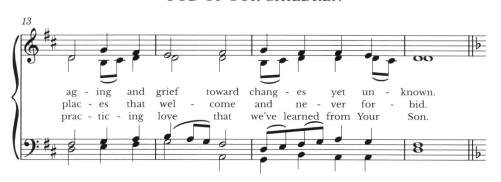

ag - ing and grief toward chang - es yet un - known.
plac - es that wel - come and ne - ver for - bid.
prac - tic - ing love that we've learned from Your Son.

Fa - ther, Mo - ther, help us feed your lambs. Teach us how to

lift the droop - ing hands. You know all our hun - gers and our

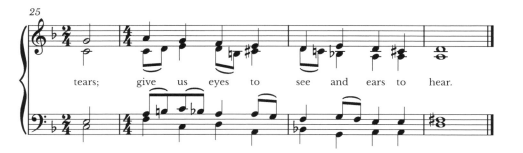

tears; give us eyes to see and ears to hear.

BEE-HIVE GIRLS·

·GIRLS·

·1915·

·Y·L·M·I·A·

HAND BOOK

FOR THE

BEE-HIVE GIRLS

OF THE

Y. L. M. I. A.

FIRST EDITION
1915

PUBLISHED BY

THE GENERAL BOARD OF
THE YOUNG LADIES' MUTUAL
IMPROVEMENT ASSOCIATION

BISHOP'S BUILDING,
SALT LAKE CITY, UTAH

DOWN BY THE BROOK.

The Bee-Hive Girls.

EVER since the organization of the Young Ladies' Mutual Improvement Association, something over forty years ago, the officers have been endeavoring to place before the members those things which are most essential to the building of a perfect womanhood. We have a splendid organization and its influence has been powerful in the lives of thousands of girls who have filled its ranks, powerful in helping them to be better daughters, better sisters, better wives and better mothers. For several years past the idea has been growing that we need to make our work concrete, to give our members an opportunity to work with their hands, to show results from the training they receive. Some months ago, with this purpose in view the General Board appointed a committee to study the subject and to submit plans. The plans have been submitted and approved. They are necessarily crude but we feel that with the blessing of our Heavenly Father, whose aid we invoke, this work may become not only a joy to our girls but a great force in the development of their womanhood.

The Committee wishes to acknowledge its indebtedness to the Girl Guide Movement, The Boy Scouts, and the Camp Fire Girls; and to Maurice Maeterlinck whose poetic version of the "Life of the Bee" has been a constant source of inspiration and joy.

I.

The General Plan.

THE NAME is to be the "Bee-Hive Girls."

THE PURPOSE is to perfect our womanhood,—to hold the faith of our fathers and to develop it in our individual womanhood, drawing from all good sources to do so.

THE ORGANIZATION is to be presided over by our regular Y. L. M. I. A. officers. Each Ward should organize one or more swarms, according to the number of its members. A swarm consists of from eight to twelve; it may be larger if necessity requires, but the officer in charge can keep in touch with her girls better if the swarm is small. The swarm is to be in charge of a Bee-Keeper and an Assistant Bee-Keeper; it is to have a name and a symbol.

MEMBERSHIP is open to all Y. L. M. I. A. members and to any others who desire to join and are willing to comply with the requirements.

RANKS. When a girl first joins she is called simply a "Bee-Hive Girl". When she earns a certain number of awards, or, in other words, fills a certain number of cells she is promoted to the rank of "Builder in the Hive"; a certain number more, to that of "Gatherer of the Honey"; still certain others, to that of "Keeper of the Bees". Generally one rank will be attained each year, but there is no time limit set; if a girl fills her cells rapidly, she may advance rapidly. From the third rank in the future Bee-Keepers will likely be chosen; but a girl may have this rank without being chosen to become a Bee-Keeper.

MEETINGS. Once each month, during the summer, it is designed to have a gathering of all the ward swarms, presided over by the ward president of the Y. L. M. I. A. Some officers may choose to distribute the seals at this meeting, but the General Board leaves this matter in the hands of the stake and local officers. The swarms should meet separately once a week except in the week when the regular monthly swarm gathering is held. The programs should vary, according to the need of the girls; they may have out-door games, a cooking class, a sewing circle, a meeting to learn stenciling or clay-modeling; take a long tramp, studying flowers, trees, birds, rocks; present an out-door play, have a breakfast party, an evening to study the stars. Suggestions as to programs will be printed from time to time in the "Journal".

The ACTIVITY of a hive is from May to September, but the swarms keep alive during the entire year. Opportunity should be given the girls to receive their awards once each month, as a large portion of the work can be carried along during the regular M. I. A. season, and in some cases, it takes one year to earn the award, for instance in attendance at Mutual, Sunday School, etc.

AWARDS. As a hive is made up of cells filled with different kinds of honey, pollen, eggs, larvae, so are our bodies made up of cells filled with the different elements taken into them, so is womanhood built and perfected by the different things we gather through our experiences in various fields. The Bee-Hive Girl will fill two kinds of cells: Foundation cells, those required to be filled by each member before she can advance to a higher rank; Structural cells, those which she will select and fill from seven fields. Of the Structural cells there are also two kinds—new and continuous. A cell is "new" the first time it is filled. It is "continuous" (marked c) when it may be re-filled again and again, as in the case of Nos. 19 and 146. It is also continuous, like Nos. 102 and 108, when it may be repeated but must be done in a different way (marked "c. d.") The seven fields are Religion, Home, Health, Domestic Arts, Out of Doors, Business, Public Service. An award is made for each cell filled. The girls receive awards from the time the swarm is organized; the Executive officers of the Y. L. M. I. A. and the Bee-Keepers may have credit for past attainment. It is desirable for the Bee-Keepers, and other officers, to take an active part and to fill the cells for themselves, as it will tend to unite them with their girls.

THE DRESS. For the present it is optional whether or not the girls have a special dress. For those who desire it, it is to be a rather short skirt, (or bloomers for a hike), with middy-blouse and neck tie. Brown skirt, khaki-colored middy, and light blue tie might be chosen; or it may be varied to suit the desire of the swarm, except that we must keep to the colors of the organization—brown, light blue and gold.

The WATCHWORD is Womanho (pronounced with a long o; the a as in father; and an accent on the second syllable). "Wo" stands for work; "man" for mankind; "ho" for home; and the three taken together spell "Womanhood" except for the last two letters which are dropped.

SONGS. Some have been specially written for us; they will be found in this book, and the April and May numbers of the "Journal".

The Womanho Call.

Music by TRACY Y. CANNON.

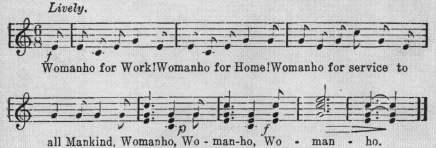

Lively.

Womanho for Work! Womanho for Home! Womanho for service to all Mankind, Womanho, Wo - man-ho, Wo - man - ho.

The Call of Womanhood.

Music by Tracy Y. Cannon.

Slowly and with deep feeling.

Faith in Woman- hood! Joy in Wo-man - hood! Splen - dor in Wom-an-hood, Strong and se-

* Note—Here, and at the corresponding place in the second verse, a swell on the note D, is effective, taking only a quick breath before the next word.

II.

Membership and Rank.

In order to become a Bee-Hive Girl the applicant must:
1st, Know the purpose of the organization.
2nd, Have read the hand-book.
3rd, Express her desire to become a member, and to abide by the Spirit of the Hive, which she must repeat from memory.

Spirit of the Hive.

Have Faith
Seek Knowledge
Safeguard Health
Honor Womanhood
Understand Beauty
Know Work
Love Truth
Taste the sweetness of Service
Feel Joy

Having become a Bee-Hive Girl, she begins to direct her efforts toward filling those cells which will entitle her to advancement.

To become a

BUILDER IN THE HIVE

a girl must fill the following

Foundation Cells.

1. Have been a Mutual Improvement or Bee-Hive Girl at least two months.
2. Select a name and a symbol.
3. Take an average of at least one-half hour's daily exercise out of doors for two months.
4. Sleep out of doors or with wide open windows for two months.
5. Know the vertical line test for correct posture of body. (See "Young Woman's Journal", May, 1915).
6. Set a table tastefully, having dishes clean and properly arranged, with clean linen and some simple seasonable decoration.
7. Mend at least one piece of her own clothing each week for two months, not delaying it until ready to wear the article.

8. Pay her dime fund for the current year.

9. Every day for one month do at least one good turn, quietly and without boasting. It may be done at home, to a member of the family, as well as elsewhere.

Structural Cells.

Fill in addition, eighteen new structural cells and eighteen continuous ones. At least two cells must be filled in each field and not more than ten in any one. In case of a shortage of continuous cells new ones may be substituted. And she must memorize and repeat

The Builder's Purpose.

As bees bring to their building
Obedient and purposeful service,
So, into the Hive of Life,
I enter to do my part.
Faith I have from my fathers,
Faith to move me to action.
Health I hold in my keeping,
Health to guard and to cherish,
That Life may come to my children
Pure and in limitless power.

Having fulfilled the above requirements, and repeated the "Builder's Purpose" the girl may have conferred upon her the rank of "Builder in the Hive". The color for this rank is brown and the one who has attained it is entitled to wear the following emblem on her sleeve.

To become a

GATHERER OF THE HONEY

a girl must fill the following

Foundation Cells.

1. With assistance of one other person prepare and serve at least two family meals, setting the table tastefully with

brightly polished dishes, clean linen, and some simple, seasonable decoration.

2. For at least one month, refrain between meals from candy, chewing gum, sundaes, sodas, and commercially manufactured beverages.

3. During two months take an average of at least one-half hour daily out-door exercise.

4. Sleep out of doors or with wide open windows for two months.

5. Know about the proper use of hot and cold baths, care of the hands, teeth, cleanliness of the hair and its appropriate dressing.. (See "Young Woman's Journal" for Jan., 1915).

6. Mend at least two pieces of clothing each week for two months, and do it in time to save the proverbial nine stitches.

7. Pay her dime fund for the current year.

8. Study the revelation containing the Word of Wisdom (Sec. 89, Doc. & Cov.) Explain its meaning (See "Young Woman's Journal," Vol. 15, page 41, or "Joseph Smith as Scientist," Chap. 13). Obey it for at least two months.

9. Read one book of the M. I. A. Reading Course.

10. Know and sing all the words of her National Anthem.

Structural Cells.

Fill in addition eighteen new structural cells and eighteen continuous ones chosen as mentioned above.

She must also memorize and repeat

The Honey Gatherer's Song.

Out in the dew sparkling dawn I dart
Straight to the fragrant flower heart.
Skies are blue and days are fair
Honey lies hidden everywhere.
      Joy to gather my share!

Youth is fair as the dewy morn.
Sing the gladness of having been born
When the sun of knowledge is shining clear,
Where nature's beauty is calling near.
      Joy to see and to hear!

Knowledge is sun of youth's bright day.
Gather and store its golden ray
To light the mind, whose hidden fire
Burns in growth of the soul's desire.
      Joy to kindle this fire!

A girl having fulfilled all the requirements and repeated the words of the "Honey Gatherer's Song", may have the rank of "Gatherer of the Honey" conferred upon her. She is then entitled to add the blue flower to the emblem she already wears; the blue violet is chosen because it means "faithfulness," and the color (light blue) is chosen for the rank because it is the favorite color of the bees.

To become a

KEEPER OF THE BEES

a girl must fill the following

Foundation Cells.

1. Keep her own clothing in repair for at least two months, doing the mending on time and not leaving it until ready to wear it.

2. Prepare and serve two family meals without assistance, and on time, doing the necessary purchasing, setting the table tastefully, having the dishes clean.

3. Outline two programs for enjoyable family home nights.

4. Keep a written account of all money received and spent during one month, classifying it under heads of food, clothing, amusements, tithing, reserve fund, etc.

5. Read Maeterlinck's "Life of the Bee".

6. Commit to memory poem of not less than twenty-five lines.

Structural Cells.

Fill in addition eighteen new structural cells and eighteen continuous cells, chosen as mentioned in Chapter one.

She must also memorize and repeat

The Bee Keeper's Service.

I love the Bees. I recognize the power of that unseen Spirit of the Hive to which each bee re-responds. To work in harmony with that spirit,— loving girlhood, honoring womanhood, guarding motherhood, working in joy today, and with faith turning my eyes ever toward the future— herein lies my bee-keeper's service and its recompense.

Having now won a sufficient number of awards, the highest rank—that of the "Keeper of the Bees" is conferred upon the candidate, and she is entitled to add the queen bee to her emblem. The color of this rank is gold.

WATCH THE OFFICERS NOTES in the "Journal" every month for additional suggestions and announcements.

III.

Awards.

As soon as a girl fills a cell the Bee-Keeper awards her a seal, indicating the field in which she earned it. The colors of the various fields are: purple, for Religion; orange, for Home; red, for Health; brown, for Domestic Arts; green, for Out of Doors; gold, for Business; red, white and blue, for Public Service; and light blue for the Foundation Cells. A special seal marked C is provided for the continuous cells.

Immediately upon receiving the seal, the girl should open her handbook, of which every girl must have a copy, turn

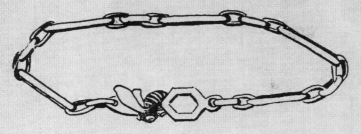

Bracelet.

to the individual record page of the field in which she earned it,
and fasten the seal on that page. She should then write opposite the seal the number of the cell which she filled, and a
brief statement that will serve to remind her of what it was.
The handbook should be preserved in good condition and become one of the most valued books in the girl's library.

These seals, taken in connection with the emblem described in Chapter II, make a system of awards, complete in
itself. However, we have designed something else which each
girl is permitted to buy and wear, as she attains the different
ranks, providing she, herself, earns the money to buy it. It can
be purchased only through the General Board, and on the
written certification of the Bee-Keeper, who must certify that
the girl has won the rank and has earned the money for the
purchase.

In selecting this larger award, we were guided by our
desire to provide something of permanent value to the girl; to

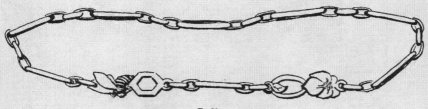

Collar.

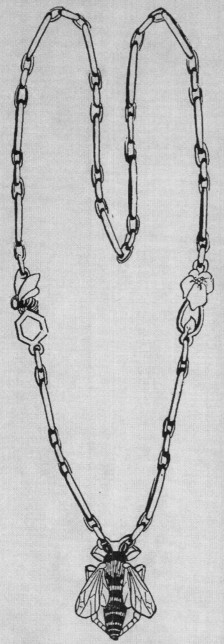

have it the best thing of its kind, and yet something that is not too expensive. We finally decided upon a silver chain, the links of which represent the awards,—one small link for each new structural cell and one large link for three continuous cells. This will make eighteen small links and six large links for each rank. Upon attaining the first rank the girl may purchase the first section of the chain, including a motif representing a bee at work on a cell—a Builder in the Hive; this section to be worn as a bracelet. When she wins the second rank, she may purchase another section, with the violet as a motif; the two sections to be joined and worn as a collar. The third rank sees the completion of the chain with the queen bee as a pendant, the whole to be worn as a necklace.

The cost of the chain cannot be stated positively at present, but will be announced later in the "Journal". To any girl who can weld her own links the chain will come much cheaper; she will also be allowed an award in the Domestic Art field for the welding.

GENERAL BOARD AWARDS. In addition to the regular awards the General Board will make awards for photographs, songs, plays, stories, etc., that may be of value to them in the general work. In taking photographs, those showing the girls actually at work or in action are the most desirable.

IV.

Bee-Keepers and Their Duties.

The success of the Bee-Hive will depend, largely, upon the Bee-Keepers; accordingly it will be necessary to select them wisely. Generally it will be well to choose people who have not been bearing the brunt of the regular Mutual Improvement work. Sometimes it will be a mother, even though she may not have been a regular M. I. member; sometimes a girl; sometimes an older woman; but always she should be in sympathy with girls, and capable of leading them to love the right kind of things.

The Bee-Keeper is not expected to know everything herself, but she should be glad to learn with her girls and capable of enlisting the help of others to teach them. Having looked over the people of her neighborhood and decided upon those who can teach the various things the swarm wants to learn, she should talk with those individuals, awaken their interest, secure their services and co-operate with them in arranging what is needed to enable them to demonstrate their work. She may need the instruction of a scout-master, a doctor, a nurse, an artist, a musician, a housekeeper, or a cook; or she may need them all at various times; but let her remember that it is intended for the girls to do things at the meetings rather than to be talked to. Her success will depend largely upon her ability to find out what the girls want to do, and her power to guide them in the doing of it, leading them gradually from less desirable things to those which are most truly beautiful and worthy.

The Bee-Keeper should help her girls to select a name and a symbol for the swarm and an individual name and symbol for each girl. Flower names will be appropriate as it is from the flowers the honey is gathered; but names may be made up from the qualities the girls desire to possess, for instance: one girl is desirous of having strength which will help her to be full of gladness—she might choose "Strengla".

The Bee-Keeper should read the Handbook carefully, studying the cells which are to be filled; she should make a list of the cells each girl elects to fill, and then opposite each number should write the date on which the award is made. In this way she will have the individual record of her girls which must correspond with the record each girl keeps. All awards must pass through her hands, or, if they are made by the ward president at the monthly gathering, must be given on her certification.

It will be part of the Bee-Keeper's duty to help the girls plan a means of earning money for the necessities of the swarm. Each girl may buy the handbook individually, or the swarm may earn the money for it, as well as for the necessary awards, but each girl must own a handbook.

A tremendous task? No. Dear Bee-Keeper, it will prove a delight to be with young and growing girls, to feel your own youth renewed in their joys and sorrows, to broaden their view, to increase their love for work, for home, for service to all mankind.

A SONG OF THE BEES.

By Ruth May Fox.

(To be sung to the tune of "Up-i-dee", found in most any collection of College songs, or on page 88 of "Heart Songs.")

The day dawns fresh and glorious
Busy bees, busy bees,
The lamp of loves hangs over us,
Busy, busy bees;
While on the wing our songs we'll sing,
With joy we'll make the echoes ring.
Busy bees, O, busy bees, busy bees, busy bees.
Happy we, O, happy we, happy, happy we!
*Bzzzzzzzzzzzzzzzzzzzzzzzz
Buzz, Buzz, Buzz, Buzz.

A lillie bell, now, don't you tell,
Busy bees, busy bees,
Lisped to me where the fairies dwell,
Busy, busy bees.
They're gay and fair, beware, beware;
They'll lure your hearts, take care, take care!
Busy bees, O, busy bees, busy bees, busy bees;
Happy we, O, happy we, happy, happy we!
*Bzzzzzzzzzzzzzzzzzzzzzzzz
Buzz, Buzz, Buzz, Buzz.

From doubt be free, and you shall see,
Busy bees, busy bees.
An elf dance with a honey bee,
Busy, busy bees;
We'll laugh and skip, their nectar sip,
Then down the hills and dales we'll trip,
Busy bees, O, busy bees, busy bees, busy bees,
Happy we, O, happy we, happy, happy we!
*Bzzzzzzzzzzzzz zzzzzzzzzzzz
Buzz, Buzz, Buzz, Buzz.

*Buzz like a bee.

REFERENCES.

Back volumes of the "Young Woman's Journal".
"Handbook of The Boy Scouts of America", (25c)
Bulletins of the Agricultural College, Logan, Utah.
Bulletins of the Department of Agriculture, Washington. D. C.

IN THE HIVE "THERE IS ONE MASTERPIECE, THE HEXAGONAL
CELL, THAT TOUCHES ABSOLUTE PERFECTION, _ A PERFECTION →
THAT ALL THE GENIUSES IN THE WORLD, WERE THEY TO MEET
IN CONCLAVE, COULD IN NO WAY ENHANCE." ┼ ┼ ┼ ┼ ┼
LIFE OF THE BEE.

No. 1

No. 2

No. 3

No. 4

No. 5

No. 6

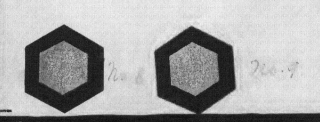

No. 8   No. 9

LIFT UP YOUR HEARTS AND BE GLAD, FOR I AM IN YOUR
MIDST, AND AM YOUR ADVOCATE WITH THE FATHER; AND
IT IS HIS GOOD WILL TO GIVE YOU THE KINGDOM
— DOCTRINE & COVENANTS

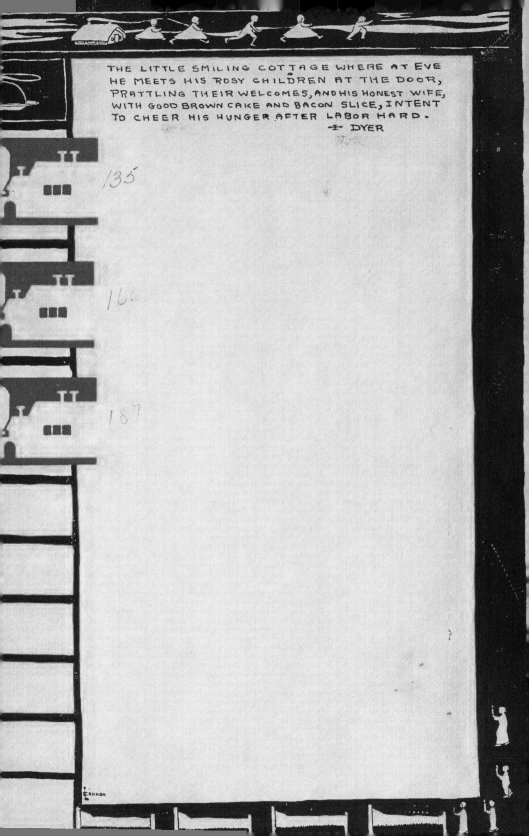

THE LITTLE SMILING COTTAGE WHERE AT EVE
HE MEETS HIS ROSY CHILDREN AT THE DOOR,
PRATTLING THEIR WELCOMES, AND HIS HONEST WIFE,
WITH GOOD BROWN CAKE AND BACON SLICE, INTENT
TO CHEER HIS HUNGER AFTER LABOR HARD.

— DYER

135

160

187

HEALTH

BETTER TO HUNT IN FIELDS FOR HEALTH UNBOUGHT

THAN FEE THE DOCTOR FOR A NAUSEOUS DROUGHT

THE WISE FOR CURE ON EXERCISE DEPEND;

GOD NEVER MADE HIS WORK FOR MAN TO MEND.

DRYDEN

401

416

416

4 62

423

NATURE NEVER DID BETRAY ❧ THE HEART THAT LOVED HER; 'TIS HER
PRIVILEGE ❧ THROUGH ALL THE YEARS OF THIS OUR LIFE, TO LEAD
FROM JOY TO JOY ⬗⬖ ⬗⬖ WORDSWORTH ⬗⬖ ⬗⬖ ⬗⬖ ⬗⬖ ⬗⬖

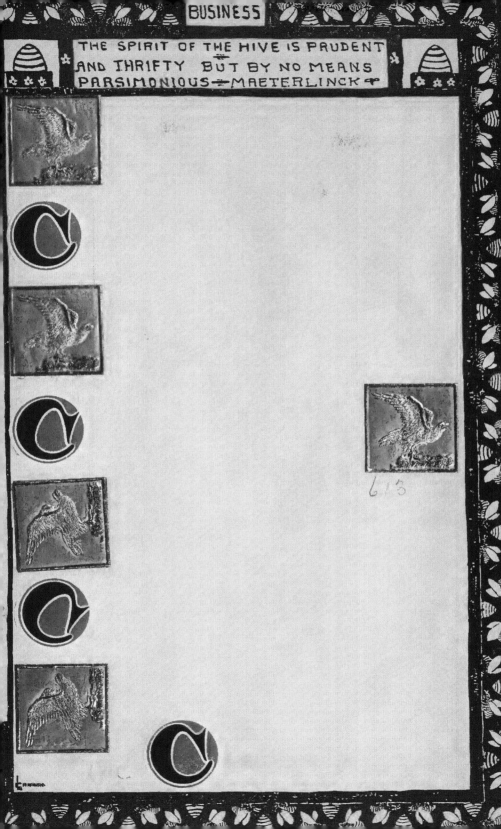

BUSINESS

THE SPIRIT OF THE HIVE IS PRUDENT
AND THRIFTY BUT BY NO MEANS
PARSIMONIOUS—MAETERLINCK

Structural Cells.

FIELD OF RELIGION.

(Purple Seal.)

The god of the bees is the future. When we, in our study of human history, endeavor to gauge the moral force or greatness of a people or race, we have but one standard of measurement—the dignity and permanence of their ideal, and the abnegation wherewith they pursue it.—Life of the Bee, by Maurice Mæterlinck.

1. Be able to repeat the Ten Commandments, the Beatitudes, and the Articles of Faith.
2. Know and be able to show in what fundamental principles the faith of the Latter-day Saints differs from that of other Christian denominations.
3. Give brief account of the work of the Apostles Peter and Paul, making special note of their prophecies regarding the Apostasy.
4. Give brief account of the work of Martin Luther, John Knox, and John Calvin.
5. Give brief account of the Restoration of the Gospel through the Prophet Joseph Smith.
6. Name and give brief sketch of the lives of each of the Presidents of the Church of Jesus Christ of Latter-day Saints.
7. Name the present General Authorities of the Church of Jesus Christ of Latter-day Saints—First Presidency, Quorum of Twelve, Seven Presidents of Seventy, Presiding Bishopric, Patriarch.
8. Give brief account of the life and labors of Elmina S. Taylor and Martha H. Tingey, presidents of the Y. L. M. I. A.
9. Give brief account of the life and labors of four other local women who have done much good in Church service. c. d.
10. Commit to memory Sec. 59, Doc. and Cov.; give proper observance to the Sabbath day for three months. c.
11. Attend sacrament meeting at least eight times in three months. c.
12. Belong to Sunday School for one year, and miss no more than six sessions. c.
13. Belong to the Y. L. M. I. A. for one year and miss no more than six meetings.
14. Prepare every lesson in the Y. L. M. I. A. Senior Course for one year. c.
15. Prepare every lesson in the Y. L. M. I. A. Junior Course for one year. c.
16. Write an essay on the organization of the Y. L. M. I. A.
17. Observe the law of tithing for one year, paying it monthly or at the time your pay is received. c.
18. Memorize verses 5-21 of Sec. 89, Doctrine and Covenants; explain meaning; observe the Word of Wisdom for two months. A "continuous" seal may be awarded for each six months thereafter.
19. Teach a class of not less than ten for three months in connection with a ward organization. c.
20. For three months respond to all calls made upon you in the ward organizations to which you belong. c.
21. Write out prayers suitable for three different occasions; for in-

stance, opening or closing a meeting, family prayer, for a group on a camping trip, a blessing on the food; during three months offer prayer whenever called upon.

22. Each day for one month, commit to memory a quotation from either Bible, Book of Mormon, or Doctrine and Covenants. c. d.
23. Memorize five hymns from L. D. S. Hymn Book, selecting those which you like best. c. d.
24. Read ten books of the Old Testament. c. d.
25. Read the New Testament.
26. Read the Book of Mormon (two awards). [This does not mean the "Story of the Book of Mormon."]
27. Read the Doctrine and Covenants.
28. Read the Pearl of Great Price.
29. Have a talk with some pioneer of 1847, of a hand-cart company, of the Mormon Battalion, of your town or state; write down facts obtained and read at Bee-Hive meeting. c. d.
30. Attend practice and sing weekly at religious services, in choir, chorus, quartette, or other musical organization, for not less than three months. c.
31. Play the piano or organ for at least one Sabbath service each week for three months. c.
32. Every day during one month repeat mentally the first and second great commandments (Mark 12:30, 31).

FIELD OF HOME.
(Orange Colored Seal.)

The queen * * * we shall most fitly describe by declaring her to be the captive heart of the city, and the centre around which its intelligence revolves.—Life of the Bee.

Cooking.

101. Make two kinds of bread and two of cake. c. d.
102. Cook meat in four ways. c. d.
103. Cook left-over meat in four different ways. c. d.
104. Cook each of three common vegetables in three ways. c. d.
105. Prepare two kinds of soup with meat and two with milk. c. d.
106. Prepare four salads, making at least two different dressings.. c. d.
107. Cook eggs in five ways. c. d.
108. Make bread and combine into five kinds of sandwiches. c. d.
109. Make four desserts—jellied, boiled, baked, frozen. c. d.
110. Prepare a gruel, a cereal, an egg, and milk or water toast as for an invalid (this may be done at different times); arrange tray attractively.
111. Gather two quarts of wild berries or fruits and make into jam or dessert. c. d.
112. Can or preserve three different kinds of fruit, at least two quarts of each. c. d.
113. Can three kinds of vegetables, at least two quarts of each. c. d.
114. Use fireless cooker successfully on meats, vegetables, cereals. c. d.
115. Use chafing dish successfully, preparing four appetizing dishes. c. d.
116. Write an appetizing, balanced vegetarian diet for one week.
117. Write a menu for two weeks for a girl in her teens, inclined to be too stout.
118. Write a menu for two weeks for a girl in her teens, inclined to be too thin.
119. Give examples of five expensive and five inexpensive nourishing foods, suitable for a person who does office work; for one who

does manual labor; give also five kinds of vegetables of value to all people.

120. Give examples of five foods with a laxative value, and five of the opposite kind.
121. Superintend cooking for two months in home, providing balanced menu, planning it for at least one week at a time. c. d.
122. Do cooking for one month in a home, providing well-balanced meals. c.
123. Assist in housework and cooking in some other home than your own for two months. c.
124. Three times make delicacies for the sick and send where needed under direction of the Relief Society. c.
125. Take care of milk and make two pounds of butter a week for two months. c.
126. Pluck, dress, and cook a fowl. c.

Marketing.

127. Describe characteristics and identify six cuts of meat; state market price of each.
128. Supply the table for one week (with all foods except flour and potatoes) at a cost of $1.00 per person, keeping accounts and records of menus.
129. Same as above, for $2.00 per person.
130. Know the best season for fruits and vegetables to be found in your locality, and a reasonable price for each.
131. Know the dangerous and common adulterations, also prices, of flour, sugar, rice, cereals, crackers, and bread.
132. Be familiar with the Pure Food laws of your State, and know how to secure full weight.

Laundering.

133. Do a washing for a family of six, using modern labor-saving devices, if possible; or twice assist, doing one-half of the work. c.
134. Iron six hours in one month. c.
135. Wash and iron a shirt-waist, a skirt, and a lingerie dress. c.
136. Clean and press a suit, or a skirt and coat. c.
137. Remove four common stains from wash material and two from non-washable material.
138. Use two methods each for softening water, bluing, bleaching; two kinds of soap and two of starch for different uses.

Housekeeping.

139. Do three hours of housework daily for one month. c.
140. Take complete charge of household for one week while mother has a vacation.
141. During two weeks keep the house free from flies, or destroy twenty-five flies daily. c.
142. Houseclean one room, caring well for floors, walls, carpet, rugs and furniture. c.
143. Sweep and dust a house of five rooms, using two kinds of sweeping or dusting compounds (or vacuum cleaner), and dust-absorbing or moist cloths. c.
144. Properly dispose of waste and garbage from the home; know its proper disposal by the city or if you live outside of city see that it is fed to animals, buried, or burned as the case requuires.
145. Know the proper airing and changing of bed; make up a bed for a baby, and one with a draw sheet for a very sick patient.

146. Air properly and make one bed daily for two months, or two beds daily for one month. c.
147. Wash and dry dishes and leave dining room in order after one meal a day for two months. c.
148. Take entire care of one room for one month, including all necessary cleaning, sweeping, dusting, washing of windows, etc.; also care of flowers and plants if there be any. c.
149. Air and store away clothing, furs, rugs, bedding for the summer.
150. Thoroughly clean the dining room, giving especial care to cupboards or buffet, silverware, china and glass. c.
151. Thoroughly clean the kitchen, giving proper care to pots, pans, aluminum and copper ware, lamps, sink and stove, including nickel trimmings on latter. c.
152. Take entire care of pantry for one month. c.
153. During two months scrub a floor once each week.c.
154. During two summer months clean ice chest thoroughly twice a week.c.
155. During two months take care of milk and cream from at least one cow; see that the pails, pans, strainer, are thoroughly cleaned. c.
156. During one month care for at least two kerosene lamps daily. c.
157. Successfully put a new washer on a faucet.
158. Build a furnace fire and care for it for one week. c.
159. During three months keep clothing in proper places, bureau drawers in order, and comb and brush clean. c.

Family Rights.

160. During three months honor the rights of other members of the family, by not using their personal belongings without their permission. c.
161. Name and observe three ways in which you can give consideration and proper respect to your mother as center of the home.
162. Name and observe three ways in which you can give consideration and proper respect to your father as head of the family.

Invention.

163. Invent a useful household device. c. d.
164. Contrive something to lessen a portion of the house work in your own home. c. d.

Care of the Sick.

165. Arrange a sick room to be sanitary, pleasant and comfortable for patient, and convenient for doctor and nurse.
166. Learn to use a clinical thermometer to find temperature of an adult and an infant; tell what temperature indicates normal, high and dangerous fever conditions.
167. Learn common symptoms as well as home care and prevention of chicken-pox, measles, scarlet fever, diphtheria, whooping cough and tuberculosis.
168. Learn some simple home treatment for prevention and cure of colds, including use of hot and cold water, and without use of drugs; for bronchitis, for pneumonia.
169. Learn simple home treatment for spasms, convulsions, nosebleed, cuts, bruises and sprains, inflammation, constipation.

Care of the Baby.

170. Learn the chief causes of infant mortality in summer; give methods for reducing the same.
171. Know the proper preparation of milk for a baby six months old; for a baby one year old; know how it can be tested.

172. Know how much a baby should increase in weight each week for the first six months, in height for each month of the first year; the relation of weight to health.
173. Know and describe three cries of a baby.
174. During one month care for a baby an average of one hour a day. c.
175. Make three playthings for a child. c. d.

Home Entertainment.

176. Memorize and sing alone five ballads or folk songs. c. d.
177. Play from memory five piano pieces of the difficulty of the "Bach Two Part Inventions," or "Chopin .Valtz, Op. 69, No. 2." c. d.
178. In any one month practice fifty hours on a musical instrument. c.
179. Know and tell five standard stories. c.
180. Recite from memory 500 lines of standard poetry. c. d.
181. Recite from memory an equivalent am unt of standard prose. c. d.
182. Write a play and have it presented. c. d.
183. Have a party of from eight to twelve persons, with refreshments that cost no more than one dollar; keep accounts. c. d.
184. During two months entertain two cr more little children for two hours a week. c.
185. Plan and give some social entertainment of a cultura: value. c. d.
186. Read three books of the M. I. A. Home Reading Course, one at least being not fiction. c. d.
187. Read three standard books, one at least being not fiction. c. d.

FIELD OF HEALTH.
(Red Seal.)

They carefully sweep the floor, and remove, one by one, twigs, grains of sand, and dead leaves; for the bees are almost fanatically cleanly.—Life of the Bee.

First Aid.

301. Know what to do for a person whose clothing is on fire; who is in deep water and can not swim, either in summer or through ice in winter; for an open cut; a frosted foot; fainting.
302. Know what to do to resuscitate a drowning person; to revive one from suffocation; for sun-stroke; for a punctured wound, like stepping on a nail; for poisoning by poison ivy, from snake-bite, from carbolic acid, from lye.
303. Know what to do for hemorrhage or bleeding; fractures· dislocations and sprains; burns and scalds; foreign bodies in eye, ear, or nose.
304. Demonstrate the principles of elementary bandaging, and how to use surgeon's plaster.

Personal Health.

305. Be entirely free from a cold for two consecutive months. c.
306. During three consecutive months do not miss school on account of ill-health. c.
307. Every time you can remember it, during one month, assume and maintain correct posture of body as tested by the vertical line test.. Learn knee-chest position; during three months put into practice some simple home treatment for prevention of pain during menstrual period. (See Young Woman's Journal, Vol. 23, pages 62-4. Read entire article.) c.

Diet.

308. During three consecutive months abstain, between meals, from candy, ice cream, sundaes, sodas, commercially manufactured beverages, and chewing gum. c.

309. For one month masticate your food so thoroughly that it slips down without any visible effort at swallowing. c

Sleep.

310. For any two months of the summer, sleep out of doors; the remainder of the year (October to April, inclusive) for any two months sleep out of doors or with wide open windows. c.

311. If a Senior girl, go to bed by 10 p. m. and arise by 6 a. m.; if a Junior girl, by 9:30 p. m. and arise by 6:30 a. m., for at least four nights of each week, during two consecutive months. c.

Games.

312. Play any of the following games (either out of doors or with open windows) for not less than fifteen hours in any one month: Circle Race, Circle Relay, Corner Spry, Curtain Ball, Round Ball, Square Ball, Circle Zigzag, Hide and Seek, Pussy Wants a Corner, Three Deep, Blind Man's Buff, Drop the Handkerchief, Red Rover, Fox and Hounds, Run Sheep Run, Quoits, Duck on the Rock, Tennis, Golf, Volley Ball, Base Ball. Emperor or Captain Ball.. c.

313. Play singing or dancing games (out doors if circumstances permit) for not less than fifteen hours in any one month. c.

Swimming.

314. Swim one hundred yards in fresh or sea water.. c.

315. Swim one mile in six days, not necessarily consecutive. c.

316. Bring up a cup from the bottom in eight feet of water.

317. Do any two standard dives in good form: Front, Side, Back, Twist, Jack, either running or standing or from spring board. c.d.

318. Swim any four standard styles: breast, side, over-hand, single over-hand, crawl, back, etc.. c. d.

319. Propel yourself 440 yards in Great Salt Lake. c.

Boating.

320. Row or paddle twenty-five miles in any six days, not necessarily consecutive. c.

Skating.

321. Skate twenty-five miles in any six days, not necessarily consecutive. c.

Coasting and Snowshoeing.

322. Coast, ski, or toboggan for not less than fifteen hours in any one month. c.

323. Cover twenty-five miles on snowshoes on any six days, not necessarily consecutive. c.

Horsemanship.

324. Saddle, bridle, mount and ride a horse in good form, using at least three gaits.

325. Ride fifty miles in six days, not necessarily consecutive. c.

326. Take care of horse for at least one month.

Mountain Climbing or Walking.

327. Climb a mountain, attaining a point at least 2000 feet above starting point, and return.
328. Walk an aggregate of forty miles in any ten days, not necessarily consecutive. (This may include walking to or from school or work.) c.

Exercise.

329. Ride a bicycle forty miles in any five days, not necessarily consecutive. c.
330. During three months take seven hours of out-door exercise a week. c.
331. Without help or advice, operate and care for an automobile for five hundred miles during one season. c.

Dancing.

332. Know any six standard folk dances. c. d.
333. Know any six of the following dances: Virginia Reel; Pop Goes the Weasel; German Hopping Dance; Varsouvienne; Hewett's Fancy; Plain, National, Triangular, or Rage Quadrille; Lancers.

DOMESTIC ARTS.

(Brown Seal.)

Whatever the human truth on this point may be, life in the hive is not looked on as a series of more or less pleasant hours, whereof it is wise that those moments only should be soured and embittered that are essential for maintaining existence.—Life of the Bee.

401. Model from clay an individual bowl, plate or cup and saucer, bearing an original design.
402. Make some article from brass or copper bearing an original design.
403. Make three pieces of jewelry from silver or copper, with original designs.
404. Design and make a raffia basket or one equally difficult. c.
405. Make a piece of furniture. c.
406. Make needed repairs around your home, doing any painting or staining necessary to make a good job.
407. Dress dolls, or make picture books or toys; send through the Relief Society where needed.
408. Make a doll house of four rooms with furnishings.
409. Take, develop, and print one dozen photographs.
410. Paint on china, stencil or wood block, three serviceable articles with original designs.
411. Make three articles in cut leather, at least one to be lined with silk.
412. Bind a book, sewing the back and lining the cover and decorating with original designs.
413. Make a water-color, charcoal, pen and ink, or oil sketch from nature.
414. Knit, crochet or tat three articles, like a bag, a collar, or two yards of lace (One large article, like a sweater, may be equal to three ordinary ones; the Bee-keeper may judge).
415. Mend six pairs of stockings, two knitted undergarments, and hem six dish-towels. c. d.
416. Make two articles of underwear by hand or on a machine, or using both. c. d.
Note.—Any article on which an award is made must show skill and taste.

417. Make two shirt waists or make and embroider one. c.
418. Make a dress. c.
419. Trim two hats. c.
420. Make a hat. c.
421. Hem by hand six napkins. c.
422. Do embroidery equivalent to a dresser-scarf, using original design.
423. Do double above amount of embroidery if design is not original.
424. Use all attachments for a sewing machine, keep machine clean and in order for three months.
425. Make a home-made rug.
426. Know prices, widths and uses of six common cotton, four common linen, four common woolen, and four common silk materials.
427. Know how textiles are commonly adulterated; give the simple microscopical and chemical tests for wool, cotton, silk and linen. (See Utah Agricultural College Bulletin, Vol. 14, No. 2.)
428. Identify twelve kinds of lace and tell reasonable price and appropriate use of each.
429. Dye three small articles or one large one.
430. Make any article as difficult to make as those above listed.

OUT DOOR FIELD.
(Green Seal.)

Events in which bees take part happen only when skies are pure, at the winsome hours of the year, when flowers keep holiday. * * * They teach us to tune our ear to the softest, most intimate whisper of these good, natural hours.—Life of the Bee.

501. Identify any fifteen trees and describe them in a way to assure recognition in summer.
502. In winter.
503. Do the same for ten other trees.
504. Plant trees where they are needed, and get at least five to grow. (Honor may be awarded three months after planted.)
505. Identify twenty wild flowers, including the state and national; describe them.
506. Fifteen other wild flowers.
507. Identify any ten ferns and describe them.
508. Ten grasses.
509. Ten mosses.
510. Twenty local birds.
511. Fifteen other birds.
512. From personal observation and notes, tell the value of two kinds of birds to man.
513. From personal observation make notes of the raising of a family of birds.
514. Build and supply a lunch counter for birds; at close of season, report how many kinds of birds you have seen use it.
515. Describe the sea gulls and their habits; tell of their historical importance in Utah.
516. Describe ten butterflies; identify them.
517. Ten moths.
518. Describe three pests that infest apple trees and give methods for eradicating them.
519. Point out the planets and seven constellations; tell their stories.
520. From your own observations while walking, make notes on mountains, strata of the earth, rocks, trees, streams, etc., that may be of value later.

521. Raise at least one kind of flowers or vegetables successfully.
522. Keep written record of method of procedure, time of digging, planting, etc., and time when products mature; also financial accounts.
523. Write history of garden and give suggestions for improving it next season.
524. Describe and identify ten common weeds; tell how to eradicate them.
525. Describe and identify ten garden bug or insect pests; tell how to combat them.
526. Describe eight varieties of apples; tell the ones best suited to your locality, time when ready for use, etc.
527. Do the same for six varieties of peaches.
528. For six varieties of pears.
529. Care successfully for a hive of bees for one season; know their habits.
530. Hatch and raise to six weeks at least ten chickens.
531. Give distinguishing characteristics of ten varieties of hens; tell good and weak points of each.
532. Of six varieties of cattle.
533. Point out, name, and tell something interesting about each canyon in your vicinity.
534. Tell briefly the history of Great Salt Lake and point out and name important islands.
535. Select a location and erect a tent (May have the help of one girl).
536. During week keep tent in order.
537. With material found in the woods or canyons make a shelter and bed.
538. Build a tree house sufficiently large for two girls to sleep in.
539. If you are unprovided with a sleeping porch, contrive a shelter that will take its place (See Boy Scout's Handbook).
540. Pack a horse successfully.
541. Build a fire in the open, in spite of wind and rain, from material found out of doors; build a good brisk fire and keep it going at least half an hour. No fire is to be credited until properly put out.
542. Make two good devices for holding a frying pan and two for holding a pot over a fire.
543. Start a fire without either fire or matches.
544. Without help or advice, do all the the camp cooking for one day, for four or more persons (or two may share the labor for eight persons). Get the wood; furnish suitable character and amounts of food; write the menu, quantities and price of food.
545. Make a bean-hole at least 18x18 inches; cook beans for one meeting of the Bee-Hive.
546. Know the meaning of weather signals; the general meaning of clouds, wind and temperature in your locality.
547. Read some good article on tracking (See Boy Scout Hand-book). Track two miles.
548. Know six blazes used by the Indians.
549. Make a willow bed such as Indians use.
550. Tie at least ten standard knots.

FIELD OF BUSINESS.

(Gold Seal.)

It is actually estimated that more than a hundred thousand varieties of plants would disappear if the bees did not visit them.—Life of the Bee.

601. Be employed at regular work for three months, earning $10 or less a week. c.
602. Be employed at regular work for three months, earning more than $10.00 a week. c.
603. Though not employed regularly, earn at least $5.00, through raising chickens, bees, flowers, vegetables, or doing any other legitimate work. c.
604. Earn $3.00 and give it to some worthy cause. c.
605. Save ten per cent of your allowance for four months. c.
606. Open a bank account, and during three months save at least ten per cent of your salary (besides your tithing); apportion the balance under heads of food, clothing, recreation, books, miscellaneous, and spend accordingly. c.
607. During four months, make your personal expenses come within an amount previously determined upon; consult parents or guardian as to how much it should be. c.
608. Act as treasurer of the Y. L. M. I. A. or your Bee-Hive group for one year, keeping accurate written account of all money in your care. c.
609. During three months, be "on time" at all meetings attended. c.
610. During three months be on time for business, morning and afternoon of every working day. c.
611. Do not borrow money or any article of wearing apparel for two months. c.
612. Attend lectures (at least six) with a view to making your services to your employer or in the home more valuable. c.
613. Keep a bank account for three months; draw and endorse checks; make deposits; balance check book with bank statement or book each month. c.
614. Write a paper of from 1500 to 2000 words on vocations for women, and read it at Bee-Hive meeting.
615. Write a paper of from 1500 to 2000 words describing your state labor laws as they affect girls, women and children, including age restrictions, hours of labor, wages, etc., making suggestions to improve working conditions in your own community; read at Bee-Hive meeting.
616. Make a ten-minute talk at Bee-Hive meeting, telling of mining and industrial operations in your vicinity.
617. At a regular Bee-Hive meeting, write the following:
    a. A business letter ordering some article from a catalogue; fill out an application blank for the money order to be enclosed.
    b. A telegram of a business nature.
    c. An application for a position.
618. Write 500 words on a typewriter from printed copy in ten minutes.
619. From dictation write twenty letters in short-hand and transcribe notes at rate of thirty words or more a minute.
620. Have a vacation away from home of not less than two weeks, spending money you have earned yourself.
621. Get three new subscriptions to the Young Woman's Journal. c.
622. Assist in getting up one or more entertainments which shall net at least $10.00 for the expenses of your Bee-Hive group.
623. Earn enough money and buy one section of your Bee-Hive chain. c. d.

FIELD OF PUBLIC SERVICE.
(Red, White and Blue Seal.)

The love of the race of today for the race of tomorrow.—Life of the Bee.

701. Know and sing all the words of America, Star Spangled Banner, and your state hymn.
702. Know the history of any one national holiday; assist in organizing and carrying through a proper celebration of the same.
703. Know the history of some state holiday; assist in organizing and carrying through a proper celebration of the same.
704. See that the streets and alleys adjoining home are kept reasonably clean for three months.
705. Beautify the front yard.
706. Beautify the back yard.
707. Co-operate with your town authorities in using water supply to the best advantage.
708. Create a bird sanctuary (See "Protect the Wild Birds," Young Woman's Journal, April, 1915.)
709. Co-operate with your town and state authorities in planting and protecting trees. Hardwood trees are desirable for future generations (See "Arbor Day," in Young Woman's Journal, April, 1915).
710. During three months, assist the Relief Society in their work of caring for the poor and sick.
711. Spend the equivalent of six afternoons in visiting the sick or entertaining some elderly persons.
712. Tell the history of each historical spot in your own locality.
713. Give the history and meaning of your national flag and of the flag of the country from which your ancestors came.
714. Know and explain the customary forms of respect due to the flag; repeat the pledge to the flag (See Handbook of Boy Scouts of America, pp. 376-7).
715. Name all the counties in your state with their principal cities; bound your own county.
716. Name 10 institutions in your state devoted to public service, religious or otherwise; describe the work of each.
717. Name and explain briefly two public services rendered the people of your locality by the National government, the State government, the city or township government.
718. Write a paper of from 1500 to 2000 words describing immigration to this country, its advantages and disadvantages, and problems connected therewith.
719. Give the laws in effect in your locality in regard to public safety from fire.
720. Give the laws in effect in your locality in regard to sanitation and ventilation of public buildings, stores and factories.
Give sketches of the lives of:
721. Five educators.
722. Five great men.
723. Five great women.
724. Five statesmen.
725. Five scientists.
726. Three inventors.
727. Five musicians.
728. Five artists.
729. Identify two masterpieces of each of five great musicians.
730. The same for five great artists.
731. Repeat from memory the preamble to the Constitution; the first two paragraphs of the Declaration of Independence; Lincoln's Gettysburg Address.
732. Know the genealogy of your grand parents and great-grandparents, including the maiden names of grandmothers and great-grandmothers; give homes and occupations.

733. Sing in a quartette, duet, trio, or chorus for not less than eight hours in any two months. c.
734. Play a musical instrument in an orchestra for not less than eight hours in one month, reading the necessary music. c.
735. Play the accompaniment for some school exercise for not less than eight hours in one month. c.
736. Write a story, a poem, or words or music for a song which is either accepted for publication or adopted for use in some organization. c. d.
737. Have entire charge of two weekly meetings of the Bee-Hive, or share that labor with one other girl for four meetings. c.
738. Tell three good anecdotes and teach or lead in a good outdoor game.
739. Be a faithful Bee-Keeper or assistant Bee-Keeper during one summer.
740. Each member of a Bee-Hive swarm who participates in carrying out a wholesome party or outing, including at least as many others (either boys or girls), may be given an honor if the work is well planned and carried out, each member having special duties; the plans to be approved by the Bee-Keeper.
741. Each member who participates in giving a party, in which the boys and girls are about equal in numbers, and in which at least two of the following dances are learned by all, may be given an honor: Virginia Reel, Pop Goes the Weasel, German Hopping Dance, Varsouvienne, Hewett's Fancy, Plain Quadrills, National Quadrille, Rage Quadrille, Lancers.
742. Name the Indian tribes that originally inhabited your state, the tribes and number of members now living there, and their economic and religious condition.
743. Own a genuinely Indian made article; know to what tribe its maker belongs, what materials were used in its construction and how it was made, and the meaning of its designs or symbols. c.d.
744. Know the location, history, present economic and religious condition of the tribe where your Indian article was made. c. d.
745. Describe or identify ten Indian symbols or designs and know their meaning.
746. Give the characteristics of five different Indian tribes.
747. Be able to distinguish between the blankets of five different Indian tribes.
748. Be able to distinguish between the baskets of five different Indian tribes.
749. Know and sing six genuine Indian songs. c. d.
750. Learn one genuine Indian song; write words and music and send to Bee-Hive committee of the General Board Y. L. M. I. A. c.d.
751. Write and send to the Bee-Hive committee a genuine Indian legend. c. d.
752. Write and send to the Bee-Hive committee three true incidents from the experiences of yourself or acquaintances, showing traits of the Indian character. You must be able to vouch for their authenticity.
753. Write and send to the Bee-Hive committee an account of the life and activities of one notable Indian with whom you or your people have been acquainted. You must tell the source of your information. c. d.
754. Write and send to the Bee-Hive committee a brief account of the life and activities of one Indian missionary who has lived among the Indians. It must be one with whom you or your people have been acquainted; tell source of your information. c. d.

Off for a Ride.

Near the Shore of Great Salt Lake.

The Joy of a Swim.

A Camp in the Glade.

The End of the Climb.

A Hayrack Ride.

En route to Emigration Canyon.

A Game in the Water.

Liberty Glen Camp.

Liberty Glen Camp.

MIKAYLA THATCHER lives in a yellow-and-green house in St. Paul, Minnesota. She enjoys baking cakes with yummy fillings, talking endlessly with her partner, and attempting to answer all of her child's questions. She teaches anatomy and physiology at a local university, even when it snows a lot. Other than caring for her family and close friends, her main priorities are reading books and going for walks in the forest.

Made in the USA
Middletown, DE
25 March 2023

27670598R00208